STUDIES IN HISTORY, ECONOMICS AND
PUBLIC LAW

Edited by the
FACULTY OF POLITICAL SCIENCE
OF COLUMBIA UNIVERSITY

NUMBER 184

THE FRENCH ASSEMBLY OF 1848 AND AMERICAN CONSTITUTIONAL DOCTRINES

BY

EUGENE NEWTON CURTIS

THE FRENCH ASSEMBLY OF 1848 AND AMERICAN CONSTITUTIONAL DOCTRINES

BY

EUGENE NEWTON CURTIS

OCTAGON BOOKS

A DIVISION OF FARRAR, STRAUS AND GIROUX

New York   1980

Originally published in 1917

Reprinted 1980
by special arrangement with Columbia University Press

OCTAGON BOOKS
A DIVISION OF FARRAR, STRAUS & GIROUX, INC.
19 Union Square West
New York, N.Y. 10003

Library of Congress Cataloging in Publication Data

Curtis, Eugene Newton.
   The French assembly of 1848 and American constitutional doctrines.

   Bibliography: p.
   Originally presented as the author's thesis,
Columbia, 1917.
   Reprint of the 1917 ed. published by Columbia Univer-
sity Press, New York, which was issued as no. 184 of
Columbia studies in the social sciences.
   1. France. Assemblée nationale constituante, 1848-
1849. 2. France—Constitutional history.   I. Title.
   II. Series: Columbia studies in the social sciences;
   no. 184.
JN2539.C8   1980   342.44′0292   80-17596
ISBN 0-374-92011-7

Manufactured by Braun-Brumfield, Inc.
Ann Arbor, Michigan
Printed in the United States of America

To

ATHERTON CURTIS

IN AFFECTIONATE GRATITUDE

PREFACE

THIS study was begun at Paris in 1913, before France and the United States were allied in war a second time. In the light of this alliance, it becomes peculiarly gratifying to find that a close friendship existed between the two countries in the early days of the Second Republic. The extent to which this friendship was based on a like attitude toward constitutional problems and issued in an endeavor to find similar solutions has seemed a question worthy of investigation.

I wish to express my gratitude to M. Emile Bourgeois, professor of diplomatic and political history at the Sorbonne, to M. Georges Renard, professor at the Collège de France and editor of *La révolution de 1848* for helpful suggestions at an early stage of my work and for invaluable assistance in gaining access to the archives of the Chamber of Deputies and to the archivists of the Chamber for their unfailing courtesy. I am indebted to Professors James Harvey Robinson, James T. Shotwell and Charles A. Beard of Columbia University for kindly encouragement, to Professors Charles D. Hazen, William A. Dunning and William R. Shepherd for useful criticisms, to Professor Hazen for unstinted aid in correcting proof, and to my wife, Blanche O. Curtis, for faithful coöperation in overcoming the mechanical difficulties of the task and for continued inspiration.

CONTENTS

CHAPTER III

WHAT FRANCE THOUGHT ABOUT AMERICA

CHAPTER IV

THE REPRESENTATIVES

CHAPTER V

THE CONSTITUTIONAL COMMISSION

CHAPTER VI

THE ASSEMBLY DEBATES

CHAPTER VII

CONTEMPORARY COMMENT

CHAPTER VIII

CONCLUSIONS

APPENDIX

CHAPTER I

Europe and America in 1848: A Contrast

To a generation like our own, whose emphasis has been increasingly transferred from the individual to society, whose deepest problems lie in the relations of employer and wage-earner, the year 1848 stands out from the background of its insignificant neighbors with a special meaning. Down to 1848, economics, so far as it affected politics, had been pre-eminently the science of the production of wealth; from then on it began to address itself seriously to the problem of its distribution. The year 1848 marks the appearance of the wage-earner as a serious political force; it is the starting-point of labor's effort to make for itself a place in the sun. It is distinctly a year of revolution, of bloody fighting, mostly in the streets of great capitals, a translation of the industrial conflict into terms of barricades and bayonets. But it would be a grave error if one were to think of 1848 solely or even primarily as a conscious struggle between clearly distinct, bitterly hating social classes. It became that to some extent, but never entirely; it was certainly not that at all in the beginning. On the contrary, 1848 began with and never quite lost a certain idyllic charm of universal brotherhood, a passionate sense of human equality. To some extent this was a hypocritical pose; the selfish capitalist of Louis Philippe's time could not and did not suddenly change his skin, as was amply proved before the year was out. But the mere fact that the pose was necessary, that rich candidates for office gave *ouvrier* as their profession in order to have a chance for victory at the polls, shows how general the enthusiasm for social justice had become. All Europe, catching fire from France, burned with radical fervor. No doubt it was an impractical time; age-long abuses cannot be suddenly solved by a burst of sentiment. Uncalculating, generous emotion formed the essential atmosphere of the moment, but the vice of impracticality caused its failure. The year 1849 was an equally universal time of reaction, whose edicts of banishment gave America one of the most valuable of its immigrant strains.

But however transitory the constructive work of 1848 seems to have been, its importance is undiminished as witnessing the beginning of the practical study of the social problem, in a modern way. The ideal reconstructions of the Utopians, of St. Simon and Fourier began now to yield to definite schemes for the improvement of society as it is. This marks the first aspect in which 1848 has permanent social meaning. As one of the leading French authorities on the period, M. Renard, said to the writer, " For me, 1848, even more than 1789, is the mother of revolutions. The latter was a political struggle for individual rights, the former a struggle for social rights. Many of the concrete schemes for social betterment which are now on the statute-books of Europe, were suggested then." [1] The French Revolution of 1789 was concerned with the Rights of Man in the singular, the Revolution of 1848, in the intent of its more thorough exponents at least, sought to realize social justice. In this respect it was more, not less, practical than its great predecessor, for modern man has moved out of Rousseau's Garden of Eden into the cities. And there was hard thinking on concrete problems, though it was too confused with visionary schemes to get much of a hearing. In brief, 1848 did not accomplish as much as its reformers expected

[1] For a detailed statement of modern labor laws traceable to the inspiration of 1848, see G. Renard, *La République de 1848*, pp. 383 *et seq.*

of it; their enthusiasm was rudely dealt with by the triumphant forces of reaction. It was, however, a seed-time of ideas, whose fruit has been the great modern body of legislation for social betterment. Herein lies its success.

The second aspect in which 1848 has permanent historical meaning is in its failure. Disillusionment followed hard on rosy dreams of a millennium, and with that disappointment came bitterness. In France, the new order of things was hardly more than a month old, when such posters as the following were affixed to the walls of Paris:

THE COMMITTEE OF THE DEMOCRATIC RADICAL CLUBS
TO THE
POPULAR SOCIETIES

The Republic, quite as well as the Monarchy, may harbor servitude under its banner.

Sparta, Rome, Venice were oppressive and corrupted Aristocracies. In North America, slavery is an institution of the State.

LIBERTY! EQUALITY! FRATERNITY!

This device which gleams on the front of our buildings must not be a mere theatrical adornment [*une décoration d'Opéra*.] Let us not permit it to become a lie as celebrated as that of the Charter: "All Frenchmen are equal before the law."

There is no *liberty* for those who lack bread!

There is no *equality,* when opulence flourishes at the side of misery!

There is no *fraternity,* when the woman of the people drags herself, famished, with her children to the doors of palaces.

No sterile formulas! It is not enough to change words, it is necessary radically to change conditions.

The Republic for us is the complete emancipation of the workers! It is the coming of a new order, which will sweep away the last form of slavery, the proletariat.

The tyranny of capital is more pitiless than that of the sabre and the censor. It must be broken.

The February Revolution has had no other aim. This aim is ours, and each of the members of the democratic Committee engages himself to pursue it without relaxation, until it be attained.

PARIS, APRIL, 1848.[1]

This dawning despair was destined to increase, not to diminish. When the fearful insurrection of June had been quelled with equally savage ferocity, Lamennais exclaimed " The Republic is dead," while George Sand wrote, " I am horrified. I believe no longer in the existence of a republic which commences by killing its proletarians." [2]

This loss of faith in the republic as the outward expression of universal harmony ushered in a narrower, but intenser loyalty, that to one's social class as such. Proudhon and Blanqui had steadily stood for that idea as against Louis Blanc and Pierre Leroux. But the classic exponent of the doctrine of essential antagonism is Karl Marx, whose star begins to rise at this time. From now on Marxian socialism becomes the orthodox form of radicalism, whose leadership passes from France to Germany.[3] This definite rise of class-consciousness is one of the permanent legacies of the failure of 1848.

No doubt can exist that while the train of revolution throughout Europe was already laid by the romantic, liberty-loving tendencies which had dominated thought and had found expression in art, literature, music and political aspiration through the whole first half of the nineteenth century, yet the spark was ignited by the February revolution in France. The specific form taken by the movement varied everywhere according to local conditions. In some countries, it was a

---

[1] Proclamation of Blanqui's club, just before April 16. Printed in *Les Affiches Rouges.*

[2] G. Renard, *op. cit.*, p. 86.

[3] *Cf.* G. Renard, *op. cit.*, p. 380 *et seq.*

struggle for constitutionalism, in others for nationalism, whether centripetal as in Germany or centrifugal as in Hungary. The definite impress of the French rising is to be found in Baden and elsewhere. But the line was not yet sharply drawn between political and economic radicalism; it could not be until the failure of 1848 brought a sharper class-consciousness into being. Thus it happened that in most of these revolutions, the more advanced economic program of the Paris movement was entirely lacking, while their general spirit of radicalism was manifestly akin. At that time all men looked to political reform as the panacea for social ills.

Turning from the general causes that lay back of the European revolutions of 1848 to a closer analysis of the movement in France, let us consider briefly the economic and political situation in the reign of Louis Philippe. Speaking generally, the social and economic structure of the country resembled more closely the France of the eighteenth century than the France of to-day. Life was still relatively simple. As late as 1850, more than three-fourths of the population lived in communities of less than two thousand inhabitants. Except Paris, which had 1,053,000 at that time, only Lyons, Marseilles and Bordeaux exceeded 100,000; Rouen just touched that number. There were no great industries in the modern sense; manufacturing was carried on in small establishments, often in a family atelier. The country was essentially agricultural. Agriculture itself was backward. The rotation system (*assolements*) was practised, 25,000,000 hectares being worked, while 5,000,000 were kept idle to rest the soil. There were few means of locomotion. Macadam roads were just beginning to be built, the majority of roads were still paved. Railroads were rare; the diligence transported passengers, wagons carried articles of commerce to the market. Food crises still occurred, especially in the provinces, as in the eighteenth century. There was little popular education. Newspapers (subject to a *cautionnement*, or bond for political good behavior) were expensive luxuries. Public life was restricted to the *pays légal*, which meant that only those voted who paid 200 francs in direct taxes (not more than 200,000 were so qualified), while only those who paid 500 francs in taxes were eligible to sit in parliament. There were few shares listed on the Bourse; mostly Government *rentes*, *titres* of the Banque de France and canal-shares, little else. Limited companies were almost unknown. France was strongly centralized, but very slightly unified. Social distinctions, for example, were strongly marked. The *blouse* marked the workman, the *habit* the bourgeois; the former wore a *bonnet,* the latter a *chapeau;* the latter was a *monsieur,* the former an *homme.*[1] Such was the case despite the monarch's supposed democratic tendencies. The old hereditary aristocracy, based on birth and land, had, it is true, lost control with the downfall of Charles X, but it had merely been replaced by the new aristocracy of wealth. Bourbon legitimism had yielded to bourgeois capitalism, insignificant as yet if measured by modern standards, but growing ever more powerful through the favor of the Orleanist régime.[2]

[1] *Vide* C. Seignobos' lectures, "Histoire politique de la France contemporaine depuis 1848," in the *Revue des cours et conférences* for 1907-08, vol. i, esp. pp. 175 and 176. *Cf.* E. Levasseur, *Histoire des classes ouvrières et de l'industrie en France de 1789 à 1870,* vol. ii, bk. iv.

[2] " Posterity, which sees only striking crimes and whose notice, ordinarily, vices escape, will perhaps never know to what degree the government of that time had, toward the end, taken on the features of an industrial company, where all the operations are made with a view to the profit which the stockholders may draw from them. These vices sprang from the natural instincts of the ruling class, from its absolute power, from the very character of the age. King Louis-Philippe had perhaps contributed to their increase." A. de Tocqueville, *Souvenirs,* p. 7.

It is this great and sudden growth of wealth that forms the chief significance of the Orleanist period to the student of 1848, for without it the revolution in the form which it assumed would have been impossible. It is interesting to see how undeveloped the age still was, in contrast to the twentieth century; it is even more important, however, to note the new tendency which had gripped and mastered it and was rushing it away from the quiet past into new and complex problems. For France was in the throes of a vaster movement than that of 1848; she was in the full tide of the Industrial Revolution.

The political philosophy of Louis Philippe was essentially that of his favorite minister, Guizot, whose power lasted uninterruptedly from 1840 to 1848. It was a policy of external peace and internal economic development. Having managed to go through the Oriental crisis without warfare, though without much glory, the government's caution in foreign affairs became more and more pronounced. It reached its extreme point in the Pritchard affair (1844), when France humbled herself before England. This was so much the easier to do, because England's constitutional and social structure was the model which Orleanist France admired and strove to emulate. The entente cordiale with the England of Adam Smith was as fixed an article of political faith with Guizot as was the entente cordiale with the Austria of Metternich. These two ideals furnish the key to the last years of Orleanist France. *" Enrichissez-vous "* [1] cried Guizot to his capitalist friends, while turning a stony impassivity to the opposition in its efforts to extend the *pays*

----

[1] Guizot denied ever making use of this expression, attributed to him by a hostile newspaper in its report of a speech made by him to his electors in 1846. It became famous, however, and even if unhistorical, adequately expresses his economic philosophy. *Cf.* Hamel, *Histoire de France depuis la révolution*, vol. 8, p. 573 and note.

légal ever so little. The glorification of property, both land and fluid capital, in the fifth chapter of his *Démocratie en France* was written from Guizot's heart. To this official policy, the new capitalist aristocracy responded with zest. Mechanical inventions, new industrial processes, but especially railroads, gave opportunities for speculation and enrichment at a rate previously unknown. Guizot points with justifiable pride to the fact that the increase in the ordinary revenues of 1847 over those of 1829 amounted to 349,413,-354 francs. Of this increase, a part was indeed due to new direct taxes, but the growth in revenue from indirect taxation, amounting to 243,317,400 francs or nearly three-fourths of the whole, was "almost solely the result of the continuous progress of general well-being and national wealth." [1] As early as 1842, a proposed trade agreement between France and Belgium was abandoned by the government at the behest of the great manufacturers and mine-owners of the north. On February 7th, 1842, Guizot launched his vast railway scheme. Up to that time, little had been done, though much had been said. According to the new scheme, France, then far behind other countries in railroad construction, was to be covered with a network connecting Paris with Lille, the Channel, Bordeaux, Marseilles, Lyons, Strasburg, in fact all the important cities of the kingdom. 2500 kilometers were thus to be built by joint public and private effort; the roads (which were owned by private capital) were to furnish the equipment, complete the construction and operate on a long franchise. There were scandals and speculations, but the roads were built, in part at least. At the end of 1841, France had only 877 kilo-

---

[1] Guizot, *Mémoires pour servir à l'histoire de mon temps*, 1867 ed., vol. 8, p. 609 *et seq.*

meters of railroads, of which 566 were in operation. In 1847, there were 1832 kilometers.[1]

The era of speculation and prosperity was followed by the panic of 1847, which started in England. The period of expansion began there about 1843. In 1844, the deposits of the Bank of England passed fifteen millions, while the discount rate fell to two per cent, even to one and one-half per cent. Then the railroad-building fever came there too. *The Economist* calculates that the new lines, receiving concessions at that time, called for £200,000,000. There was great speculation in other new enterprises. Such was the position of affairs when, in 1846, a potato disease and a bad wheat crop required heavy food importations which necessitated considerable exports of specie in the spring of 1847. Credit was violently shaken in January, but, during the summer, gold began to return, and the danger was considered past. Towards autumn, the drainage of gold began again and the Bank of England was compelled to raise its rate of discount abruptly. Panic ensued. Bankruptcies commenced with those of the wheat merchants. The quarter fell from 102 shillings in January to 49 shillings in September. In October, the crisis was at its height. Discount was then at eight per cent. Factories were closed, railroad workmen discharged, construction ceased for lack of capital. Misery was universal.[2] This situation was not without a parallel in other countries. France and Germany saw their

---

[1] Articles "Chemin de fer" and "France (Industrie)" in *La Grande Encyclopédie*. Guizot states, however, that on Dec. 31, 1847, there were 2059 kilometers in full operation and 2144 under construction. (*Mémoires*, vol. 8, p. 626.) That this is an overestimate seems probable from a comparison of the figures given in the text with those of A. de Foville (in *La Transformation des moyens de transport*, p. 18 et seq.). Foville gives for 1841, 571 km.; for 1847, 1829 km.

[2] Art. "Crise," by Emile de Laveleye in *La Grande Encyclopédie*, vol. 13, p. 383.

unsubstantial cloud-castles come crashing to the ground in turn. In France, government expenses had been mounting steadily. From 1840 to 1846, in spite of an average annual increase in receipts of 40 millions, the total excess of disbursements over receipts had reached 433 millions. The failure of the wheat crop in 1846 affected France as well as England; here, too, grain had to be purchased abroad, at the cost of heavy specie exportations. Floods in 1846 caused much damage. The railroad project drained the resources of the state heavily and, as the defeated partisans of government ownership grumbled, all for the benefit of private corporations. In less than two years the companies had contracted loans to the amount of 1300 millions, and the treasury a loan of 200 millions, or 1500 million francs for railroad construction. The public was swept away by the mad fever of speculation in these securities, which rose to fabulous quotations. Meanwhile the Bank of France, unable to cope with these heavy demands, saw its balance diminish by 172 millions from July 1st, 1846 to January 1st, 1847. It was compelled to borrow 25 millions in bullion from London. Discount commenced to rise. Credit was tightened and the market began to totter. The budget for 1848 foresaw a further deficit of 243 millions in the national treasury. To cover it, a new loan of 350 millions was contracted in July, which added its weight to depress the already overburdened market. Wheat continued to rise; in January, it was already up to 29.92 francs a hectolitre, by June in certain places it touched 49.70. Riots broke out, bands of armed peasants opposed the movement of crops, and blood was shed, before the military could restore order. Railroad construction was suspended, workmen saw themselves discharged or their wages reduced, industry came to a halt, it was a time of panic and privation.[1]

[1] Garnier-Pagès, *La Révolution de 1848*, vol. i, ch. i and ii.

Perhaps if the economic crisis of 1847 had stood by itself, there would have been no revolution in France, any more than in England. But it did not stand by itself. It was aggravated by a political crisis.

To begin with, the two causes of popular discontent, the economic and the political, were unhappily linked by the revelation of a number of grave scandals affecting men in high position. Corruption was uncovered in the supply departments of the army and navy, particularly in connection with Algeria, whereby inferior food for the men and horses and poor coal for the ships had been accepted by the authorities.

A still greater sensation was caused by the publication of letters which had passed between M. de Cubières, lieutenant-general, and a mine-owner at Gouhenans, whereby the former demanded and obtained 45 shares, worth 100,000 francs, to gain for the latter the necessary support in the council of ministers for certain coal and salt-mine concessions. The man higher up in this scandal turned out to be M. Teste, a former minister, then sitting in the Chamber of Peers and acting as *président de chambre* at the Court of Cassation. In July the trial was held before the Chamber of Peers, the defendants found guilty, and sentenced to a heavy fine and imprisonment.

These sporadic scandals, however, though more spectacular, were in reality of far less importance than the insidious and thorough-going corruption of the parliamentary majority by the government. As has been indicated above, the parliament was elected on an extremely restricted franchise and was thus already the choice of the property-holding and well-to-do classes. It was thus almost entirely conservative in its composition, as a result of such an election. But to make its control absolutely sure, the government appointed no fewer than 200 out of a chamber of 459 to posts in the civil service.[1]   These office-holders, who owed their places to the cabinet, always voted for it solidly and constituted the main strength of the government party.   There were hence two lines of action on the part of the opposition, electoral reform and parliamentary reform.   The first line was taken in the proposition presented by Duvergier de Hauranne in March 1847; it called for a lowering of the voter's qualification from 200 to 100 francs, the addition of the " capacities " to the list of voters (i. e. a limited number of intellectuals, whose education would be a sufficient safeguard of their conservatism), and an increase in the number of deputies from 459 to 538.   The other line was taken in M. de Rémusat's project of April, which would establish the ineligibility to the chamber of all officers of the army and members of the military and civil households of the king and the princes.   Both of these projects were defeated, the latter by a smaller majority than the former.

There soon followed the famous campaign of the banquets, which began at Paris, July 9th, and continued throughout the remainder of the year in all parts of France.   At these banquets, organized by the opposition, the principles of reform were patiently propagated among the people.

It was this campaign which led directly up to the Revolution of 1848.   The prohibition of the final banquet, planned for February 22, the popular uprising on that and the succeeding day, the dismissal of the Guizot ministry, the public rejoicing interrupted by a fresh clash with the troops, the renewal of the struggle on February 24 with heightened bitterness, the abdication and flight of the king and the vain effort to establish a regency are too well-known to need repetition here.

Republican propaganda had been going on all through

---

[1] E. Hamel, *Histoire de France depuis la révolution*, vol. 8, p. 499.

Louis Philippe's reign in the clubs and secret societies. Of late it had taken a distinctly socialist turn, due in large part to the economic distress traced above, and to the miserable condition of the working-classes in the early days of the Industrial Revolution.[1] It is to be noted that the Revolution of 1848 was carried through in the cities; the country-districts, still strongly agricultural, followed their lead, but with lukewarm interest, and later formed the strength of the reaction that carried Louis Napoleon into power. The 23rd of February was the day when the political interests of the lower middle class were uppermost in the public mind; the battle-cry was *Vive la réforme;* that night, with the choice of the Barrot ministry, they had gained their cause. The 24th of February was the day when the economic grievances of the wage-earning class held the stage; the workers won their victory that afternoon when in a stormy session, invaded by the populace, the chamber rejected the regency and chose a Provisional Government consisting of Dupont (de l'Eure), Arago, Lamartine, Ledru-Rollin, Garnier-Pagès, Marie and Crémieux, the majority of whom were

---

[1] A careful study shows that workmen took little part in the republican societies and propaganda until 1834. Both during the Restoration and the first four years of the July monarchy, the membership of the societies was bourgeois, students and journalists playing an important part. The secret societies from 1834 to 1848 were, however, largely composed of workmen, the *Saisons* being entirely so. Workmen were, however, rarely leaders of the societies. It is to be noted also that the workmen interested in politics formed only a small minority of the total working population, and consisted chiefly of those living in Paris, Lyons and a few large towns, the industrial north and east being largely indifferent. The majority preferred the strike as a weapon for industrial grievances, and many of these strikes were violent. *Cf.* G. Weill, *Hist. du parti républican en France de 1814 à 1870*, I. Tchernoff, *Le parti républicain sous la monarchie de juillet*, but especially the contemporary sources referred to in the latter's excellent bibliography, particularly the *Revue retrospective*, no. 1 and the reports of the various political *procès* of the time, published in the pamphlet literature of the period.

moderate republicans.   Their number was soon after increased at the Hôtel de Ville, which became the new seat
of government, by a socialist and radical group, Louis
Blanc, Marrast, Flocon, and Albert, a workman, who were
first accepted only as secretaries, but presently tacitly admitted as full members.   These groups represented, roughly
speaking, the more moderate *National* and the more radical
Réforme, the two chief republican newspapers in whose
offices the preliminary caucuses on names had been held.
Here was a line of cleavage destined ultimately to destroy
the republic.   For the moment, however, all was harmony.
Social distinctions were forgotten, political oppression had
reached its close.   The people were light-headed with the
intoxication of their painless victory, so sudden, and so in-
credibly complete.   *Tous les hommes sont frères* was a
phrase repeated again and again in official and unofficial
proclamations.   The atmosphere men breathed was sur-
charged with sentiment.   " It was as though one swam in
a sea of milk," says M. Renard.   Lamartine, the poet, was
the natural head of such a movement.   " We are making today the most sublime of poems," he cried in a sort of Delphic
ecstacy to the enraptured throngs who mistook his eloquence
for statesmanship.   Idealism, radicalism, brotherhood were
on the tongues, if not in the hearts, of all.

Such was France in 1848.   America presents a striking
contrast.   In the first place, the United States was at that
time in the full swing of an era of territorial expansion.
For some years there had been a growing sentiment, especially in the south, in favor of the annexation of Texas.   In
1844, Andrew Jackson wrote a letter of introduction for the
Texan commissioner to the United States, in which he said
that " the present golden moment to obtain Texas must not

be lost," [1] though Texas was still claimed by Mexico, a friendly state. The annexation fever spread like wildfire and the election of 1844 turned on it. James K. Polk was nominated by the Democrats on a platform calling for annexation. President Tyler, the original annexation man, was renominated by a faction with the slogan " Tyler and Texas," but his personal unpopularity was too great to be overcome by the catchword of the hour. Van Buren, the favorite, lost his chance for the Democratic nomination by coming out against annexation, and Clay, the Whig nominee, hedged. Mass meetings were held all over the south demanding annexation; at many of them there were threats to secede rather than abandon Texas. The interests of the cotton-trader and the desire for more slave territory were at the bottom of this Texas enthusiasm, but the spirit of imperialism in north and south alike kept it from being a purely sectional issue. Polk, though relatively obscure, was elected over his more distinguished opponents and on March 1st, 1845, as one of his last official acts, Tyler signed a joint resolution of Congress annexing Texas.

Meanwhile, the Oregon claims provided an opportunity to restore the political and economic equilibrium of north and south. Oregon was a region between California, which belonged to Mexico, and Alaska, which belonged to Russia. For twenty years, the delimitation of this territory had been in dispute between the United States and England. The question was partly one of discovery and partly one of occupancy; the crux of the matter was who was to control the fur-trade of the Columbia River. If Texas meant cotton, Oregon meant fur, and both meant money as well as the satisfaction of national pride in extended boundaries. The latter motive was perhaps uppermost in the popular war-cry

---

[1] McMaster, *History of the People of the U. S.*, vol. vii, p. 323.

of the time, "Fifty-four forty or fight," 54° 40' being the southern border of Alaska. But the realization of the fact that the Rockies could be crossed and that the Far West was open country to such settlers as chose to come, lent another economic motive to the patriotic impulse. The Polk platform declared "that our title to the whole of the Territory of Oregon is clear and unquestionable; that no portion of the same ought to be ceded to England or any other power, and that the re-occupation of Oregon and the re-annexation of Texas at the earliest practicable period are great American measures, which the Convention recommends to the cordial support of the Democracy of the Union." [1]

If war with England over Oregon was averted, war with Mexico over Texas was not. In consequence, military pride at that time became a marked characteristic of America in our period. It is only fair to say that there was a strong anti-war party among the northern Whigs and that Congress was flooded with petitions to stop the unrighteous contest. But the dominant sentiment was shown by the Whig nomination of General Zachary Taylor for President in 1847, so little a politician that there was some doubt as to whether he was a Whig or a Democrat. But he was the incarnation of the victorious army and that was enough. "All parties, and all the politicians might combine against Taylor; abolitionism, Fourierism, and radicalism might unite to cry him down; the North and the South might rally as they pleased on the Wilmot Proviso, and the cry of 'slave-holder' might be uttered by every Abolition press and throat in the land, but it would not avail. A great, generous, and grateful people would unite, and with one accord put Zachary Taylor in the seat of him who had not scrupled to plan his destruction." [2] The Democrats could do no better than put up

---

[1] McMaster, *op. cit.*, vol. vii, p. 355 *et seq.*

[2] *New York Courier and Enquirer*, quoted by McMaster, *op. cit.*, vol. vii, p. 541.

another man with a military title, General Cass, who, however, was more eminent in politics than in war. The *London Times* in an editorial of October 20, 1848, says, somewhat exaggerating the General's military exploits: " Cass
is nothing more than a military rival. Glory just now is
the fashion and the President must at least be a distinguished General. The Whigs have set up one and the
Democrats another. The achievements of the two candidates are compared step by step, their killed and wounded
reckoned up, their marches timed and measured, and the
value of their captures reduced to hard cash." Taylor was
elected. Van Buren polled 291,000 votes as the candidate
of the Free-soilers, the only party that stood definitely for
higher things. The curious circumstance that a Whig could
be elected in 1848 as the exponent of a war policy which
sprang directly out of the Democratic triumph four years
before shows how little theoretical party allegiance signified
when contrasted with such dominant national ambitions as
those for territorial expansion and military glory.

A third factor of great importance in the general situation was the economic prosperity and consequent self-satis-
faction of the time. To illustrate both points it is hardly
necessary to do more than quote a portion of President
Polk's fourth annual message to Congress, dated December
5, 1848:

Peace, plenty, and contentment reign throughout our
borders, and our beloved country presents a sublime moral
spectacle to the world. The troubled and unsettled condition
of some of the principal European powers has had a necessary
tendency to check and embarrass trade and to depress prices
throughout all commerical nations, but notwithstanding these
causes, the United States, with their abundant products, have
felt their effects less severely than any other country, and all
our great interests are still prosperous and successful.

In reviewing the great events of the past years and contrasting the agitated and disturbed state of other countries with our own tranquil and happy condition, we may congratulate ourselves that we are the most favored people on the face of the earth. While the people of other countries are struggling to establish free institutions under which man may govern himself, we are in the actual enjoyment of them— a rich inheritance from our fathers. While enlightened nations of Europe are convulsed and distracted by civil war or intestine strife, we settle all our political controversies by the peaceful exercise of the rights of freemen at the ballot box.

The great republican maxim, so deeply engraven on the hearts of our people, that the will of the majority, constitutionally expressed, shall prevail, is our sure safeguard against force and violence. It is a subject of just pride that our fame and character as a nation continue rapidly to advance in the estimation of the civilized world.

To our wise and free institutions it is to be attributed that while other nations have achieved glory at the price of the suffering, distress, and impoverishment of their people, we have won our honorable position in the midst of an uninterrupted prosperity and of an increasing individual comfort and happiness.[1]

In a history of the Polk administration published two years later, one reads "There is something so just and equitable in the constitution and laws of the United States, that no one can have cause for dissatisfaction. . . . Let the boundaries of the Union then be extended; let contiguous territory be incorporated with our own, let all the *keys* to our rivers and harbors be secured; let the model republic increase in greatness until its political, moral, and physical power shall be felt and acknowledged throughout the civilized world."[2]

---

[1] J. D. Richardson, *A Compilation of the Messages and Papers of the Presidents*, vol. iv, p. 629. The entire message was translated in the *Journal des débats* of Dec. 23, and was published in whole or in part, in most of the leading Paris newspapers.

[2] Lucien B. Chase, *History of the Polk Administration*, pp. 109, 110.

America, of course, was unanimous as to the desirability
of political liberty; it was hard for her to see her own self-
contradictions. The *London Times*, not then inclined to be
gentle with us, helped us to see them in a leader of October
26, 1848. We read: "Political slavery is an abomination in
the eyes of our friends on the other side of the Atlantic . . .
social slavery an unobjectionable condition of humanity.
The figure of a spare, yellow, sinewy man, holding in one
hand a red banner, inscribed with the words, ' Death to
Tyrants,' and in the other a cat-o'-nine tails, would afford a
not inapposite image of the present condition of the American mind as reflected in the press." [1]

To ignore the social enthusiasm of the time would be a
gross error. The Abolitionist movement was, of course, in
full swing. By 1840, there were 2,000 antislavery societies
with a membership of 200,000. Afterward, though they
continued to be of great importance, the unity of their
counsels suffered from a split on the advisability of political
action.[2]

There were other fine efforts to better human conditions.
The Fourierists were never more active than in the 40's.
They gained the interest of Horace Greeley and the use of a
column in the *Tribune*. They founded nearly forty
phalanxes, one of which, at Red Bank, N. J., lived thirteen
years. The majority lasted two or three. Brook Farm, with
its distinguished group, began as a community in 1841, became a phalanx in 1844 and died in 1847. One cannot say
that the communistic theories of Europe failed to touch
America at this time. On the other hand, they were more
thoroughly tried out here than anywhere else. One can only
say that they all promptly failed and that the overwhelming

[1] *Cf.* J. R. Lowell, *Biglow Papers*, 1st series, nos. 5 and 6.
[2] *Cf.* J. F. Rhodes, *Hist. of the U. S.*, vol. i, ch. i, esp. p. 74.

majority of Americans never took them seriously.   There
was labor reform, educational reform, and prison reform.
Dorothea Dix was engaged in her great work for the insane.[1]
But these were the few.   As we have seen the main interests
of American life lay in other directions.   America was in
the full exuberance of material growth with all the vanity
and indifference of healthy youth.   Let older civilizations
wrestle with the complex issues of industrial life; America
had plenty of room for all her people; if they were not satisfied, they could move elsewhere.

Such was the contrast between Europe and America in
1848; the old continent seething from end to end with revolutionary spirit, the new continent complacently materialistic,
wedded to political immobility, the old world radical, the
new world conservative, the former dissatisfied, the latter
self-satisfied.   Given this contrast, our curiosity can hardly
fail to be aroused when we discover that a strong interest in
American institutions and particularly in American constitutions existed in the France of 1848.

There had been such interest at other important crises in
the past, it is true.   It was keen from 1789 to 1791.   Jefferson, who was in Paris when the Estates-General met in 1789,
was not above suggesting helpful ideas out of the fullness of
American experience.[2]   He was most optimistic about the
proposed French constitution.   The leading members, according to his information, had in mind a federal system,
with a royal executive, a House and Senate, the latter
" chosen on the plan of our senate by provincial assemblies,

---

[1] For a comprehensive account of social reform activity at this time,
see McMaster, *op. cit.*, vol. vii, ch. lxxiv.

[2] Jefferson's *Writings* (Ford ed.), vol. v, pp. 99-104 (Letters of June
3 and July 19).

but for life," their powers limited to those of " a mere council of revision like that of New York; " there was to be an
order of judges, " a good deal like ours " and provincial assemblies analogous to the American state governments.
" In short ours has been professedly their model, in which
such changes are made as a difference of circumstances rendered necessary and some others neither necessary nor advantageous, but into which men will ever run when versed in
theory and new in the practice of government, when ac-
quainted with man only as they see him in their books & not
in the world. . . . It is impossible to desire better dispositions towards us, than prevail in this assembly.   Our proceedings have been viewed as a model for them on every
occasion; and tho' in the heat of debate men are generally
disposed to contradict every authority urged by their opponents, ours has been treated like that of the Bible, open to
explanation but not to question."   Jefferson goes on to fear
that this interest in us will be checked by our placing them
" on a mere footing with the English." [1]

The actual position of affairs has been summarized as
follows.[2]   In 1778, the state constitutions of Pennsylvania,
New Jersey, Delaware, Maryland, Virginia and South Carolina, the Declaration of Independence, the Articles of Confederation and certain Acts of Congress were collected in
one volume and published in French.   In 1783 a more complete collection was issued at Franklin's request. Démeunier,
the royal censor, made a still better collection in his
Encyclopédie Méthodique, 1784-8.   He published them also
separately with comments. These constitutions were studied
with great interest by French statesmen.   Turgot in 1778

[1] Letter to Madison, Aug. 28, 1789, *Writings* (Ford ed.), vol. 5, pp.
108-110.

[2] H. E. Bourne, " American Precedents in the National Assembly,"
Am. Hist. Review, vol. 8, p. 486.

attacked the American bicameral system; John Adams' famous Defence was read at Paris in its English version even before it was translated in 1792, while William Livingston's rejoinder was translated at once, (1789). After the American Revolution, however, the weakness of the Confederation caused a decline in America influence; the early collapse of the system was predicted. The new constitution of the United States was much admired by philosophers, according to Lafayette. But Condorcet wrote to Franklin, " I see with pain that the aristocratic spirit seeks to introduce itself among you in spite of so many precautions" (July 8, 1788). It was thought that the English constitution had been too much imitated. The abandonment of the Declaration of Rights created displeasure. Jefferson wrote: "The enlightened part of Europe has given us the greatest credit for inventing this instrument of security for the rights of the people and have been not a little surprised to see us so soon give it up." The strength of the central power and the division of Congress into two houses was disliked. In the National Assembly, there were many references to American example in the discussions on the Declaration of Rights (where the practice of state constitutions was freely cited), the veto power of the king and the bicameral system, though the people who upheld the American example had an even greater weakness for that of England which was regarded as a still stronger government. This conservative group, represented by Mounier, met with Barnave and the radicals (who opposed two chambers and an absolute veto) at Jefferson's house in a conference, August 27th, 1789. It was after this meeting that Jefferson wrote the over-enthusiastic letter to Madison quoted above. In September, the matter was brought to a vote; the single chamber and a suspensive veto triumphed, the enlargement of the provincial assemblies into Americanized state governments was not seriously discussed.[1]

Another writer draws three main conclusions: (a) that the influence of America was so powerful between 1776 and 1789, that the American Revolution may be called a "proximate cause" of the French Revolution, (b) that it was distinctly traceable, though to a less degree during the latter movement, from 1789 to 1791, (c) that during the Legislative Assembly and the Convention it was almost imperceptible.[2] In other words an increasingly radical France found American precedents less and less to its liking.

It is impossible within our limits to trace the American influence in each of the later constitutional changes in France. The probabilities are that it was very slight. Most of the changes were made under circumstances of stress and urgency, and were not the product of calm deliberation. It is interesting to note, however, that when the Revolution of 1830 had placed Lafayette in a position of authority, he came to the Duke of Orleans in the Palais-Royal, being instructed by the republicans to procure from him a guarantee of popular rights. During the conversation, Lafayette said, "You know that I am a republican and consider the American constitution the most perfect." To which the Duke answered, " I am of the same opinion: no one could have been two years in America and not share that view. But do you think that that constitution could be adopted in France in its present condition with the present state of popular opinion?" "No," Lafayette replied, "what France needs is a popular monarchy surrounded by

[1] This was substantially the result as embodied in the Constitution of 1791. *Cf.* C. H. Rammelkamp, "French Constitution of 1791 and the U. S. Constitution: a comparison," *South Atlantic Quarterly*, vol. 2, p. 56 *et seq.*

[2] Lewis Rosenthal, *America and France*, pp. 296-298.

republican—thoroughly republican—institutions." " There I quite agree with you," said Louis Philippe.[1] Thus the head of the House of Orleans expressed his approval of American ideas. It has been shown above how he admired even more the ways of England.

But independently of the dramatic contrast between the France and America of 1848, there is another reason which gives French interest in American ways at that time peculiar importance. For this was the first time in history that the American constitution was deliberately studied by a great European country since it had become a practical success. In 1789, it was at best a hopeful theory; sixty years of trial had now given an opportunity for some definite appraisal of it as a working institution. What judgment did the critics across the sea pass upon it? How did it impress them? And above all, who were the men chiefly impressed? Was it those who were anxious to set up a bulwark of republicanism as opposed to reaction toward monarchy, or those who were seeking a support for conservative institutions as opposed to radicalism? For both of these groups were desperately in earnest; they were not idle, academic theorists, and if they praised or blamed American ways, it was with a very sharp eye to their own interests. Who praised, who blamed American example, and why?

These are the questions which this study attempts to answer.

[1] W. Müller, *Political History of Recent Times*, sec. 7, p. 109.

CHAPTER II

Composition of the Assembly

THE Provisional Government, as has been already said, consisted of two groups, one more radical than the other. Notwithstanding this divergence, the record shows an honest effort to coöperate in thorough-going reforms. "At what epoch and in what country," asks Louis Blanc, " will one find a government which in two months,—in two months!— has issued so many decrees favorable to liberty and stamped with respect for human dignity? In two months, to abolish the death penalty, to establish universal suffrage, to proclaim the right to employment, to give a tribute to the proletariat, to decree the emancipation of the slaves, to suppress corporal punishment in the maritime code, to prepare a plan of universal and free education, to extend the jury system, to suppress political oaths, to abolish imprisonment for debt, to assert the principle of judicial suspension and recall, to facilitate the naturalization of foreigners, to organize the immediate representation of the working-class, to inaugurate the great principle of association, and to denounce the wage-system as the last form of slavery, was all this nothing?" [1]

Nor is this list exhaustive. As instances of further social legislation, we find the following decrees: that of March 2, reducing the hours of labor for all workers in Paris to ten a day, in the provinces to eleven, and abolishing the hated system of sub-contracting (*marchandage*); that of

---

[1] L. Blanc, *Histoire de la révolution de 1848*, preface, pp. v and vi.

March 7, establishing national discount banks (*comptoirs nationaux d'escompte*) for the extension of credit, in all industrial and commercial cities; that of the 7th, fixing the rate of interest to be paid by savings-banks at five per cent, this being the rate of treasury-bonds; that of the 8th, establishing an employment bureau in every *mairie*.[1]

In spite of all this legislation (some of which was inadequately carried out), a sense of disappointment began to creep over the working-class as time went on. As early as the 25th of February, the republic began to have its *journées révolutionnaires*. On that morning, a crowd of workmen gathered in the Place de l'Hôtel de Ville, demanding the proclamation of the *droit au travail*, but were forced to be content with a skilfully worded formula by which the government *s'engage à garantir du travail à tous les citoyens*.[2] In the afternoon, a still more alarming demonstration in support of the red flag was discomfited by Lamar-

[1] A complete list of decrees passed by the Provisional Government is to be found in E. Carrey, *Recueil des actes du gouvernement provisoire de 1848*, Paris, 1848.

[2] The importance of this formula has not received the attention it deserves. Louis Blanc proved himself an extremely able politician by devising and carrying through this compromise and thus saving the government. A complete refusal of the *droit au travail*, such as Lamartine wished, would have driven the working-class, whose barricades were still standing, into a new revolution: a complete acceptance of the principle, which of course Louis Blanc would have preferred, but which he was clear-sighted enough not to insist upon, might have caused the resignation of Lamartine and a split with the conservative element of the government and the community. However, the compromise, successful at the time, proved in the end disastrous, because it opened the way for Marie's national workshops, which were doomed to failure from the start, while Louis Blanc's ateliers, if accepted in their entirety, might have succeeded. The Clichy tailor enterprise, at least, carried out on his lines, had sufficient success to show his scheme to be not impracticable. The inevitable failure of Marie's ateliers dragged the republic down with them. Thus, from one point of view, this compromise formula holds the key to the future history of the republic.

tine's oratorical glorification of the tricolor.   The 28th witnessed a gathering, which in concert with Louis Blanc, demanded the creation of a ministry of progress, instead of which the government organized a commission to sit at the Luxembourg and consider plans for improving social conditions; of this commission, Louis Blanc and Albert were made the heads.   Whether or not this was a clever scheme to shelve the two socialists by putting them at the head of a debating society, is perhaps uncertain; at all events, their duties at the Luxembourg kept them thereafter from taking much part in the councils of the government.   The substitution of a commission for a ministry had the further effect, as Louis Blanc justly complained,[1] of giving the cause of social betterment an ineffective parliament instead of an executive department with power to act; it might discuss and recommend as much as it pleased, provided it did nothing to disturb the *status quo*.   It served thus as a safety-valve for inconvenient radical energy.

The next *journée révolutionnaire* was March 17th.   Its object was to secure a postponement of the elections for the Constituent Assembly, in order that more time might be allowed for the republicanization of the country districts.   It turned into a sort of field day for Louis Blanc, who made a speech that sent the crowd away satisfied.   The result was the decree of March 26, adjourning the elections to April 23.   This was one of the few demonstrations that resulted in a radical victory, and the public was much impressed. Afterward, however, the radicals complained that the postponement then made was for too short a time really to effect any considerable change in the popular mind.

A month later, the radicals met a decisive defeat that completed the alienation of their sympathies from the govern-

---

[1] *Vide* L. Blanc, *op. cit.*, vol. i, pp. 134 *et seq.*

ment. The real purpose of the manifestation on April 16th remains obscure; whether or not the great procession that bore banners calling for the " abolition of the exploitation of man by man " intended to overturn the government is not clear.[1] The facts seem to be that there undoubtedly was something serious in the air, though it is hard to trace the responsibility to anyone, as all the leaders made haste to exculpate themselves after the fiasco.   It is certain that for some time prior to the 16th, Ledru-Rollin was being urged by radicals to consent to a *coup d'état* by them, and to allow his name to figure in the composition of a new Provisional Government, that Flocon and others were urging him not to, that he was in sore doubt and perplexity, and that it was not until the morning of the 16th that he went to Lamartine and frankly announced his intention to stand with the government.   Whatever revolutionary purposes the gathering might have had were frustrated by the national guard, which occupied all the square before the demonstrators appeared at the Hôtel de Ville, and only permitted them to pass in small groups through narrow lanes in the ranks.   Thus the effect of the manifestation was totally destroyed and it broke up without accomplishing anything.   The sight of the Place de l'Hôtel de Ville full of bayonets and the angry cries of " *À bas les communistes* " from the troops, together with the very cool reception of their delegates by the government, strengthened their growing conviction that the republic of February was to be in no sense the *République démocratique et sociale* of their dreams.   It is easy to believe Lamartine, furthermore, when he says that from this time on, the in-

[1] For divergent explanations, *vide* L. Blanc, *op. cit.*, vol. ii, ch. 16, Lamartine, *Hist. de la révol. de 1848*, vol. i, bk. 13, secs. 14-21, and the conservative historians, Pierre and de la Gorce. But *cf.* the careful study of Suzanne Wasserman (*Les Clubs de Barbès et de Blanqui en 1848*, Paris, 1913), which shows clearly the relatively minor influence of these leaders and their clubs in all the social uprisings of the time.

formal confidence that had ruled within the government itself, yielded to suspicion; the simple friendly atmosphere of their meetings gave way to a strict officialism.

With the election of the *Assemblée Constituante* the term of the Provisional Government came to an end. It had worked hard and done as well as it could under very trying circumstances. Its lack of greater success was partly due, no doubt, to the administrative inexperience of its members, but even more to its lack of a unified political philosophy and program, which merely reflected a similar lack in France at large. No conceivable platform could have been agreed to by the socialist workman in Paris, the capitalist manufacturer and the peasant monarchist. The diversity in their ideals could not but be reflected, though less acutely, in any government which tried to please everybody. If all the members had represented one social class, they might have forced through a strong policy, but it would have been the success of 1793; lacking sufficient unity and energy to be tyrannical, the government tried to be fair to all and satisfied nobody. The solitary idea that held it together was *la république*; when it came to defining the content of that word, chaos entered. It is on the whole surprising that it accomplished as much as it did and finished its term, as Lamartine earnestly desired that it should, with a record unstained by bloodshed.

On the tenth of May, its place was taken by an Executive Commission of five elected by the new Assembly. The choice fell on five members of the old government. Arago headed the list with 725 votes, Garnier-Pagès had 715, Marie 702, Lamartine 643 and Ledru-Rollin 458. The vote shows in part the loss in popularity of the two last named (Lamartine's decline being to some extent due to his insistence that Ledru-Rollin be included in any government); it also shows the relative strength of the parties in the Assembly, to which reference will be made later.

The executive commission was no more successful than
its predecessor in checking the rapidly growing cleavage between bourgeois conservatism and working-class radicalism.
The latter class was growing more and more desperate as it
saw the reins of power slipping completely from its grasp.
It began to feel that the control was getting back into the
same hands from which it had been rescued only three
months before.

Less than a week after the Executive Commission came
into office, the first of its two great tests took place. Poland
was at that time just losing the last fragments of its independence. France had always been interested in Poland and
there were many Poles in Paris who endeavored to get material aid and official recognition. The Assembly made an
interpellation on the subject an order of the day, to be de-
bated May 15. The clubs arranged a demonstration for the
same day. Barbès and Blanqui, the chief club-leaders, dis-
approved of it, but lesser lights, Sobrier, Huber and Raspail,
from various motives, favored it. A petition demanding
French intervention on behalf of Poland was to be brought
to the bar of the Assembly by a procession of the clubs,—
this was the only ordered program; whether some of the
more violent leaders intended to carry out a revolutionary
design under cover of the resulting confusion, is uncertain,
but not improbable. The result of the elections and the
military repression of the election disorders at Rouen had
lately revived the painful memories of April 16th. The
Assembly was already unpopular among the workmen; it
would take very little to make them hostile. The military
guard and its leader, General Courtais, proved unable to
prevent the demonstrators from entering the Assembly.
For three hours, a scene of utter confusion took place, in
which all the popular orators took turns in trying to make
themselves heard above the clamor of the mob. Finally the

more radical betook themselves from the Chamber of Deputies where the Assembly was in session, to the Hôtel de Ville and there constituted a new Provisional Government. Various lists were drawn up, most of which contained the names of Louis Blanc, Albert, Ledru-Rollin, Barbès, Raspail, Pierre Leroux and Thoré.[1] The Assembly, however, retained control of the troops; the new government was not supported by the populace and fell still-born. The result was disastrous for the radicals. Barbès, Albert and Raspail were imprisoned in the dungeons of Vincennes. Blanqui escaped arrest until the 27th, Huber fled to England, Sobrier was seized. The Assembly decided that Louis Blanc (who was a member) had not been seen at the Hôtel de Ville on the 15th, and voted against his prosecution for complicity, by the narrow margin of 369 to 337.

From this time on, the bitterness between the classes became pronounced. The government was openly condemned by the radicals as reactionary, who in turn were called *les factieux* by the conservatives. The Executive Commission satisfied the working-class even less than the provisional government. " Were MM. Arago, Lamartine, Garnier-Pagès, Ledru-Rollin, Marie no longer the same men? Ah, the trouble is that a great change had taken place around them; what had changed was the air they breathed. Once subject to the rule of the Assembly majority, they saw themselves condemned to live in the atmosphere of a bourgeois coterie, while the Provisional Government had lived in the atmosphere of the people." [2] Making allowance for personal pique, this judgment of Louis Blanc is not without foundation.

It was six weeks later that all these *journées révolution-*

---

[1] Pierre, *Hist. de la République de 1848*, p. 296, note.
[2] L. Blanc, *op. cit.*, vol. ii, p. 113.

naires and the mutual hatred they had gradually engendered found final expression in an outburst of such horror that it ranks with 1793 and 1871 in sad pre-eminence.   The final decision to close the national workshops and to distribute their members among the army, the railroads and private factories where possible was to the populace a final, definite surrender of the *droit au travail* even in the attenuated form in which it had been attempted.   The republic had plainly abandoned any thorough-going social reform and had fallen completely into the hands of the bourgeoisie.   Industry had not been able to recover from the economic crisis of the preceding year;[1] constant agitation had prevented the return of confidence and Garnier-Pagès' addition of 45 per cent to the taxes, while it saved the state from bankruptcy, was extremely unpopular;[2] the misery caused by unemployment and inadequate employment was acute.   The members of the national workshops had formerly furnished, under Marie's guidance, a sort of possible counter-army to the delegates of the Luxembourg; now, enraged by their summary dismissal, they made common cause with the latter. The workshops had indeed become a sort of Frankenstein; they had been created, they could no longer be maintained; the question was how they could be peaceably dissolved. The government's solution was a complete failure; it was a dangerous thing to place over 100,000 desperate, hungry

---

[1] The revenue from customs in the first six months of 1847 (a year of crisis) was 65,000,000 francs; for the same period in 1848 it fell to 38,000,000 francs. Using these two periods as a basis of contrast, cotton imports fell from 220,000 metrical quintals to 182,000; wool from 57,000 to 34,000 quintals; raw silk from 3842 to 1662; spun silk from 2824 to 1279; olive oil from 156,000 to 70,000; sugar from 433,000 to 200,000; cast iron from 512,000 to 234,000, etc. (Figures from the *Constitutionnel* of July 26, 1848, quoted in *Niles' Register*, vol. 74, p. 229 *et seq.*)

[2] Especially among the peasants, whose consequent disaffection carried Louis Napoleon into power.

men between serfdom and dismissal. Their absolute refusal to accept the plan made the June insurrection a matter of hours.

Those three frightful days of street-fighting, in which the whole eastern section of Paris was involved from the 23rd to the 25th of June, without obvious leadership yet with evidences of careful preparation, had several results of the first magnitude. In the first place, it compelled the resignation of the Executive Commission, as inadequate to the situation, replacing it with the one-man government of General Cavaignac, which lasted (Paris being officially in a state of siege for a major part of the time) until the inauguration of the newly elected president, Louis Napoleon Bonaparte, on December 20, 1848. Cavaignac's authority sprang from the Assembly, by which he was chosen as president of the council of ministers and chief of the executive power. In the second place, the brotherhood in arms of all who stood for *l'ordre*, the popular catchword of the time, minimized the importance of all previous political distinctions between legitimist, Orleanist and moderate republican in comparison with the sharp line henceforth drawn between conservative and radical. This definite adhesion of the republican government to the side of conservatism and the stamp of social approval consequently placed on it by the west half of Paris are facts of prime importance for our study. In the third place, the ten thousand dead bodies of June formed an impassable barrier between conservative and radical. The June insurrection is the dividing line between the two phases of the Second Republic, the phase of harmony and the phase of hatred. Although, as we have seen, the harmony began to be disturbed more and more from the very first days, yet it was in theory *le peuple* which had triumphed and was ruling, and any mistakes on the part of the authorities (from the radical point of view) were mistakes of the head and not of the heart; there was always hope that the true light would be more clearly seen next time. In May, this idea became seriously suspect; after June it became definitely impossible. The bloody fighting and the stern reprisals mark a change, not only in French politics, but in the history of economic radicalism. Before, socialism had been Utopian in one form or another; its key-note was brotherhood expressed in coöperation. From now on, socialism becomes Marxian; its motto, class-consciousness embodying itself in the class-struggle. Besides these far reaching results, a special consequence important for us is the control of the Assembly by a terror-stricken spirit of reaction. Measures of repression were taken by Cavaignac with its approval, whose application lasted from the end of June to the end of August. Twelve to fifteen thousand arrests were made; half of the prisoners were released without judgment, most of the rest were transported to Algeria en bloc. A decree of July 3rd closed the national workshops. Louis Blanc went into exile; Ledru-Rollin was isolated on the extreme left of the Assembly. Those legions of the national guard which had not fought against the revolt were disbanded; the bourgeoisie thus acquired complete control of the armed forces. The best-known clubs were closed; the rest remained under police surveillance, must be public, open at certain hours only, free, the subjects of discussion limited, petitions were forbidden; henceforth the clubs lost all influence. Many newspapers were suppressed; the bond for the rest was fixed at 24,000 francs for Paris, 6000 and 3600 for the provinces, thus rendering cheap, popular organs impossible; attacks on property or the family, were forbidden. Thus of all the new freedom of '48, only the republic and universal suffrage remained, and these were not unmenaced.[1]

[1] A clear summary of this repressive legislation may be found in Seignobos, *op. cit.*, in *Revue des cours*, vol. I, pp. 801-4, 810.

Our aim in recounting this preliminary history has been to show the gradual cleavage in the French body politic between the radical and conservative groups, a knowledge of which is indispensable to a correct understanding of the Constituent Assembly. Without such knowledge, one might conceive the Assembly as working in that atmosphere of idealism and fraternity, which remains for us, as indeed it was originally, the spirit of 1848. No error could be more capital; between February and June, a gulf lies. In feeling they are decades, not months, apart.

In sketching the character and composition of the Assembly, we must go back to April, when the electoral campaign was in full swing. In that campaign several of the electoral addresses, issued by candidates, already introduce the thought that American example ought to be considered. Thus we have the circular of Charles de Montalembert, the Catholic, whose progressive sentiments had involved him with Lacordaire and Lamennais in the pre-Modernist failure of *L'Avenir*. The circular, dated April 3, contains this passage: " If this republic, in improving the lot of the workers, guarantees, like that of the United States, to religion, to property, and to the family their supreme benefits, it will have no partisan more sincere, no son more devoted than I. If, on the contrary, it follows the steps of its predecessor, if it proceeds by way of exclusion, of suspicion, of persecution; if it does not recoil from violence and confiscation, then it may well have me as adversary or as victim, but never at least as instrument or as accomplice." [1]

Lucien Murat's address declared: " Banished by the enemies of France, I bring you from the United States twenty-two years of experience and of republican opinions." [2]   Ambert wrote from Nantes to the electors of

---

[1] *Vide L'Univers*, April 6, 1848.

[2] Garnier-Pagès, *op. cit.*, vol. 2, p. 312.

Lot: " I visited the republicans of the United States. A conscientious study of democratic organization taught me that true liberty was the daughter of order. It is then order which must be established, in order to arrive at liberty, at equality, at fraternity." He speaks of himself as " ready to protect property, the family, the Church, quite as much as the workshop, the house of the rich quite as much as the cottage of the poor." [1]

E. Pacini, a naval officer, thus addressed the electors of the Seine : " Commanding a steam frigate in the transatlantic service, I have had commercial as well as maritime interests in my hands, and I have been able to observe in the United States the happy results of a government truly democratic and liberal. As for my principles, behold them : Liberty for all ! I will, therefore, combat every retrograde tendency, but I will likewise struggle against violence with the energy which I have had to employ against ocean tempests." [2]

Blanchet, advocate at the court of appeals, wrote to the electors of the Seine : " Soon after, my republican instincts led me to America, where I devoted nearly two years to the study of the different democratic constitutions of the New World, the observation of their governmental mechanism and the drawing up of a body of legislation for the Haytian republic." [3]

Eugène Guillemot of Pont-Saint-Maxence, first deputy-mayor of the first Paris *arrondissement* and an editor of the *Réforme*, gave this account of himself to the electors of the Oise :

I was quite young when the July Revolution broke out ,yet already full of love for the democratic principle, full of grief

[1] *Dictionnaire des parlementaires français, s. v.* "Ambert."
[2] *Murailles révolutionnaires*, vol. I, p. 441.
[3] *Ibid.*, vol. 2, p. 19.

at seeing it trampled under foot by royalty, I went to America to study republican institutions. There I remained three years, occupied with the study of the political and economic problems solved by the sagacity of the citizens of the United States. I returned, thinking only of making my country profit by these studies. The spectacle of the complete well being I had found everywhere, in the cities as in the newly cleared fields, had impressed me. Convinced already of the greatness and beauty of the democratic principle, I saw and touched in a certain sense its *useful* side. . . . Profiting by what my travels and my experience have taught me, I would oppose a centime's leaving the coffers of the republic for unproductive works. In the *Réforme* for Sept. 18th and 23rd last, I reminded the government that for a sum much less than that used by it in scientific labors [*travaux d'art*] on the railroads, the United States had covered their vast territory with rails.[1]

M. Maillefer, writing March 18 to the electors of Seine-et-Oise, announced: "For thirty years I have served the cause which has just triumphed. In France, in both Americas, [where he wrote for the New Orleans *Abeille*], in Ireland, in Italy, in Spain and in Portugal, I have written, fought and suffered for the rights, whose full possession you have at last acquired. . . . For me, the republic has nothing new, nothing terrifying or intoxicating, even in practice, for I have taken part in these virile exercises in the country of Washington and of Bolivar; travels and experience have doubled in me the results of study and meditation."[2]

A bit of the old February spirit of cosmopolitan fraternity flares up in the radical newspaper, *La Commune de Paris*, which is quoted with approval by *Le Démocrate* of April 19, 1848: "Not only should Lamennais, Cabet, P. Leroux,

[1] *Murailles révolutionnaires*, vol. 2, p. 89 *et seq.*

[2] *Ibid.*, vol. 2, p. 422.

Proudhon, Considérant, Louis Blanc form part of the national representation but Robert Owen, Emerson and various other foreigners, if it were possible, ought to figure in that council."

The election took place on Easter Sunday, April 23rd and on the 24th. The polls were established at the chief towns of the cantons. In the country districts, in many cases the whole male population of the commune attended early Mass, and then marched in a body to the voting-place, the curé and the maire at the head. Such splendid discipline had its roots too deep to be shaken by a few carpet-bagger commissaries from Paris, eminent neither for ability nor character. Ledru-Rollin's educational propaganda failed, partly because the time was too short (it might well have taken years!), but also because it was not well carried out. Another of his pet ideas produced a more successful result. The election of 1848 was the first real application of the principle of universal suffrage. It had been provided for in the abortive Constitution of 1793, but this was its first practical test. The vote was enormous; of 9,636,000 enrolled on the registers, 7,893,000 or 82 per cent voted. Except at Rouen and Limoges, where regrettable disorders occurred, the two days passed off quietly, without disturbance.

The victory went to the moderate republicans, the men who dominated the Provisional Government and the Executive Commission. Of the 900 new members of the Assembly,[1] the majority were bourgeois, principally lawyers and landlords. The vote was taken by *scrutin de liste, i. e.,* each elector voted for the total number of representatives to which his department was entitled according to its population (1 to every 40,000), and there was neither residence qualification for the candidate nor limit to the number of

[1] There were really 885, though 900 is the number usually given. See complete list of names in Lamartine, *op. cit.,* vol. 2, p. 230 *et seq.*

departments from which he might be chosen. As there were no strict party organization or party nominations in the modern sense (a candidate's name being suggested either by a group of political friends, a newspaper or even by himself), it is very hard to form an exact idea of the result. Almost every estimate differs in its classification. Of contemporary historians, for example, we find Odilon Barrot saying: "They [the radical republicans] represented at most a quarter of the Assembly; the legitimist party, about the same number; the rest were divided between moderate republicans and former constitutional liberals. There was the true force of the Assembly; to these last especially belonged the principal influence, by reason of their experience in assemblies and of their already established political notoriety. One may judge of this by the fact that of the *nineteen* presidents elected for the first time in the bureaux, *seventeen* were former members of parliament. Although beaten, they were naturally called to direct or at least to moderate this revolution." [1] As an ex-Orleanist (under the late régime he had been a leader of the liberal opposition), Barrot might be expected to over-emphasize the influence of his party in the new Assembly. But we find Louis Blanc asserting that " there was something not very reassuring in the fact that out of 900 members, the legitimist party claimed 150, and the Orleanist party 300." [2]

Without presuming to give figures, the *Vraie République,* Thoré's radical newspaper, indicates its bitter disappointment in these terms:

Since one can guess the composition of the Constituante, we have the right and the duty to say that *the Republic is compromised!*

[1] Barrot, *Mémoires posthumes*, vol. 2, p. 166.

[2] L. Blanc, *Histoire de la révolution de 1848*, vol. 2, p. 67.

Today, the party which seems to triumph is that which often made a coalition under Louis Philippe, and which reached a cordial understanding toward the end of the monarchy. That bourgeois coalition commenced on the outskirts of the conservatives, of whom several even passed to the ranks of the opposition and became almost its chiefs; examples, MM. Duvergier de Hauranne, Lamartine and some others. It included all the ambitious or disappointed *dynastiques,* aiming for power, or even having concurred in all the tyrannies of the court; examples, MM. Thiers, de Malleville and others, of the left center. It was allied with the left of Barrot, Crémieux, Bethmont and the radical left of [1] Carnot, Marie and Garnier-Pagès, who contented themselves for the moment with the Constitutional Charter. It fraternized with the *National* and all together wanted to organize the *parliamentary system,* that is, the rule of the bourgeois class. Their common enemy was not so much the institution of monarchy, as the *personal system.* The dynasty removed, one and all, with only a few differences in affections and regrets, will persist in what was the profound conviction of their whole lives, the government of the *country* by the privileged, and for the profit of the privileged.

It means little that the name of the political form is changed and that the Bourbon personalities are replaced by lawyers or bourgeois. The foundation of society will be the same. The lot of the *laboring classes* will be improved. There will be much talk of the sovereignty of the people. But the rich, the capitalists, the skilful, will remain the sovereigns in fact, and Equality will be stricken from the flag as in 1830. Citizens of the social and popular republic, do you think that the candidates of the *Siècle,* the *Constitutionnel* and the *National* united, who are going to represent Paris in the National Assembly, do you think that citizens Lasteyrie, Bethmont, Vavin,

---

[1] These designations apply, of course, to the parties under the July monarchy. The radical deputies of that time were the conservatives of the republic.

Cormenin, Wolowski, Berger, Peupin, Corbon, Smith, Garnon, Coquerel and others, represent the young French Republic? [1]

Later writers confirm the impression gained from Thoré's editorial, so far as the popular disappointment at a moderate republican victory is concerned, but also fail to agree on details. De la Gorce says that the legitimists won 130 seats, that all the ex-monarchists together amounted to about a fourth of the total, that the rest were republican, dominated by the moderate wing.[2] Pierre maintains that the legitimists secured 100 seats, and makes no effort at a summary of the rest.[3] Seignobos declares that the moderate republicans were the best represented, having elected all their notables and gained more than 300 seats; about 100 belonged to the party of the *Réforme*; the rest were legitimists or former partisans of the *gauche dynastique* (the O. Barrot group); there were no Orleanists, even Thiers lost (though subsequently chosen at a by-election).[4] Berton gives the legitimists not more than 150. As for the strict Orleanists, he says that they, like the legitimists, were not numerous; they were, however, according to this writer, closely united, and succeeded in electing the ablest of their party, who were determined to regain the leading position. The greatest part of the Assembly called themselves republican (he includes O. Barrot, Duvergier de Hauranne and others in this group rather than among the Orleanists). The pure democrats of the Mountain had only about 100 representatives.[5]

Renard's estimate of the situation is probably as near as

---

[1] *Vraie république*, April 29, 1848.

[2] P. de la Gorce, *Hist. de la seconde répub. française*, vol. 1, p. 214.

[3] V. Pierre, *Hist. de la république de 1848*, vol. 1, p. 239.

[4] Seignobos, *op. cit., Revue des cours*, vol. 1, pp. 749-752.

[5] *Annales de l'école libre des sciences politiques*, Nov. 1897. H. Berton, " La Constitution de 1848," pp. 683 *et seq.*

we can get to the facts: "Lamartine, head of the poll at Paris, was named ten times, and the republicans of his nuance seemed the most numerous, so far as one could discover in the very confused results, as happens when the vote has been cast on men rather than on measures. But the legitimists were numerous (130 to 150), the Orleanists of the dynastic opposition were returned en masse; two Bonapartes were sent by Corsica; the Catholics had Montalembert, Lacordaire, de Falloux, several bishops, without counting hostages in all the parties; the radicals, except in two or three cities, were beaten; the socialists crushed." [1]

The astonishing divergence in the estimates of the number of Orleanists returned is due to the fact that the number of irreconcilables was very small; the great majority accepted the republic nominally, while inwardly preferring a constitutional monarchy; some tried to pave the way for a return of the Comte de Paris; the greater number set to work through alliance with the moderate republicans, to give the republic a content in harmony with their ideas. Thus it becomes difficult to distinguish Orleanists from moderate republicans; the former were to be recognized chiefly by a heightened conservatism. The different estimates appear to arise from the circumstance that some historians reckon only professed Orleanists of the unreconstructed type while others include all who had accepted the July Monarchy when it was in power, no matter what they called themselves in the new régime.

The first reference to the United States after the election occurs in a shout of victory from the moderate *Havre Courrier*, on the local election of the list headed by Lamartine over the radicals, headed by one Deschamps. " The cause of order is won. . . . No more of '93; nothing of that

---

[1] G. Renard, *La République de 1848*, p. 40.

hideous epoch. One may, without drenching oneself with blood, pure or impure, be an excellent republican; there are already more than fifty millions of that kind in the United States. Let the French rally to these. In New Zealand and in other savage countries of the world, one finds enough republicans like those of citizen Ledru-Rollin and his companions." [1]

Before leaving the elections, it is impossible to resist quoting from Lamartine's account of his own triumph. Lamartine did in fact quite overshadow every one else by being returned from ten departments. This moves the excellent poet to the following comment. As is his custom, he refers to himself in the third person. " If he had said a word, insinuated a desire, made a sign, he would have been named in eighty departments; his popularity was boundless at Paris, in France, in Germany, in Italy, in America. For Germany his name was peace; for France it was the guarantee against the Terror; for Italy it was hope; for America it was the republic. He had really at this moment the sovereignty of the European conscience. He could not take a step in the street without arousing acclamations. They followed him to his house and interrupted his sleep," etc. [2]

Just two weeks after the vote was counted, Lamartine came out a bad fourth in the election of the Executive Commission.

The first meeting of the new Assembly witnessed a momentary revival of the February spirit, a wave of emotional enthusiasm for the republic and for the principles of equality and fraternity. The members of the retiring Provisional Government marched arm in arm through the thronged and decorated streets; there was cheering, drum-beating, trum-

[1] *Havre Courrier*, Apr. 27, 1848.
[2] Lamartine, *Hist. de la révol. de 1848*, vol. 2, p. 229.

pets and cannon; then when the Assembly had come to order
in the huge temporary structure erected in the court of the
Chamber of Deputies to seat the great number of delegates,
it must needs adjourn to show itself on the peristyle to the
people in the streets below. Nor was this enough; intoxicated by the enthusiasm of the moment, the deputies rushed
down to " fraternize " with the populace, and all spectators
were greatly edified at the view of Lacordaire, the monk-
deputy, in his Dominican black and white robe, clasping
hands through the grille with blouse-clad workingmen.[1]

The moderates were of course full of confident expectation in the Assembly's success. The radicals differed. A
few were temporarily swept away by the current of popular
enthusiasm, but not for long. One of the most extreme
newspapers describes the occasion in the following terms:

Good people, I saw you day before yesterday, and on the faith
of Père Duchêne, I, too, nearly forgot myself to the point of
breaking out in frenzied exclamations. Yes, your intoxication won me; I already felt my heart beat with violence
and my eyes wet with tears. . . . Enthusiasm is almost always
dangerous. It has caused us to fail in all our revolutions. With
enthusiasm one converts a republic into a monarchy as easily
as a monarchy into a republic. . . . What is the new Chamber?
An assemblage of heterogeneous elements, a mosaic whose
badly assorted colors, whose thousand pieces, disposed as by
the hand of chance, shock the eye and fatigue the spirit, a
chaos where the shadows absorb the light until the hand of
the people comes to disentangle it. That is the National
Assembly. I ask you, can a fine, regular constitution proceed from its midst? Will great and generous ideas germinate

---

[1] *Vide* Garnier-Pagès, *Hist. de la rév. de 1848*, vol. 2, p. 360 *et seq.;*
also interesting selections from a contemporary diary of the provisional
minister of education published under the title of *Mémorial d'Hippolyte Carnot*, as vol. viii of the *Bibliothèque de la Soc. d'histoire de la
révolution de 1848*.

in the heart of a majority fashioned according to the royalty of Orleans? What difference do you find between the National Assembly of today and the Chamber of Deputies of former times? None. There are the same usages, the same habits, the same dispositions, and, *mille diables!* there is still the same language. How many imbeciles, among these canton-representatives who cannot articulate clearly the word *citizen!* Be assured, ex-deputies, you will have to pronounce and to hear words which will seem to you much harder than that. Great struggles are about to begin, burning dicussions are about to take place between the last defenders of tyranny and the young tribunes of the Republic. What will be the final word?[1] You will know before a month.[2]

Victor Considérant's paper, *La Démocratie pacifique*, was willing to give the Assembly a fair trial. " Let us hope to-day that the National Assembly has accepted the Republic with enthusiastic unanimity; we are through with the reservations of certain papers, which were pleased to sow irritation between the various classes of citizens; let us hope too that the Assembly will justify by its frankly democratic attitude the confidence which the people has placed in it since its first acts, and that it will repair by prompt and energetic measures the time unfortunately lost in half-measures by the Provisional Government." [3]

The majority of the radicals, however, were hostile from the start. Thus we have an editorial by Proudhon in the *Représentant du peuple*, which shows a keen comprehension of the spirit of '48. It begins in this wise: " The National Assembly has formed itself to the sound of the cannon, the drum, fanfares, surrounded by all the pomp of war. In

---

[1] The text reads *mois*, apparently a misprint for *mot*.

[2] *Père Duchêne*, May 7. The last sentence has a sinister sound, in view of May 15 and June 23, and raises the unanswered question of how far ahead these movements were planned and organized.

[3] *Démocratie pacifique*, May 5.

these days when the imagination is seduced by the senses, the heart drawn on by the imagination, reason absorbed by sentiment, when the mind thinks itself infinite because it is empty, the soul has no more attraction except for the unfolding of sensibility, for the illusions of hope. Reflection seems to have lost its rights, judgment to have laid down its authority. It is the work of Lamourette kisses, it is the moment of perfidious reconciliations. But soon enthusiasm wanes; sentiment vanishes like a caress; in place of congenial ideas, reason returns to put its redoubtable questions." [1]

The *Réforme*, somewhat later, says that nothing vital is being accomplished, " because the chamber elected is not a serious assembly; because it does not comprehend the severe duties of this time; because, in talent and in vigor, it is inferior to the chambers of the monarchy; because it is wasting its hours (last hours of hope!) in personal debates, in useless colloquies, in frivolous prayers." [2]

Thoré's *Vraie république* in its bitterness, throws an interesting light on the question already referred to, as to who are to be classed as Orleanists.

Do you believe in conversions? The whole National Assembly has cried together: *Vive la République!* We watched carefully the hands which have for so long weighed down upon us; all were raised today for the Republic. Here the Dominican Lacordaire and Monseigneur the Bishop of Langres; there M. the Marquis de La Rochejacquelein and M. Berryer; then M. de Hauranne, M. de Lasteyrie, M. de Rémusat, M. de Malleville, M. Barrot, M. Dupin and all the friends of all the odious régimes which have crushed France since the end of the eighteenth century. All cried: *Vive la République.* Not a single man was met who had sufficient conscience to declare

[1] *Représentant du peuple*, May 5.
[2] *Réforme*, May 21.

that he was not and that he never had been a republican. . . .
An assembly is like a man. One may judge it at first sight
by its physiognomy. The social and popular republic, the
republic of equality and justice, how many adorers does it
count in that reunion of bourgeois who considered it yesterday
a crime or a folly? On leaving the hall, real republicans
thought perhaps of that fine scene in Hamlet: Words, words,
words.[1]

One of the principal ex-Orleanists referred to, admits the
justice of Thoré's stricture. " In all political bodies there
is a certain dissimulation, which is not hypocrisy nor false-
ness, but a concession forced by this or that circumstance of
the moment. Thus to judge from the outside demonstrations of the new assembly one would have thought that it
was entirely composed of profoundly convinced republicans,
which was far from being the reality: the great majority
felt, it is true, the necessity of rallying to the republic and
lending itself with a good grace to the experiment which was
about to be made; but for a large number, this was only a
concession made to circumstances, a pure marriage of reason, as one spoke of it at the time." [2]

The legitimists were little friendlier than the radicals.
"Those who regularly attend the debates of the Assembly,
have already the conviction that a constitution cannot come
out of this Assembly and that it conceals nothing but storms.
Nothing has come out of it but disputes, in place of discussion, and questions of personalities in place of questions
of principles." [3]

To complete the picture of the first meeting of the Assembly, we have the impressions of two outsiders. One
was an American. " Even in modern maiden parliamentary

[1] *Vraie république*, May 5.
[2] O. Barrot, *Mémoires posthumes*, vol. 2, p. 166 *et seq.*
[3] *Gazette de France*, May 10.

meetings, be it by accident or design, some place consecrated by the occasion will be visited in time to come; but the great, or *monstre* temporary shed in which the National Assembly of France first met, with its pasteboard figures without and its pasteboard presidential canopy within, its endless tri-colored flags in *faisceaux*, and its scenic decorations, par-taking partly of the circus, and partly of the *Bal Morel*, will disappear like a mimic stage scene, carrying with it no unapt commentary on the no less fragile performance beneath its roof." [1]

We have also the remarkable letters of Mme. d'Agoult, who wrote under the pseudonym of Daniel Stern. Her *History of the Revolution of 1848* is one of the best accounts of the early period from the moderate republican angle. " Let us enter the National Assembly together, if you please. Our first impression will be one of surprise. Bald heads, gray hairs, bent backs, heavy steps, broken voices, that is what one sees and hears, when one plunges, from the height of the tribune, into the gathering of the first choices of revolutionary France. Let us say it politely, the National Assembly is of a *certain age*. . . . Everybody agrees to-day, if the National Assembly has a defect, it is assuredly not excess of revolutionary ardor. . . . The great breath of February has not penetrated that enclosure." [2]

The Assembly contained 99 lawyers, 51 commissioners and sub-commissioners of the government, 47 magistrates (including former judges and those still on the bench), 25 physicians, 21 workmen, 16 priests (including three bish-ops and a Protestant minister), 16 generals of brigade and division (including two admirals), 18 cultivators, 21 pub-licists and editors, 11 present or former notaries, 6 members

---

[1] J. F. Corkran, *History of the National Constituent Assembly*, p. 14.

[2] Daniel Stern, *Lettres républicaines*, " Lettre ii: Physionomie de l'Assemblée Nationale. À Fanny Lewald, June 4, 1848."

of the Institute, 4 dramatic authors, 4 colonels, 3 sons and nephews of an emperor and of kings, 1 pharmacist, 1 innkeeper, 1 confectioner, 1 chief of an institution, 1 baker, 1 street-porter.[1]

One may fairly distinguish four main parties in the Assembly, the moderate republicans, the radical republicans, the socialists and the legitimists. The moderate republicans should again be divided into what were called at the time *républicains de la veille* (republicans of the eve) and *républicains du lendemain* (republicans of the morrow), or as we should say, original republicans and converts. The line between them is very obscure, but the existence of the two elements is highly important for our study.

The former element was the majority party in the Assembly, as it had been in the government from the start. Lamartine,[2] Marrast, Garnier-Pagès and the other heads of the provisional régime were its parliamentary leaders; Cavaignac soon became its executive representative. *Le National* was its official organ. This party represented the capitalist bourgeois class of liberal political opinions. It wanted a republican form of government as a greater safeguard of the reforms won in 1789 and not well maintained under subsequent governments. It desired freedom of speech, press and person, a wide extension of the suffrage,

---

[1] This curious and somewhat miscellaneous list is taken from *La Vraie république* for May 16, 1848, which also prints the names of the deputies practising the professions enumerated. It is obviously extremely incomplete.

[2] While acting with this group politically in 1848, Lamartine had previously been an independent, affiliating with no party during the Orleanist régime, willing to support any government whose spirit was democratic. " It will appear that in Lamartine's view, the question as to form of government was rather one of circumstances than of principles. . . . While his conscience forbade him to excite a revolution, yet should circumstances produce one, he would gladly accept it." Lamartine, *Hist. of the revol. of 1848*, bk. i, p. 46.

the abolition of parliamentary corruption. Lamartine and, to a somewhat less extent, his political friends, had all the virtues and vices of the Girondins whom they admired so much.

The *républicains du lendemain* were ex-monarchists; some had been followers of Charles X and then of the Duc de Bordeaux, more had been adherents of Louis Philippe. In general, the legitimist cause had deeper roots in sentiment and tradition than the Orleanist, and its supporters were more stubbornly loyal in the hour of defeat. There were some legitimists, indeed, who rallied to the republic (not of course as an ultimate form of government, but as a temporary *modus vivendi*) with savage satisfaction at the downfall of the usurper's throne; better a republic than a false royalty, they declared. In certain legitimist journals appeared a deadly parallel, illustrating the remarkable coincidence in the external episodes of the revolutions of 1830 and 1848 as an instance of divine retribution upon the traitorous Duke of Orleans. But the majority preferred not to compromise their pure devotion to their king merely to gratify their spite. The Orleanists, on the other hand, being attached to their dynasty by a past of eighteen years instead of one of thirteen centuries, had fewer misgivings about leaving the ship when it was manifestly sinking. It was they, therefore, who formed the bulk of the *républicains du lendemain*, some no doubt with the secret purpose of working for the return of the constitutional monarchy, others content with any form of government, provided its substance guaranteed the safety of their economic interests. Like the *républicains de la veille*, they too represented the capitalist bourgeois class, but rather that portion which held conservative political opinions. Barrot was their most distinguished representative in the Assembly, until Thiers later joined him. *Le Constitutionnel* was the faithful journalistic exponent of this type of mind. Its emphasis was on a strong executive, whereas the other wing of moderate republicans would prefer to see the power in the hands of the legislative. Being essentially cautious, however, it sought for the preservation of peace and property in a system of checks and balances.

The radical republicans were rather a group apart. They had for their political masters, not the Girondins, but the Jacobins. Ledru-Rollin and Flocon stand as typical of this party: *La Réforme* should be read to secure their political point of view. A concise statement of their platform is to be found in one of Ledru-Rollin's circulars to his commissaries, with reference to the approaching elections. After exalting the French republican trinity, liberty, equality, fraternity, he continued, " From them are deducible: the abolition of every privilege, the division of taxes according to fortune [income-tax], a proportional and progressive inheritance-tax, a freely elected judiciary and the most complete development of the jury system, military service weighing equally upon all, the instrument of labor assured to all, the democratic reconstitution of industry and of credit, voluntary association everywhere substituted for the disorganized impulses of egoism." [1]   Despite the slightly socialistic sound of a few of these phrases, which are to be attributed to the atmosphere of the times and the desire to catch the proletarian vote, the radical republicans were in no sense socialists. They were made up of the small shopkeeper class, who in their reverence for property and the wage-system, were as firmly bourgeois as the large capitalists. They already had their feet on the lower rounds of the ladder of fortune and had no wish to overturn the ladder and construct a new one, but merely to be assisted to mount

[1] *Représentant du peuple*, April 8.

more quickly. They believed in the " democratic," but not in the " social " republic, in Robespierre, but not in Babeuf.[1]

The socialists, then as always, but perhaps even more then than now, were united only in dissent. Louis Blanc, Proudhon, Cabet, Leroux were among their chief leaders; no two of them could agree on a constructive system. Blanc's system of coöperative workshops was as different from Proudhon's anarchism as Cabet's community on the banks of the Mississippi was from either. No newspaper could rank as " the " socialist organ par excellence; most were purely personal; Cabet spoke through *Le Populaire* as individually as Proudhon through *Le Représentant du peuple*. The bulk of the socialist strength lay in the workingmen of Paris; the proletariat of other large industrial cities contributed, though less ardently.

Finally came the legitimists, of whom we have already spoken. Berryer and La Rochejacquelein were two of their most conspicuous leaders in the Assembly; *La Gazette de France*, strongly Catholic and royalist, was their chief journal. They found the officers of their army in the Faubourg St. Germain, the privates in the peasantry of France.

A few deputies like Barbès, a few newspapers like *Le Père Duchêne*, represented the clubs of Paris; lacking a definite program, they sympathized more with the socialists than with any other party, but were more at home in street-demonstrations for the purpose of upsetting abuses than in constructive administration.

A few others, like Lacordaire and Montalembert, represented the Roman Catholic Church, and were willing to forward its interests by republicanism or monarchism as

---

[1] Strictly speaking, this party, too, should be ranked among the *ré-publicains de la veille*, having as good a right to the title as their more moderate brethren.

might seem most convenient. *L'Ère Nouvelle*, Lacordaire's paper, was the standard-bearer of these *dévots*.

The strong parties were, however, those sketched above, of whom the legitimists may be called the right, the *républicains du lendemain* the right center, the moderate *républicains de la veille* the left center, the radical republicans the left and the socialists the extreme left. These parties were rather common tendencies of political thought than organizations as we understand party organizations. Such common action as they had was usually for some temporary purpose.

There were, however, certain " groups " of a more or less permanent character into which the Assembly presently divided itself. These groups were named from the location of their meeting-places and were each composed of men of similar political beliefs. The leading ones were five in number: (a) the *Réunion du Palais National*, the coterie of moderate *républicains de la veille*, with more than 300 members; (b) the *Groupe de la rue de Poitiers*, mostly legitimists and Catholics, joined after June by the old dynastic opposition, the Barrot and Thiers ex-Orleanists, who made up the core of the *républicains du lendemain*; (c) the *Réunion de la rue de Castiglione* and (d) the *Réunion de la rue des Pyramides*, both composed of deputies of the left; (e) the *Réunion de l'Institut*, made up of the members of the Executive Commission and a few of their friends, who seceded from the *Réunion du Palais National* after June, the larger body supporting Cavaignac. The latter was of course the most powerful group.[1]

Even these groups were not in the least political party machines, but rather rallying points for common counsel

[1] For a summary of the various combinations attempted by these groups, see Seignobos, *op. cit.*, *Revue des cours*, 1907-08, vol. I, pp. 804-806.

outside the walls of the Assembly. There was, no doubt, some effort at common action as well, but not of a highly organized character.

Such was the party-system in the new Assembly. It should be added that before getting down to work, the Assembly divided itself into fifteen permanent committees of sixty members each for the study of such bills as might appropriately be referred to them; special commissions of reference might also be appointed. The Assembly was also divided by lot into fifteen bureaux, the personnel of which was changed monthly. The bureaux were simply so many subdivisions of the Assembly to which every important bill must be referred for discussion, before being voted on in the Assembly as a whole; a vote was taken in each bureau, (though this was not binding on the Assembly) and a reporter chosen to express the views of the bureau to the Assembly. This was merely a device for expediting the consideration of a measure and giving everybody a chance to express himself withont delaying all other business till each in turn had had the ear of the whole Assembly, a manifest impossibility in so large a body. Every report must be distributed twenty-four hours before discussion. Amendments must be voted on before the principal question, the articles then voted separately, finally the bill as a whole. The vote was taken by rising or by a public division (on demand of twenty members), or *par appel nominal à la tribune et au scrutin secret*, each member depositing his secret ballot before the presiding officers, (on demand of forty). Five hundred were necessary for a quorum. Every motion was submitted to a preliminary vote of *prise en considération*; if the subject was deemed worthy of discussion, such could not take place until five days after. Every amendment presented during the discussion was sent to the committee in charge of the bill, on demand of its reporter. Matters could always be expedited by a vote of *urgence*, which required only a simple majority. Each committee must make a weekly report of petitions addressed to it. The president had the right to requisition an armed force to guard the Assembly. All recommendations and requests relative to private interests were forbidden to representatives.

Such were the Assembly's chief working-rules, adopted May 20.[1] The presiding officer was one of the members, elected monthly. Buchez was chosen May 5, Sénard June 5, A. Marrast held the post by continued re-election, July 19, 1848-May 26, 1849. Finally, a few words must be said on the chronology of the constitution. The first step was the election of a *commission de constitution* of eighteen members, which was done on May 17 and 18. On the first ballot, Cormenin received 657 votes, Marrast 646, Lamennais 552, Vivien 517, Tocqueville 490, Dufaure 395 and were declared elected, none of the numerous other candidates having an absolute majority (393, there being 784 present).[2] The next day on the second ballot, 374 being necessary to a choice, Martin (de Strasbourg) received 550 votes, Woirhaye 474, Coquerel 453, Corbon 459, Tourret (de l'Allier) 414, G. de Beaumont 388 and Dupin 388. On the third ballot, with 332 votes necessary to elect, Vaulabelle had 390, O. Barrot 368, Pagès (de l'Ariége) 353, Dornès 352 and V. Considérant 339.[3] Of the personalities of these men, something will be said later.

The history of the formation of the constitution may now be briefly indicated in tabular form:

---

[1] *Vide* F. Hélie, *Les Constitutions de la France*, p. 1113 *et seq.*

[2] *Moniteur*, May 18.

[3] *Ibid.*, May 19. Woirhaye here misspelled Voirhaye.

[1] This first draft was read to the Assembly by Marrast. *Cf. Moniteur*, June 20.

[2] The revised text of the constitution was read by Woirhaye, Marrast being indisposed. The following day, Marrast formally presented the report of the commission's work, but did not read it; it was ordered printed, together with the text of the constitution and furnished the basis for the Assembly debates. *Cf. Moniteur*, Aug. 30 and 31.

[3] Beginning with Sept. 4, the Assembly held two sessions daily, from 11 a.m. to 1 p.m., for the discussion of ordinary legislation, and from 2 to 6 p.m. for the discussion of the constitution. *Vide Moniteur*, Aug. 31.

[4] It was not read as a whole, but printed and distributed to the members at their homes, on the evening of Oct. 31. *Cf. Moniteur,* Oct. 31.

CHAPTER III

WHAT FRANCE THOUGHT ABOUT AMERICA

HAVING considered what France was thinking about herself at the time she started constitution-making, it is now time to find out what France thought about America. That will put us in a position to see why the American constitution appealed very strongly to some Frenchmen and not at all to others.

That the attention of France was early directed toward America in the February days is beyond dispute. The official friendliness of the two governments went rather beyond the merely formal courtesies of diplomatic recognition.

The interchanges begin with an act of the American minister, Richard Rush, so unprecedented in its nature that his official report of it to the Secretary of State betrays no little anxiety. It is addressed to the Hon. James Buchanan, Secretary of State, and dated "Legation of the U. S., Paris, March 4, 1848." After describing the fall of the monarchy and the establishment of the republic, the dispatch continues:

Of a revolution so total and sudden, I am not now to speak. The journals of the world are still teeming with it. Nor can I yet speak of the acts of the new government, except to say that they have been characterized so far by moderation and magnanimity in the midst of triumphs of a nature to have intoxicated minds less pure and firm than happily are believed to be possessed by its leading members.

I press to what, foremost of all at present, I am bound to report to you—namely, the part which, as representing the

United States, I have taken under the new duties that encompassed me.

On Saturday, the 26th, I received an intimation, earnestly given, that my personal presence at the Hotel de Ville, to cheer and felicitate the provisional government, would be acceptable. The information was not officially sent, but I believed it to be true.

I asked a short interval for reflection.

Before the day was out, I imparted my determination to take the step. Monday morning, the 28th, was the time appointed for it; and accordingly I repaired to the Hotel de Ville, the Secretary of the Legation accompanying me. To the provisional government there assembled, I delivered the address, a copy of which is enclosed.

It was cordially received, and M. Arago, on the part of the members, replied to it.

He remarked that they heard without surprise, but with lively pleasure what I said; France expected it from an ally to whom she now drew so close by the proclamation of the Republic. He thanked me, in the name of the Provisional Government, for the wishes I expressed for the greatness and prosperity of France; and in alluding to the words it had called up from General Washington's address in 1796 on receiving the French colors, he expressed a confidence that they would be not merely a desire, but a reality. M. Dupont (de l'Eure) as President of the Provisional Government, then advanced, and, taking me by the hand, said, " The French people grasps that of the American nation." Here the ceremony ended. In coming away, three of the members of the Government conducted us out of the building; the guard presented arms, and cries went up of " *Vive la République des Etats Unis!* " Major Poussin, a French officer, who accompanied General Bernard to the United States, and who, from his attachment to our country, was naturalized there, also attended me.

On Sunday, the 27th, I received the note of that day's date from M. Lamartine, as Provisional Minister of Foreign

Affairs, which announced to me, in official form, the existence of the new government. I answered it on Monday. Copies of the note and answer are enclosed.

The Provisional Government published my answer the morning after its reception. My address of Monday has also appeared in the newspapers—not, however, in its exact form.[1] I had written it out, to guard against inaccuracies on an occasion so grave, and left the paper in the hands of the Provisional Government; a transcript of which you now have.

This succinct narrative will accurately apprize the President of what I have done. I shall anxiously await his judgment upon it all. The events were as new as momentous. They had transcended all expectation. In recognizing the new state of things, as far as I could without your instructions, and in doing it promptly and solemnly, I had the deep conviction that I was stepping forth in aid of the great cause of order in France and beyond France, and that I was acting in the spirit of my Government and country, the interpreter of whose voice it fell upon me suddenly to become. If I erred, I must hope that the motives which swayed me will be my shield. The Provisional Government needed all the moral support attainable, after a revolutionary hurricane which shook society to its base, and left everything at first portentous and trembling. In such an exigency, hours, moments were important; and the United States are felt as a power in the world, under the blow that has been struck.

I am not unaware that the course I have pursued departs from diplomatic usage, and separates me, for the time being, from the European diplomatic corps, accredited, like myself,

---

[1] The version published in the *Moniteur* and the *National*, which was identical in both papers, seems a fairly accurate translation. The principal divergences are where "this early opportunity" is translated "*la première occasion*" and where "All will ardently hope that through her wisdom the results may be beneficial to mankind, of which the magnanimous bearing," etc., is rendered "Tous les Américains auront l'ardent espoir que, grâce à la sagesse de la France, ces institutions auront pour le genre humain les heureux résultats dont la conduite magnanime," etc. See issues of these papers for Feb. 29.

to the late Government of France, all members of which will probably wait instructions before adopting any steps of recognition. Having acted under a sense of independent duty in the emergency, I am, however, not the less aware that the diplomatic corps represents countries in friendly relations with the United States, and that it will hence be as much my duty as inclination to go on maintaining that amicable footing with its members, ever dictated by reciprocal good-will among the representatives of friendly powers, whatever different forms of government they may represent.

I have the honor, etc.

RICHARD RUSH.

HON. JAMES BUCHANAN, *Secretary of State.*

The address which Rush had made to the members of the Provisional Government and which he enclosed in his letter to Secretary Buchanan was as follows:

To the Members of the Provisional Government of the French Republic:

Gentlemen: As the representative of the United States, charged with the interests and rights of my country and of American citizens now in France, and too far off to await instructions, I seize this early opportunity of tendering to you my felicitations, not doubting the sanction of my Government to the step I thus take in advance. Nor can I avoid the occasion of saying that the memory of the ancient alliance and friendship between France and the United States is ever fresh and grateful with us, and that I am of nothing more sure than that the voice of my country will be universal and loud for the prosperity, happiness, and glory of France under the institutions she has announced, subject to ratification by the national will. All will ardently hope that through her wisdom the results may be beneficial to mankind, of which the magnanimous bearing of her people in the late events affords so auspicious a promise. It is under such institutions that the United States have for seventy years enjoyed constant prosperity, with a Government of uniform stability; and whilst they invariably leave to other nations the choice of their own forms, without interference in any way, they would naturally rejoice in beholding this great nation flourish under institutions which have secured for themselves the blessings of social order and public liberty.

Allow me then, gentlemen, using the words of the great and good Washington, the immortal founder of my country, on an occasion which the present recalls, to signalize this address to you, by mingling my felicitations with a fervent aspiration that " The friendship of the two republics may be commensurate with their existence."

Rush also enclosed Lamartine's letter of February 27, announcing his succession to the portfolio of foreign affairs, and his own answer to the same, dated February 28. After felicitating France on the choice of Lamartine "as a favorable first step in the new order of things," and promising " with great satisfaction " to transmit to his government a copy of Lamartine's communication, " not doubting its cordial reception," he declares his readiness in the meantime to transact with him any business affecting America or its citizens.

He then says: " The United States, having learned from their own experience the value of free institutions, will naturally anticipate from similar institutions in France, administered with the wisdom and moderation of which the enlarged and beneficent principles announced in your note are the auspicious harbingers, nothing but the best results to the interests and well-being of both countries." [1]

An interesting comment on this despatch is afforded by the diary of Lord Normanby, the British minister, who says that on February 27th, he received a visit from Mr. Rush

---

[1] *Congressional Globe*, vol. 17 (1st session, 30th Congress), p. 579 *et seq.*

and Mr. Martin, the secretary of legation.   Mr. Rush denied the news in the morning papers, that he had already gone to the Hôtel de Ville and acknowledged the republic, but said that, because of his distance from America and the sympathy she would feel for the new government, he should probably do so to-morrow.   Lord Normanby, receiving Mr. Rush's consent to express his opinion, admitted that the latter could not wait for instructions before giving any expression of views, but thought the proposed step " unusual and premature."   This was only a provisional government, itself not yet ready for such a step, as no notice had yet been sent from the new minister of foreign affairs; it was " quite unheard-of for an individual without credentials to present himself officially to any Government which had opened no communications with his own; " probably after getting Lamartine's circular the diplomatic corps would meet at the request of its senior member and decide on some course; waiting for that customary occasion would not hamper him.

It appeared to me that would be the natural moment for him to take his own line, not confining his answer to the dry acknowledgment of its receipt, which the others without instructions would probably give, but putting himself personally upon those terms with the Government which he desired to establish; and that, as he was only accredited to King Louis Philippe, he could not well go much farther than this in the course he contemplated till he received fresh letters.   Mr. Rush listened very attentively to what I said, admitted there was much reason in it, and added that he would consider it; but I am convinced he will still do as he announced, a course to which, in fact, he is probably already committed.[1]

Lord Normanby was doubtless right on the point of diplo-

---

[1] Marquis of Normanby, *A Year of Revolution*, vol. I, p. 130 *et seq.*

matic etiquette. Yet Mr. Rush was himself an experienced statesman, then 68 years old. The son of Benjamin Rush, signer of the Declaration of Independence, he had already occupied the posts of Attorney General under Madison, temporary Secretary of State, Minister to England for seven years under Monroe, Secretary of the Treasury under John Quincy Adams and candidate for Vice-President with him in 1828. He was neither youthful nor ignorant, but he had the courage to feel that an extraordinary situation should not be decided by looking up precedents.[1]

Recognition of so conspicuous a sort from such a man greatly flattered republican susceptibilities. The *National* announces that at two o'clock, Mr. Rush " recognized the Provisional Government. It was fitting that the representative of the American Union should be the first to come and salute our young republic; there is no more powerful bond between peoples than community of sentiments. The step taken by the Minister of the United States, had, in the present circumstances, something solemn about it: although it was anticipated, it touched the members of the government deeply; and, after an interview in which the noblest words were exchanged, they conducted this representative of a great people, in a body, to the threshold of the Hôtel de Ville, to testify the cordial affection which must forever exist between republican America and republican France." [2] Allowing for the sentimental optimism of the period, it is plain that this unusual act made an impression.

---

[1] Mr. Rush, in his journal, gives an account of the Normanby interview in substantial accord with the above. The person who urged him to recognize the republic was Major Poussin, who called on Mr. Rush for that purpose on the 26th, not without the Provisional Government's knowledge, Rush surmises. A full account of the matter, including Poussin's arguments and Rush's gradual determination to accede to them, is contained in Richard Rush, *Occasional Productions*, pp. 364-376.

[2] *National*, Feb. 29. *Cf.* other Paris papers of same date.

Immediately after the action of the minister, the American consul, who had lived many years in Paris and whose judgment on French affairs Rush greatly valued, wrote the following letter to the government, which was not published in the papers.

CONSULATE OF THE U. S. OF AMERICA, PARIS.

1st March, 1848.

To the members of the Provisional Government of the French Republic,

Gentlemen: In the year 1782, the City of Paris offered to Louis XVI, a ship of war to aid him in protecting the final independence of the Americans. The generous sympathy of the French nation may be exemplified by the circumstance that the small community of St. Germain-en-Laye contributed, for the same purpose, by an extraordinary tax, the sum of forty thousand francs.

The City of Paris has just accomplished a work—the foundation of a mighty Republic—in which all Americans must feel the liveliest satisfaction and deepest interest. In testimony of these feelings, I beg to render, for the Hôtel de Ville—the temple of power and wisdom of the City of Paris— American engravings of Washington, of the Senate of the United States, and the present Chief Magistrate of the Union. Your recent glorious Revolution was begun on the anniversary of Washington's birth. May it prove in its advances to perfect liberty and order, such as shall rejoice the spirit of that illustrious friend of France, and as the heroism, moderation and philanthropy of its commencement authorize an attentive world to expect!

I have the honor to be,

Gentlemen,

with the highest consideration,

your very obedient, humble servant,

ROBERT WALSH [1]

Rue de Rivoli, No. 30 bis.   U. S. Consul.

---

[1] Archives Nationales BB^{30} 300 No. 2292. A French translation is added in the same hand. (2)

If this seems a trivial gift, offered in bombastic phrases, it should be remembered that it was the kind of thing that appealed to the people of 1848, who were unusually sensitive to romantic idealism.

The American colony in Paris was not long in following the example of its official chiefs. From February 27 to April 28 nearly 300 deputations of various kinds were received by the Provisional Government. The American colony came eighth in this list. It was presented March 6 [1] by the indefatigable Major Poussin and the inevitable congratulatory address was read by Mr. Erving, former minister of the United States to Spain. In the course of his speech, occurs this sentence: " Recognizing the right which each nation possesses to form its own government, we think however that we may felicitate France on the choice of a system, which is based on the great principles of enlightened liberty and political equality." M. Arago replied for the government, after which an emblem, consisting of the united flags of the two nations was presented and accepted by Arago with the adjuration to place it in the Hôtel de Ville and the hope that despotism would never come to tear it down.[2]

---

[1] See the list in Daniel Stern, *Hist. de la révolution de 1848*, vol. 2, p. 371 *et seq.* The only foreigners presenting themselves at an earlier date were some English Chartists, who were received the day before, bearing a congratulatory address adopted at a Chartist meeting in London on March 2d. The other foreigners received were Democrats of London and the English colony of Paris on Mar. 12th; 2000 Swiss on the 13th; Greeks on the 15th; Hungarians, the 16th; Norwegians, the 16th; Irish, the 18th; Roumanians, the 21st; Portuguese, the 23d; Poles, the 27th; Italian Association, the 28th; Irish citizens of Dublin, Manchester and Liverpool, April 4th; the Swiss colony, April 4th; the Spanish colony, April 13th.

[2] *National*, Mar. 7. The *Moniteur* for the same date gives Mr. Goodrich as the American spokesman instead of Mr. Erving and omits any mention of Major Poussin, whose activity is, however, proved by an

Not to be outdone, the American women also " offer for your acceptance the Tricolored Flag and the Star Spangled Banner, now united together by the ties of Liberty, Equality and Fraternity," as a " slight mark of the Sympathy which the daughters as well as the sons of America feel for the success and stability of the French Republic." [1]

The effect of all this on the French mind is attested by a letter from " a gentleman residing in Paris to his friend in this country," read in the Senate of the United States, in the session of April 6. The letter, dated March 8, says in part: " Believe me, the proclamation of the republic has raised you here ten ells. You already know, perhaps, that not only the American minister, but all the Americans now in Paris, have waited upon and congratulated the Provisional Government. This double compliment has had an admirable effect. Never has there been so much anxiety to draw closer the alliance, I should rather say the fraternity, with the United States." [2]

The friendliness of the United States toward the French Republic, expressed by Mr. Rush's early recognition, re-

unpublished letter in the Archives Nationales (BB $\frac{30}{(2)}$ 300 No. 2206), dated Mar. 5, signed by Hawkes, Richards and Lovering on behalf of the colony, and addressed to Dupont de l'Eure, agreeing to present its felicitations at two o'clock on the 6th, " le gouvernement provisoire ayant bien voulu accorder aux citoyens des Etats-Unis par l'entremise de Monsieur le Major Poussin, . . . la permission," etc. If Poussin was acting in this case, as Mr. Rush suspected that he was in the other, as an unofficial agent of the provisional government, his efforts to secure American recognition are peculiarly interesting. The Erving here mentioned is probably G. W. Erving, minister to Spain, 1814-18. Washington Irving was in New York in 1848.

[1] Letter dated Mar. 6, signed by Josephine Wickliffe, Archives Nat., BB $\frac{30}{(2)}$ 317, No. 214.

[2] Appendix to Congressional Globe for 1st Session, 30th Cong., p. 459. For a less favorable view, cf. D. G. Mitchell, *The Battle Summer*, ch. xiv.

ceived the endorsement of President Polk. James
Buchanan, Secretary of State, wrote a long letter to Rush,
dated Washington March 31, saying that the President approved the minister's conduct, the policy of the United
States being to recognize de facto governments. The
United States is not indifferent to France's help in the
past. " It is therefore with one universal burst of enthusiasm that the American people hailed the late glorious
revolution in France in favor of liberty and republican government." Then follows much advice to France, that she
take care not to become involved in a general war and that
she create a federal system, combining her departments to
form sufficiently large units. " I have ventured upon these
speculations, because it is certain that, in your intercourse
with the authorities of the new Republic, you will be often
called upon in conversation for information respecting our
political system, State and national, which they seem to have
adopted as their model; and also for your opinion how far
this system ought to be changed or modified, so as best to
adapt it to the peculiar position of the French Republic.
Your intimate and enlightened knowledge of our government, both theoretical and practical, will enable you to im-
part much valuable information and advice to the French
authorities." [1]

On April 26, Mr. Rush presented his official letters, ac-
crediting him to the French Republic. In his remarks on
that occasion, he expressed the hope that " when the Republic shall have passed from your hands, which have guided
its destinies, into those of the National Assembly which is
soon to meet, that great body will crown its labors by the
establishment of institutions which will assure to France the
greatest prosperity and the purest glory."

[1] *Niles' National Register*, vol. 74, pp. 98, 99.

Lamartine replied that this first official recognition of the French Republic was a fitting return for the similar honor which France had been the first to confer upon America. He was confident that the republic, despite the inevitable confusion of readjustment would leave the hands of the present government, strong and great. His confidence was based on the fact that France was now ripe for such institutions.

What, fifty years ago, was only the idea of the leading men of the nation has passed into the ideas and habits of the whole people, without exception. The Republic which it wants today, is that which you have founded yourselves; it is a progressive republic, but conservative of the rights, of the property, of the industries, of the commerce, of the probity, of the liberty, of the moral and religious sentiment of the citizens.

It was a republic which had abjured vengeance in favor of fraternity. These principles, adopted by the Assembly and strengthened by the power of the people,

will make of the French republic the glorious sister of the American republic, and one will be able to say of the French people and of the American people, what was once said of a man dear to our two countries, the republic of the two worlds. As for the sentiments which the French people transmits with emotion and gratitude to the citizens and to the government of the United States, I will express them to you, in a single word, citizen minister: every Frenchman has for the Americans, the heart of Lafayette.[1]

---

[1] *Moniteur*, April 27. A socialist newspaper, *La République*, has a remarkable editorial on this occurrence. After recounting the various evidences of American enthusiasm for the French republic, crowned by its official recognition, the editorial quotes Lamartine's words, "The republic which it wants today is that which you have founded yourselves," and continues, "These last words will obtain general assent. It is certain that the Republic of the United States is, in many respects,

Meanwhile the question of recognition had been brought before Congress by a joint resolution offered in the Senate, March 28, by Mr. Allen, a Democrat of Ohio.

Resolved, That in the name and behalf of the American people, the congratulations of Congress are hereby tendered to the people of France upon their success in their recent efforts to consolidate liberty by imbodying [*sic*] its principles in a republican form of government. Resolved, That the President of the United States be, and he is hereby, requested to transmit this resolution to the American Minister at Paris, with instructions to present it to the French Government.[1]

The second reading took place, March 30.[2]   Allen, in opposing a motion to refer the resolution to the Committee on Foreign Relations, seems to have some sense of the contrast between Europe and America in 1848, set forth in Chapter I.

It was remarked by a distinguished member of this body not long since, that we, now-a-days, hear but little said upon the great elementary truths of public liberty; that the subject seemed to be forgotten. Here, sir, is an occasion for reviving and reviewing the elementary principles of public liberty: and I

a model for European nations. Its constitution, the causes of its prosperity must be today the object of the meditations and studies of all serious men. A people which for sixty years has made the noblest use of its sovereignty and which without disturbances, without commotion, has reorganized all public services and given to labor the most precious guarantees, that is a striking, decisive fact, which should close the mouth of the detractors of democracy." *La République*, April 28. The same article was reproduced, accidentally or by design, in the issue of the 29th. This radical organ's sympathy with the United States deserves notice. The key to it is apparently in the last sentence of the quotation, though the reference is not clear.

[1] *Congressional Globe*, vol. 17, p. 549. Some of the speeches, here summarized, are given in full in the Appendix, published in a separate volume.

[2] *Ibid.*, pp. 567-570.

desire, for one, to contribute my humble efforts to remedy this evil of which we have heard so much complaint—that in our discussions here the public mind has seldom been directed to the great question of liberty—that we were distracted with ideas of conquest, and had lost sight of ideas of liberty.

The anti-slavery men caught at this and endeavored to turn the matter to the benefit of their cause. John P. Hale, of New Hampshire, wished to add after the word " government " in the resolution, "And manifesting the sincerity of their purpose by instituting measures for the immediate emancipation of the slaves of all the colonies of the republic." Calhoun now made a considerable speech, moving to lay the Allen resolution on the table, as premature. The French have decreed a republic, it remains for them to establish it. " If they shall prove themselves to be as wise in constructing a proper constitution, as they have proved themselves to be skillful in demolishing the old form of government . . . if they shall really form a constitution which shall on one hand guard against violence and anarchy, and on the other against oppression of the people, they will have achieved, indeed, a great work." Failure, however, might result in a military despotism, for the old governments could not be reinstated. In that case, there would be no ground for congratulation. Let us wait for the action of the French convention, called for April. This far-sighted plan was defeated, 14 to 29. The yeas and nays on Calhoun's motion show that 7 Whigs and 7 Democrats voted for the motion, 8 Whigs and 21 Democrats against it. A discussion now arose as to when the Allen resolution had best be considered. In the course of it Stephen A. Douglas of Illinois declared that he regretted any postponement. This was the glorious beginning of a revolution, without bloodshed. The Provisional Government's decrees were very wise; they intend a radical revolution; never except the

Continental Congress has a body shown such skill and wisdom. Why defer congratulations? Sympathy is needed now, not when success is achieved. Calhoun was wrong, in saying that liberty would be greatly hurt by failure; this is the first step, which will generate another if it fails. The dethronement of the king and the decree founding a republic, the abolition of titles and orders of nobility, universal suffrage, the moderation that has combined all classes and parties in a bond of brotherhood, inspire confidence in their success.[1] The French are keen to know what America thinks, the only real republic in the world. "All republicans throughout the world have their eyes fixed upon us. Here is their model. Our success is the foundation of all their hopes." Rush should be supported; delay would seem to criticize his action, whereas he expressed the sentiments of the American people.

The question dragged along on that and the following day, without decision. On April 3, a message was read from President Polk, enclosing the despatch from Mr. Rush, quoted above.[2] Mr. Polk shows himself an ardent champion of the new régime. " The world has seldom witnessed a more interesting and sublime spectacle than the peaceful rising of the French people, resolved to secure for themselves enlarged liberty, and to assert in the majesty of their strength the great truth that, in this enlightened age, man is capable of governing himself." Needless to say, Mr. Rush's prompt recognition of the new government " meets my full and unqualified approbation. . . . He judged rightly of the feelings and sentiments of his Government and of his countrymen, when, in advance of the diplomatic representa-

---

[1] It is interesting to notice the difference between Douglas' notion of a radical revolution and that of the French socialists. It illustrates the contrast between the two countries in 1848.

[2] *Congressional Globe*, vol. 17, pp. 579-581.

tives of other countries, he was the first to recognize, so far as it was in his power, the free Government established by the French people." Our policy has always been non-intervention, leaving foreign countries to establish the form of government of their choice. While continuing this policy toward France, we cannot help feeling great sympathy for her people, " who, imitating our example, have resolved to be free." We can never forget France's help in the past. " Our ardent and sincere congratulations are extended to the patriotic people of France upon their noble and thus far successful efforts to found for their future government liberal institutions similar to our own." The message concludes with a hope that France will cultivate with America " the most liberal principles of international intercourse and commercial reciprocity, whereby the prosperity and happiness of both nations will be promoted."

Allen then moved to take up his joint resolutions. After a wrangle over parliamentary procedure, the vote was taken, resulting in a defeat of the motion by 21 to 22. Of the 21 yeas, 19 were Democratic votes and 2 Whig; of the 22 nays, 6 were Democratic and 16 Whig. The division seems to have been on purely partisan lines; the Democratic support of the resolutions being due to a desire to follow the lead of Polk and his minister, the Whig opposition having a precisely contrary motive. A few votes were based on other considerations, as the affirmative vote cast by the Whig Hale, who approved of the anti-slavery stand taken by France, and the negative vote cast by Calhoun who was unfriendly to the Administration [1] and who doubtless drew some Democrats after him. Northern and southern votes were about equally divided. This vote (which was not on the resolutions themselves, but merely on their immediate

[1] See Von Holst, *John C. Calhoun, passim.*

consideration) was explained by the *National* of April 22 as an instance of American reserve, which must not be held indicative of hostility or indifference toward France, especially in view of the President's message, which it reproduced in full.

On April 6,[1] Hannegan, Democrat from Ohio, presented a long series of congratulatory resolutions from the Committee on Foreign Relations, which did not differ in spirit from Allen's. The French are, among other things, felicitated on " their successful efforts thus far to found for their country institutions similar to our own."

A lengthy discussion ended in the defeat of Hale's amendment 28-1, and in the passage of Allen's resolutions as simpler than those of the committee, the only change from their original form being one of improved phraseology, the final draft alluding to " the success of their recent efforts to consolidate the principles of liberty in a republican form of government." The vote was 19-13; it was immediately made unanimous.

Meanwhile, on March 28, in the House, Haskell, Whig from Tennessee, gave notice that he intended to present resolutions concerning France. He was anticipated, however by Cummins, Democrat from Ohio, who, in the session of April 3,[2] offered an even more verbose set than had Hannegan in the Senate. Two anti-slavery amendments were offered and a long, bitter debate ensued, which began on affairs in France, but ended in a general discussion of the slavery question and became intensely personal. Hilliard, Whig from Alabama, had some misgivings as to the *droit au travail*, but most of the remarks about France were sentimental eulogies like that of McClernand, Democrat

[1] *Congressional Globe*, vol. 17, pp. 590-592.

[2] *Ibid.*, pp. 572-579.

from Illinois, who "wished to see France and the United States as the two great republics of the Old and of the New World soar and culminate in the moral grandeur and glory of eternal freedom and Christian civilization." The same orator, referring to the late king, declared: "The people bear his shattered throne along the streets, hymning the song of liberty, and calling anon for a republic on the model of the United States." Ingersoll, Democrat from Pennsylvania, thought that "the mere expression of the good will of the American people and the Congress of the United States and now (with the communication of the President) of all the branches of this Government" would be so potent "that everywhere, not merely in France, but in Italy, England, Germany, everywhere, the consequence must be the peaceable establishment of something at least approximating to the public institutions of this country."

Haskell now introduced his resolutions, drawn up so as to exclude the possibility of any reference to slavery, which Cummins' frequent references to "all forms of tyranny and oppression" might perhaps admit. "It was from this country that they [the kingdoms of Europe] had caught the flame. It was by looking at us and seeing us advancing in greatness and harmony, developing our resources, accumulating wealth, and enjoying all the benign effects of civil and religious liberty . . . it was this view of our condition which animated and inspired the nations of the world." Then France was forgotten in an angry wrangle over slavery, closed only by a motion to adjourn, which required the Speaker's vote to carry it, 81-80.

On April 7 and 8, the House was asked to take up the joint resolutions received from the Senate, but objection was made each time. On the 10th,[1] the discussion was begun,

[1] *Congressional Globe*, vol. 17, pp. 598-604.

and after another long slavery debate, the Senate resolutions were concurred in and passed, 174-2, two northern Whigs alone voting in the negative.   A motion to reconsider was made in the anti-slavery interest on the next day, but was defeated 123-46, all the forty-six being Whigs.   Voting in favor of the resolutions as they stood were the Democrat, Jefferson Davis, of Mississippi in the Senate and the Whig, Abraham Lincoln, of Illinois in the House.   Everybody wanted to congratulate France, the only question was as to the form of the congratulations, as to which the radical anti-slavery men took up a separate position.

This action by Congress was officially transmitted to the Executive Commission by Mr. Rush, May 22, accompanied by an address of his own dated May 17, conveying the felicitations of the American people, as well as its government, declaring that the President hopes for France that it will enjoy internal and external tranquillity while it is occupied in giving itself new institutions and that these institutions, the fruit of calm and wisdom, will redound to the happiness of the nation.   " The people of the United States, free by right of birth, since it has existed in the Occident, found after its own revolution, that the action of time and of peace was necessary to consolidate its system of government, whose form is republican, its essence popular, and which finds stability in the elements of order which compose it."   He feels honored at being the bearer of this resolution, " so much the more keenly because it is at an epoch when the whole French people, represented by the majesty of the National Assembly, is to deliberate to found its constitution, ..."

Lamartine received the resolution as a happy confirmation of the fact that America was first to recognize the French republic.   He continued

The new government of the republic would regard with just sensitiveness foreign governments mingling advice with their good wishes. But in the very intimate relations of the French and the American republics, every word which it may address to us will be received in token of perpetual friendship. The senate, the legislative body and the executive power of the United States may be convinced that these wise counsels are already the law of the French republic; not only will it follow its course, but it will follow its examples of regular institutions, *(ses exemples d'ordre d'institution régulière),* of caution with its neighbors, of solicitude for the labor, the instruction, the prosperity of the people, substance and goal of its resolution. The names of Washington, of Jefferson, of Jakson [*sic*] are inscribed on the banner of the new Republic, and if France is so happy as to find in its future names worthy of these great names, liberty will assume its true character on the old continent as it has found it on the other side of the Atlantic.[1]

The next day, M. Bastide, minister of foreign affairs, informed the Assembly of the resolution, its reception and his haste to have the transaction recorded at once in the *Moniteur*, that it might be brought immediately to the knowledge of all French citizens.

Now, I take the liberty of remarking that this fact is entirely new in the democratic history of the republic of the United States. Up to the present, communications of this kind had always been made by the executive power alone; today it is the whole Congress, the representatives of the American republic who address themselves to the representatives of the French republic, to felicitate them on the advent of their government. You will feel, citizens, like your executive commission in the name of which I have the honor to speak, that this act, so new, so honorable, and which may be so fruitful in useful consequences, should call forth from our side an

---

[1] *Moniteur*, May 23.

act of the same nature. I will propose, then, to the Assembly
to name a committee to draw up an address in response to
the resolution of the United States Congress and this address
will be transmitted as quickly as possible through your executive commission of government to the government of the
United States.

The committee on foreign affairs was then assigned the duty
of drawing up such a resolution.[1]

On the 25th, M. Drouyn de Lhuys reported the committee's resolution in a speech which reviewed the various acts
of friendly recognition on the part of America from the
28th of February, when " the barricades opened before M.
Richard Rush." In addition to official acts, he alluded to
the numerous addresses, particularly to " that assembly at
Baltimore where thirty thousand citizens gave regular and
pacific expression to their good wishes for a friendly people,
as if a single heart had spoken by a single voice." Finally
he reached this latest step of the nation united with his own
" by an ancient alliance and by the recent confraternity of
an identical political dogma." As to this, he asserted on the
part of the committee that after consulting with care the
annals of American diplomacy, they were convinced that at
no time, with reference to no government or people, had the
United States ever taken such action before. It had always
been an executive, never a legislative act. France should
respond to this flattering exception made by the United
States by an equally unusual response. They proposed,
therefore, that a decree be drawn up by the Assembly in the
name of the French people and transmitted through the
regular diplomatic channels to the President of the United
States, to be brought by him to the cognizance of the people,
the Senate and the House. This procedure would cor-

[1] *Moniteur*, May 24.

respond with that of Congress and further, "the solemn and laconic form of a decree" is the most fitting way to express "the virile and austere friendship of two great republics." They proposed the following decree:

Art. 1. The National Assembly, profoundly touched by the sentiments which have dictated to the Congress of the United States the decree of April 13th last, offers to the American people the thanks of the Republic and the expression of its fraternal friendship.

Art. 2. The commission of executive power is charged with transmitting the present decree to the French legation at Washington, with orders to present it to the American government.

No remarks being made, the decree was passed by a unanimous rising vote.[1]

This decree was borne to the United States by G. L. Poussin, who had been so prominent in bringing about the rapprochement between the two countries at the time of Rush's recognition, and who, though a naturalized American, was now appointed French minister to the United States. The *Washington Union* called attention to the striking coincidence, so expressive of the fraternal relations of the two nations that at the same moment, the United States was choosing M. Vattemare (a rather eccentric Frenchman, who originated the idea of each nation exchanging objects of art, specimens of fauna and flora, etc. with the other), American agent at Paris for international exchanges. These reflections of the *Union*, together with an account of Major Poussin's reception by President Polk are

---

[1] *Moniteur*, May 26. The reception of the decree is acknowledged in a brief message of the President to Congress, dated August 8th; *vide Congressional Globe*, pp. 1050, 1057.

recorded at length in *Le National* of September 4,[1] quoting from *Le Courrier des Etats Unis.*

In addition to these expressions of friendship, which after due allowance for the courtesies of diplomacy and for 1848 sentimentalism, remain cordial beyond the ordinary, certain concrete offers of help were proposed in Congress.

Pierre states that as soon as the constitution began to be discussed, the United States proposed to send to France their most eminent statesmen, who were to bring the experience of a half-century's practice. The offer was not received with sufficient cordiality, and was dropped.[2] The same statement is also made by Berton, (following Pierre?) who speaks of a consultative commission, offered by the United States, but withdrawn on account of its cold reception.[3] An examination of the *Moniteur* and the *Congressional Globe* fails to reveal any trace of this offer. The nearest approach to it is in a speech in the Senate, April 6 by Hannegan, who made this proposal:

When the National Assembly, which is to convene on the 20th of April, shall have closed its deliberations by giving to France a constitution after our own model, I would go further: I would send a solemn embassage—its members composed of the snow-crowned and most honored servants of our Republic, those who have given the energy of long life to liberty and their country, and whose mellow but all-radiant light still rests upon the theatre of action. I would send such an embassy, in the name and with the spirit of our people, to fraternize with the descendants of those who shed their blood on the battle-fields of our Revolution.[4]

[1] *Cf.* also *Moniteur*, Sept. 4.

[2] V. Pierre, *Hist. de la république de 1848*, p. 479.

[3] H. Berton, " La Const. de 1848," *Annales de l'école libre des sciences politiques*, 1897, p. 685.

[4] *Congressional Globe*, App., p. 458.

This, however, is a congratulatory, not a consultative commission; if the latter was really offered, it must have been
by the executive.

A more practical suggestion was made in the House on
April 17, by C. J. Ingersoll, Democrat from Pennsylvania,
who moved this resolution;[1]

That the Committee of Ways and Means ascertain, by con-
sultation with the Secretary of the Treasury and otherwise,
and report to the House, whether the immediate reduction of
fifteen of the thirty per cent *ad valorem* now imposed as duties
on French productions imported into the United States will
not, at this crisis in the French Government, afford great and
seasonable relief to the distressed industry of that country, to
which this is so much indebted, and also be without disadvant-
age, if not beneficial, to the revenue, commerce and general
welfare of the United States.

There were several amendments and some discussion by a
member unfriendly to the resolution, of the relative merits
of " French gewgaws " and Pennsylvania iron, but the whole
subject was finally laid on the table by a vote of 99 to 85.[2]

On June 20th, Mr. Pearce, from the Committee on the

---

[1] *Congressional Globe*, vol. 17, p. 638 *et seq.; cf.* p. 343.

[2] According to the Paris *Union*, quoting from the *Courrier des États-
Unis*, Mr. George Sumner, a Bostonian, resident for some years in Paris,
had on Mar. 22 addressed a plan to Vice-President Dallas and Secretary
of Treasury Walker, proposing the reduction of duties on a large number of French products, for the excellent moral effect it would have in
France and the ensuing benefit to the commerce of the two nations.
The *Union* continues on its own account that Mr. Dallas was believed
to have studied the matter and to have been preparing a set of resolutions when the Ingersoll bill was defeated. The latter's failure was
credited to insufficient preparation, and the belief expressed that it
would be brought up again at the next session, especially if the French
government showed any intention of " replying to the good dispositions
of the Americans." *Vide Union*, July 29. George Sumner was Charles
Sumner's brother.

Library, reported a joint resolution to the Senate, authorizing the presentation to France of a series of the standard
weights and measures of the United States, which was
passed, apparently without contest.[1]

As Drouyn de Lhuys suggested in his speech, previously
mentioned, unofficial enthusiasm for the new republic had
been expressed in many American cities.

An open-air meeting was held April 3, at New York in
what the American correspondent of the *National* calls " the
immense park opposite the City Hall," where according to
his report, 30,000 people were gathered about various temporary platforms, from which speeches lauding liberty and
international fraternity were made in all languages.[2]   A
complete account of the meeting with extracts from the
speeches is taken by the *Moniteur* from the *Courrier des*

---

[1] *Cong. Globe*, vol. 17, p. 857.   The details of the bill, not found in
the *Globe*, are given by the Paris *Union* of Sept. 11, quoting from " one
of the recent numbers " of the *Washington Union*.   It is there spoken
of as the bill of July 25th; since the *Globe* contains no record of any
action relative to France in either branch of Congress at that time, the
Pearce bill is probably meant.   The measure provided that Vattemare,
as agent for international exchanges, should receive for presentation to
France seven folio volumes of American archives, a new edition of
United States laws, legislative documents published by Congress, the
report of Wilkes' voyage around the world, duplicate copies of American works not contained in the American library in Paris, and a series
of weights and measures.   To this motley collection the director of the
Patent Office added drawings of the twenty-five most recent inventions,
and the Secretary of the Navy drawings of a new warship and of " a
machine for constructing large masts."   Various maps were also sent,
including a chart of winds and currents.   Parchment addresses, signed
by senators and representatives, were added.   The Paris *Union* was
deeply moved by this transaction.   " It is with joy, we doubt not, that
the country will receive this double expression of the sentiments of the
American Congress.   Between the United States and France there has
existed for so long a time a close bond, glorious and touching memories !"

[2] *National*, Apr. 22.

Etats-Unis.[1]   Another detailed report is furnished by the
N. Y. Evening Post,[2] which says that " at dark the crowd
was so immense that no estimate could be formed of its
numbers." The mayor presided, many spread-eagle
speeches, poems and resolutions were read (one calling for
reciprocal citizenship, without probation, between the people
of France and the people of the United States), and then the
" City Hall was illuminated on all sides except the north,
with more than fifteen hundred sperm candles—one to each
pane of glass—and produced a most magnificent appearance.
Tammany Hall and the block of buildings adjoining were
also illuminated, as were most of the hotels, and especially
the residences of the French." Finally came fireworks from
the balcony of the City Hall, concluding with a set piece,
the letters *Vive la République*, flanked on either side by two
stars, " each representing the star of America enclosing the
newly risen star of the French republic. The shouts which
now rent the air were truly tremendous. Cheer upon cheer,
and hurrah after hurrah, were given, as if in perfect ecstacy
of enthusiastic joy at sight of the glorious words." [3]

Three weeks later, " one of the most brilliant and im-
posing pageants that has ever been witnessed in this metro-
polis " [4] was held in the Park Theatre, presided over by a
prominent lawyer, Theodore Sedgwick. The occasion was
a military ball, at which a velvet and gold liberty cap was
presented by the city of New York to the city of Paris and

[1] *Moniteur*, Apr. 23.

[2] *N. Y. Evening Post*, Apr. 4.

[3] *Cf.* M. Moses, *Full Annals of the Revolution in France*, for an
account of the similar celebration in 1830, when ex-President James
Monroe presided over the meeting and when " the students of Columbia College, with their President and Professors" participated in the
parade.

[4] *N. Y. Evening Post*, Apr. 26.

received by the French vice-consul.   An enthusiastic letter was read from Martin Van Buren, the purport of which was that in spite of past failures, the new republic had a good chance to last.   In due season, the *bonnet phrygien* was sent to the minister of foreign affairs, together with a manuscript book containing the speeches made, and a long letter describing the ball.[1]

What is described as " a dignified meeting " took place in the Chinese Museum, Philadelphia, at which speeches were made and long congratulatory resolutions read by William A. Stokes.   One clause contained these words: "And, whereas, during sixty years the friends of liberty in France have in each successive struggle invoked their countrymen's regard to our political institutions as models for their own imitation and adoption."[2]

Another gathering, at Boston, strikes a somewhat more radical note in one of its resolutions, " That the active efforts of the Provisional Government of France, to conciliate the rights of property with the still more sacred right to live, merit the praises of all those who esteem both life and property."[3]

Both houses of Congress adjourned their sessions on April 24, to attend the local celebration of the February Revolution. Though the Marine Band, " playing the Marseilles Hymn," the Washington Light Infantry, the mayor and aldermen and other dignitaries marched in the procession, though speeches were made before the east front of the Capitol and salutes were fired by the Columbia Artillery, the glamour of this particular occasion seems to have been somewhat dimmed by " the unfavorable condition of Pennsylvania

[1] *National,* July 12.

[2] *Phila. Public Ledger,* Mar. 23.

[3] *Journal des débats,* May 12.

avenue, which was literally a cloud of dust all the morning and at the time when the procession passed along it." [1]

Other meetings are reported [2] at Richmond, Baltimore and Rochester, and doubtless these are not all that were held.

Special addresses were voted by societies of various descriptions. The Boston typographers sent one to the printers and compositors of France.[3]   A group of New York Fourierists sent another to their brothers across the sea.[4]

But more important than any of these, the Democratic national convention that nominated Cass, inserted in its platform long resolutions of congratulation to the French Assembly, expressing wishes for the " consolidation of their liberties . . . on the basis of a Democratic Constitution." [5] The Whigs adopted no platform.

The importance to us of these meetings in American cities and these resolutions of the American Congress does not lie in their revelation of America's enthusiasm for republican France, but in the fact that they were carefully reported, often at length, in many French newspapers, and thus could hardly help having a tendency to predispose the French mind in favor of the United States.   It was something more than the international fraternity, common at the time, for a study of the newspapers fails to show any similar interchange of courtesies with any other country.

The more detailed knowledge which the educated part of the French public had regarding America was based essentially on a very few books.   Foremost among these was of

[1] *Washington Daily National Intelligencer*, Apr. 25.   *Cf. Cong. Globe*, vol. 17, pp. 664, 665.

[2] *National*, May 20.

[3] *Journal des débats*, May 12.

[4] *Démocratie pacifique*, May 8.

[5] *N. Y. Evening Post*, May 29.

course A. de Tocqueville's *Démocratie en Amérique.* He
and his friend, G. de Beaumont, studied the prison system
of the United States from May, 1831 to May, 1832, during
which time they travelled from Boston to New Orleans.
The results of this study were set forth in a book by the
two men, entitled *Système pénitentiaire aux Etats Unis et
de son application en France,* published in Paris in 1832 and
reaching its third edition in 1845. This work, which recommended the partial adoption of what was known as the
Auburn system, (modified system of silence) was crowned
by the French Academy, given the Prix Monthyon and
translated into German, English, Portuguese and other languages. From the observations made on that journey, combined with his own reflections (for he was essentially a de-
ductive thinker) Tocqueville wrote his classic on Democracy in America, which, appearing in part in January, 1835,
was the first reasoned political account of the American experiment. It created a great sensation. Royer-Collard, the
old statesman of Restoration times, said, " Since Montesquieu, nothing like it has appeared." Four thousand copies
of the first part were sold in a short time, an extraordinary
number for the period.[1]   It was widely translated. In
1836, the French Academy awarded it a special prize of
8000 francs, the ordinary maximum being 6000.[2] The author, on the strength of it, was in 1838, elected a member
of the Academy of Moral and Political Sciences and in 1841
of the French Academy. By 1848, the book had reached
its tenth edition, and was generally familiar to cultivated
people. Tocqueville's attitude was that of the early nineteenth century aristocratic liberal. He was not a democrat,

[1] Eugène d'Eichthal, *Alexis de Tocqueville et la démocratie libérale,*
p. 106.

[2] G. de Beaumont, *Correspondances et oeuvres posthumes de Alexis
de Tocqueville* (vol. 5 of *Oeuvres Complètes*), p. 48.

though not violently hostile to democracy; he regarded it as inevitable, and sought to study its workings where they had been in most successful operation. Originally a legitimist, he had sat in the liberal opposition during the July Monarchy, and was now a *républicain du lendemain.* His attitude toward the republic is clearly described by a later writer. Tocqueville, he says, about the time that Beaumont's electoral profession of faith appeared, produced a new edition of the Democracy.[1] It was preceded by an elaborate preface, which was reproduced in a great number of newspapers and "very noisily commented upon." Tocqueville and Beaumont began to be considered pronounced republicans, " while the republic had never been more than an object of study for them," nor had they voted with the republicans in the chamber of deputies. It is to them, the writer continues, that is to be traced back the distinction between the moderate and the violent republic. He then quotes Tocqueville's own words in the preface of the 1848 edition, as follows :

It is no longer the question whether we shall have in France royalty or republic, but it remains for us to learn whether we shall have an agitated or a tranquil republic; a regular or an irregular republic; a pacific or a warlike republic, which threatens the sacred rights of property and of family, or a republic which recognizes or consecrates them. A terrible problem, whose solution concerns not France only, but the whole civilized universe. . . . If we save ourselves, we save at the same time the peoples which surround us. If we fail, we lose them all with us. According as we shall have democratic liberty, or democratic tyranny, the destiny of the world will be different, and it may be said that it depends on us today whether the republic shall end by being established everywhere, or abolished everywhere.

[1] This 1848 edition is unfortunately not to be found in the Bibliothèque Nationale.

The later writer, a radical, observes somewhat bitterly that the real point was whether " under the aegis of that *regular and tranquil* republic, of which one spoke with so much enthusiasm, it was not desired to keep things practically as they were under the government of Louis Philippe. . . . It was on the 14th of March that the preface of M. de Tocqueville appeared and certainly many points of reform remained to be noticed, many improvements to be demanded." [1]

In America, Tocqueville became an ardent admirer of the system of checks and balances. The particular points of the American system, outside of the central structure itself, which appealed most strongly to him were local self-government, the independence and authority of the judiciary, and the federal scheme in general. " Such were the great remedies which Tocqueville perceived opposed in the United States to democratic excesses." [2]

Tocqueville begins his constitutional study with the New England township as the best expression of Anglo-American popular sovereignty, proceeding outward to the county and the state. When he takes up the federal constitution,[3] he finds worthy of particular attention the two chamber system in the legislative branch, the President's suspensory veto and indirect election, and the power of the Supreme Court. He considers the greater independence in the federal constitution of the three branches of government over against the people, as proof of its superiority over the state constitutions. It is in fact "the most perfect federal constitution that ever existed." [4]   European conditions, however, make its slavish imitation undesirable; it should be studied and the best parts

[1] F. Rittiez, *Hist. du gouvernement provisoire*, vol. 2, pp. 78-80.
[2] E. d'Eichthal, *op. cit.*, p. 88.
[3] Tocqueville, *op. cit.*, pt. i, ch. viii.
[4] *Ibid.*, p. 210.

of it adapted to European conditions.[1]   In fact, one of the most important features of his attitude is his dictum that of the three vital elements in American prosperity, " the laws contribute more to the maintenance of the democratic republic in the United States than the physical circumstances of the country, and the manners more than the laws." [2] Nevertheless, he was so generally recognized as an admirer of the American republic that he was dubbed *l'américain* and laughingly accepted the title.   " I have already," he writes in a letter to M. de Corcelle, dated Berne, July 27, 1836, " as an American [*en ma qualité d'américain,*] conceived a very superb disdain for the federal constitution of Switzerland, which without ceremony I call a league and not a federation.   A government of that nature is surely the softest, the most powerless, the most awkward and the most incapable of leading nations anywhere except to anarchy. . . . Then English kingdom is a hundred times more republican than that republic. . . . Enough of politics.   If Quincy Adams' speech is still in your hands, I beg you to keep it for me." [3]

Tocqueville was not alone in his interest in America, in the early days of the July monarchy.   " The idea, furthermore, that a republic, somewhat similar to that of the Americans would be one day founded in France, preoccupied many minds at that time; the duc de Broglie was thinking of it and Armand Carrel in disappointment was commencing to rally to it." [4]

At almost the same time appeared another book on which

[1] See especially, Preface to ed. of 1850 (p. liv in Century ed.) and close of ch. xvii.

[2] Ch. xvii, esp. p. 409; by "manners" (*moeurs*) he meant religion, morality, the tendency toward social equality, etc.

[3] *Correspondances; Oeuvres complètes,* vol. 6, p. 62.

[4] R. P. Marcel, *Essai politique sur A. de Tocqueville,* p. 289.

the educated Frenchman based his impressions of America, a series of letters written by Michel Chevalier, during a visit to the United States from 1834 to 1836.[1]   The author, a St. Simonien in youth, afterward settled down into a conservative professor of economics in the Collège de France; he was of the Manchester school, a great believer in individual liberty and free-trade.   The letters are written from the standpoint of a liberal Catholic royalist.   They are somewhat rhetorical in style; on the whole they are laudatory. The subject-matter is chiefly concerned with banks and railroads, then with social conditions; little is said on purely constitutional issues.   Chevalier was in America at the time of Jackson's conflict with the Bank, in which his sympathies inclined toward the latter as the most stable financial force in the country.   Like Tocqueville, Chevalier's fortune was made by his book on America (which in this case, included Cuba and Mexico).   It seems to have been widely read and Alexander von Humboldt praised it.   Chevalier received a government commission to study financial conditions in England as a result of the book's success and later was made a member of the council of state.

A third writer on America at this time was Guillaume Tell Poussin, to whom reference has been made.   In 1834, he wrote a book on canals and railroads in the United States, a subject which Chevalier later developed.[3]   In 1841, Poussin published his *Considérations sur le principe démocratique qui régit l'union américaine, et de la possibilité de son application à d'autres états.*   This was largely a review of Tocqueville and highly eulogistic of the United States.

---

[1] *Lettres sur l'Amérique du Nord*, Paris, 1836; 2 vols., 2d ed., 1837.

[2] *Travaux d'améliorations intérieures, projetés . . . par le gouvernement général des Etats-Unis d'Amérique de 1824 à 1831*, Paris, 1834.

[3] *Hist. et description des voies de communication aux Etats-Unis*, 2 vols., Paris, 1840-41.

But his principal work was *De la puissance américaine*, published in 1843 for the first time, and appearing in an enlarged third edition in 1848.[1] The first part is a history of the colonial period, the second a discussion of the "military, agricultural, commercial, and industrial resources of the United States."

Still another writer on the United States was Achille Murat, son of the marshal, an American citizen living in Florida and a strong admirer of his adopted country. He published at Paris in 1832 his *Esquisses morales et politiques des Etats-Unis de l'Amérique du Nord*, which told about everything except the constitution.

There was, however, another class of publications, which is very important for our purpose. As the meeting of the Assembly approached, collections of constitutions began to appear. In some cases, these were purely former French constitutions; in many other cases, however, the American federal and sometimes, various state constitutions were added; rarely were those of any other country included.[2]

Another class of writings is made up of ideal constitutions; here American influence is often perceptible. One of the most important writers in this class is E. de Laboulaye, a professor in the Collège de France and a publicist of the liberal school, equally hostile to socialism and to reaction. He was a strong admirer of the United States and held it up as an example in many books, mostly written after our period. He wrote an essay, entitled *Considérations sur la Constitution* (Paris, 1848), filled with quotations from American practice, to which was appended a plan for a constitution, based on the report of the commission, (then before the

---

[1] Published in English in 1850 under the title *The United States, its Power and Progress.*

[2] *Cf.* ch. vii and bibliography.

Assembly), amended largely in accordance with the United States constitution. He gave a lecture December 4, 1849, at the opening of his course on comparative legislation, entitled *De la constitution américaine et de l'utilité de son étude.*[1] This, of course, came too late to have any effect on the thought of the Assembly, but it shows what was in the minds of some of the leaders in Parisian intellectual life at the time. For other writings of this nature reference must be made to the bibiliography. There was also no little information about the political and constitutional life of America in the newspapers, as will be seen in a subsequent chapter. If now, we essay to determine the general feeling about America in the France of 1848, we must distinguish between the American ideal and the American fact.

As to the American ideal, there was general adulation. Washington, regarded as its incarnation, was constantly held up by all parties as a sort of republican superman. We find Lamartine replying to the Italian delegation, who had come to pay their respects to the Provisional Government, March 27, bidding them remove from their pantheon the name of Machiavelli and substitute for it " the purer name of Washington; there is the name which must be proclaimed to-day, it is the name of modern liberty. It is no longer the name of a politician, it is the name of the most disinterested man, the one most devoted to the people. There is the man whom liberty needs. A European Washington, that is the need of the century: the people, peace, liberty! "[2] And again, in a letter to the electors, defending his policies, he predicted, " The republic inspired by Washington will triumph over the republic of Baboeuf, of Robespierre and of

---

[1] *Revue de législation et de jurisprudence*, Dec. 1849. Published separately in 1850.

[2] Lamartine, *Trois mois au pouvoir*, p. 144.

Danton." [1] The chief radical newspaper printed an article on Washington à propos of the approaching American presidential election. His name is here said to have remained great and respected, because " that name is a synonym for honor, for courage and for devotion to the country, for disinterestedness. Never did ambition trouble the severity of that conscience, inaccessible to petty calculations and to vanity; so the errors of that great man were excused by his contemporaries, who honored in Washington political virtue, if not the most impetuous, at least the most severe." [2] The same article praised Jefferson's " firmness and noble modesty " which marked the dawn of a new era for America, the triumph of democracy. Of him might be said, what he had said of Washington, that when he died, " a great man perished that day in Israel." The royalist organs held the same opinion.

In America, Washington reveals himself. Again a man who directs all the forces of the revolution. . . . Those who follow him have confidence, those who combat him esteem him; in the councils, his opinion is followed, because his opinions are never ambiguous; in the assemblies, he is listened to, because his character gives power to his speech. So history records one more great man. . . . But this time, in your second republic, where is the man who directs it? [3]

And again, " Meanwhile, permit us to deplore that absolute void, that profound lack of leaders commanding respect, under the rule of a revolution which ought to produce the expansion of so many high intelligences. We count several candidates; but where is Washington?" [4]

[1] *Le Siècle*, Sept. 2.
[2] *Réforme*, Oct. 25.
[3] *Union*, May 22.
[4] *Ibid.*, Oct. 28.

One paper seeks partisan advantage from Washington's relations with the French monarchy.

And who then, in the history of the world, would pretend to put himself above Washington and all those illustrious founders of the American Union, for devotion to country and for jealous care given to her honor? And yet were not Washington, Franklin and all their glorious friends found in accord on the principle of asking aid in men and money from the Versailles cabinet? This aid was granted and accepted and we recall it in passing, to the eternal glory of the founder of American independence, that the grateful heart of Washington kept to its last beat, homage for the memory of Louis XVI, an instinctive and insurmountable horror for his executioners.[1]

Another royalist paper remarked that the Assembly is now discussing presidential candidates. " It is not a question of designating another Washington, named already by the glorious renown of his services: there is no man who, having long been the representative of the republican idea, has so to speak personified it in himself, and who, elected president, would be the worthiest to install in power the form of an elective government. No such man exists in France." [2] Again it is said that " the authority which this famous chief of the United States enjoyed was the result of the freest and most regular choice," [3] which would however be more difficult to obtain in so large a country as France, for which a king was more desirable than a president.

Other newspaper references might be given, but these must suffice. There are besides such statements as that of Guizot, who said of him, " Washington does not resemble

1 *Assemblée nationale*, Oct. 4.

2 *Opinion publique*, Oct. 22.

3 *Gazette de France*, Mar. 30.

Napoleon; the former was no despot. He founded political liberty, at the same time as the national independence of his country. . . . He is the model for the chiefs of a democratic republic. . . . He was of those who know that in a republic no more than in a monarchy, in a democratic society no more than in any other, does one govern from the bottom up." [1] The historian Baron de Barante writes of Cavaignac,

If M. Cavaignac had wanted to be anything except a factional republican, he would have had a fine chance. But this French soil could not produce a Washington. I read the other day his farewell to the American people on leaving the Presidency; what reason and simplicity! Has God refused the faculty of good sense to our poor nation? Shall we never know other liberal opinions than those of journalists and littérateurs? [2]

Others, however, had a better opinion of Cavaignac, as Tocqueville, who in a conversation with Nassau Senior on January 29, 1851, said " Cavaignac was the only chance of the republic. He is not a man of wide views, but an honest man who prefers glory to power. His model would have been Washington." [3] The same rôle was assigned to Lamartine a little earlier. "All France considered him as a providential mediator between parties and classes. The name and the rôle of Washington were assigned to him by the public will." [4]

While all parties joined in the expression of esteem for the great American patriot's memory, it is easier to find such references from royalist than from radical pens.

[1] Guizot, *De la Démocratie en France*, p. 28. As in the case of Laboulaye, this book, published in 1849, is cited to show the feeling of prominent men of the time.

[2] " Letter to Mme. Anisson du Perron," dated Nov. 9, 1848. *Revue de Paris*, vol. iii, p. 562.

[3] E. d'Eichthal, *A. de Tocqueville*, p. 282.

[4] Daniel Stern, *Hist. de la révolution de 1848*, vol. 2, p. 19.

For a long time there had been publicists interested in American governmental theory. On the eve of the revolution of 1830, Thiers wrote in the *National*, " We shall be content to seek our political examples and our models of government in England, across the Channel; but if you force us to it, we shall cross the ocean and go as far as America." [1]

In 1839, Guizot wrote of the American system,

In its own interior organization, the central government was well conceived and well weighed; the rights and the relations of the different powers were regulated with much sense and a strong appreciation of the conditions of order and of political vitality, at least for the republican form and the society to which it adapted itself. Comparing the Constitution of the United States to the anarchy from which it sprang, one does not tire of admiring the wisdom of its authors and of the generation which had chosen and sustained them. [2]

In 1848, Henri Martin in his course on modern history at the Sorbonne laid stress on that

imperishable monument, the Declaration of Rights [*sic*]. For the first time in modern societies, a people justified theoretically the assumption of its liberty by philosophy and universal right, and no longer by the violation of some special pact, of some ancient custom; no revolution, not even the glorious revolt which gave birth to Holland, had laid claim to that august character. Nothing was more radically opposed to the genius of old England, nothing was more in conformity with the genius of France than that declaration pronounced in the English tongue by English lips. It was not only in the name of liberty, but in the name of the natural equality of men, that America proclaimed her independence. France recognized the echo of her thought, the thought which others were realizing before her, and she arose with a start. [3]

---

[1] Spuller, *Hist. parl. de la seconde répub.*, p. 41.

[2] *Washington, Etude historique*, p. lxiii.

[3] *Moniteur*, June 1.

But it was not only intellectual leaders who were thinking of America at this time. To get any idea of the mass of material on the subject, reference must be made to the newspapers, many of which published long articles about the American constitution, (not all friendly by any means) which will be discussed in another chapter. Among the sample constitutions, which were produced so prolifically at this time, it is interesting to find suggestions for the new government by Robert Owen.[2] The letter suggests the opportunity France has for making a new experiment on true principles, some of which he lays down, as opportunity for the education and self-development of every individual, religious freedom, liberty of speech, thought and action, no taxes, except perhaps a graduated property tax, " reasonable ideas of unity and of association," a local government based on small divisions, most advantageous to secure the well-being of all, no interference by foreign powers, and the principle of being armed for defence, not for attack. His 11th clause reads: " The American government, in principle, with some essential modifications in their practice, will be a good present model with which to commence."

The notion that other countries and particularly the United States were being studied by the constitution-makers at this time and for several years after, was sufficiently popularized to give birth to a doggerel reactionary verse, containing these lines,

> Certain rêve pourtant, titré de libéral,
> N'en doit guère à celui qui se dit social ;
> Et quand, croyant pour nous faire chose qui vaille,

[1] *To the Men and Women of France.* An English copy, dated London, Feb. 27, 1848, is in the Archives Nationales (BB 30 299(1)) ; a French translation is printed as an appendix to E. Dolléans, *Robert Owen* (Paris, 1907), taken by him from a newspaper, *La Voix des Femmes*, March 25, 1848.

A nous constituer nuit et jour il travaille,
Son constituantisme aura cela de bon
Qu'il ne se mettra guère en frais d'invention;
Aux Chartes, en effet, qu'il voulut nous prescrire,
Les Grecs et les Romains ne pouvant plus suffire,
Les Anglais, sur leur sol, l'ont vu plus d'une fois
Gueuser stupidement d'inapplicables lois;
Et prétendant, de plus, d'un élan héroïque,
A défaut de la Manche, enjamber l'Atlantique,
Il n'est point de sottise, il n'est point de travers,
Qu'il n'aille mendier aux bouts de l'univers.[1]

Another rhyme in equally bad verse, but this time on the republican side, is equally interesting as an indication of popular opinion. It is fifteen pages long and is based on Napoleon's prophecy that in fifty years Europe would be Cossack or republican. It sets forth the exhaustion of the monarchies like aged men. What is to come next? Domination by Russian tyranny would be horrible. America is free. The star of empire is passing to her. Then comes a disquisition on the excellence of quadrennial presidential elections. There is no party spirit in America. Her future glory is sure; she is destined to conquer Canada and Cuba.

The lines which follow are perhaps the only ones in which James K. Polk has ever been regarded as a poetical subject.

Et l'homme qu'il érige à ce point de hauteur,
Tel que vous, monsieur Polk! un marchand ou planteur,
Cet homme sent en lui la royauté plus forte
Que si vingt régiments paradaient à sa porte;
Il concentre en lui seul toutes les volontés,
Fait la paix ou la guerre, affermit les traités,
Soutient par sa sagesse, et même développe
Un Etat aussi grand que nul Etat d'Europe,

---

[1] Claude-Simplicien Constitutionnelisky, *Considérations plus ou moins poétiques, etc.* (*'48-'52*), p. 27.

Règne enfin par les lois mieux qu'un prince absolu ;
Puis le jour le peuple appelle un autre élu,
Il vient au Capitole, avec un front austère,
Résigner le pouvoir dont il fut mandataire,
Et rentre dans la foule en simple citoyen,
Entouré de respects, s'il fut homme de bien.[1]

This is as important as a treatise by Guizot, because it shows that the American constitution had become a subject of popular as well as of academic interest.

The American ideal contemplated across the Atlantic was on the whole regarded with favor, though, as will be seen, there was strong opposition to the American political system, viewed as a model for France. When one comes to consider the America of daily life, as she presented herself in her acts, the balance of praise and blame was much more nearly divided.

The two subjects of immediate interest in American affairs at the time were the Mexican war and the presidential election. As to these, opinions differed. We find ardent defenders of the war, such as the *Réforme*, which closed a despatch recounting the conclusion of peace, by saying: "All republican France will applaud with joy the success of the Washington republicans, our friends and our brothers." [2] Another paper, in the last days of the monarchy, printed Polk's message of December 7, 1847, almost complete, with a eulogistic editorial, the whole taking up nearly ten columns. The message recalls unfavorably the king's late speech at the opening of the Chamber, " what a contrast! One would think he was really leaving Lilliput and entering a land of giants." The year has been " as fruitful and prosperous

[1] A. M. Barthélemy, *À M. J. K. Polk, Président des Etats-Unis d'Amérique*, Paris, 1848.
[2] *Réforme*, March 14, 1848.

for the New World as it has been sad for the old continent, a year of glory for the Washington government and of transition for the United States." The American victories and the approaching annexation of Mexican territory were received with complacency, the internal prosperity resumed in the words "*tout marche, tout se développe, tout s'améliore*" and the article closed with the comment, "The dignity of the acts has elevated the words which have naturally reflected the situation, quite as naturally as the speeches of our ministers reflect the feebleness of their character, the poverty of their ideas and all the miseries of their policy." [1]

Other papers took a gently critical attitude. "The year which is just closing will remain a glorious date in the history of two nations friendly to France. In the United States, it will recall brilliant victories, whose glamour lacks only a juster cause." [2]   So the following: "The war against Mexico was not a just war. The citizens of the United States, most considerable for their lights and their political renown, had been almost unanimous in blaming it. . . . The spirit of conquest is the enemy of political liberty;" [3] the rest of the article praises the United States for its generosity in purchasing the new territory, and discusses the increased complexity of the slavery question.

Still others blamed the Americans sharply. The following are typical: "The United States will not stop before counsels of moderation nor before scruples of conscience; they regard all North America as their domain and only wait the occasion to claim their rights. Mr. Polk has contributed no little to push thought into that channel. And yet all

[1] *Presse*, Jan. 2, 1848.
[2] *Constitutionnel*, Jan. 1.
[3] *Journal des débats*, Aug. 15.

the eminent men of the Union have signalized the peril." [1]
" Mr. Polk is at much pains to prove that Mexico has been
the aggressor, and that the United States have only used
reprisals; it is a task whose least defect is its uselessness;
the North Americans would do better to cast the responsibility for their conquests, as they have already done more
than once, on Providence or on fate." [2]   One of the bitter-
est enemies of the United States was F. de Courmont, who
wrote a pamphlet on the war in 1847, which contained such
sentences as these.   "A meddlesome spirit [Polk], a few
months were sufficient for him to cast the republic into a
war whose avowed object is an infamy and whose secret
object, a ridiculous project if it is not one of the most Ma-
chiavellian. . . . Personal interest being the sole motive
which acts seriously on American minds, it resulted that
every citizen has examined the question of peace and war
according to the good or the harm, which eventualities might
bring to his business," [3] and so forth, the author being convinced that underneath this infamous war lurks a secret
policy, whose mysteries it is highly important for European
diplomacy to penetrate.

The feature of the presidential campaign which chiefly
impressed French observers was of course its connection
with the war.   The *Constitutionnel* was astonished that the
Whigs, the peace-party, should nominate the general who
led the campaign.

But the Americans are, after the French, the people who show
themselves perhaps the most sensitive to the glory of arms.
America has already had for president several general officers:
Messers. Jackson, Harrison, without speaking of Washington.

---

[1] *Univers*, July 10.

[2] *Revue des deux mondes*, Jan. 15.

[3] *Des Etats-Unis, de la guerre du Mexique et de l'île de Cube*, p. 29.

The appeal which the Democratic party has the habit of making to the warlike sentiments of the nation, is one of the principal elements of its success; it is for having flattered these sentiments that Mr. Polk has arrived at presidential power. Today the Democrats have chosen for candidate a general, Mr. Cass. . . . This party dreams of the establishment of the rule of the United States over the whole extent of the American continent, by war and by conquest; it wishes to fortify the institution of slavery. If its clamors had been heeded, the United States would have seized Oregon at the risk of war with England. It is the party which required the annexation of Texas and which made an unjust war on Mexico, defending the independence of its territory. General Cass is a man to enter into all its views. If Mr. Cass is elected, he will be the representative of an arrogant and bold policy; and besides he will contribute to binding closer the chains of slavery, for slavery accords perfectly with the ideas of progress of the Southern democrats, who are, as everyone knows, the democrats par excellence in the United States.[1]

Two policies, this interesting editorial concluded, are face to face; the policy of peace, moderation and liberty, and the policy of war, turbulence and servitude; the victory of the latter was feared, from a division of the majority.

L'Univers, in its editorial of July 10, saw the same striking fact, that both candidates were generals and predicted a warlike future with no limits to " the ambition of the young republic." The other Catholic organ asserted that it seemed as though the United States government were going to belong to " a military president for life, with a military presidency and a military ministry," [2] while if Cass wins, he will do all he can to get into a war with England. The same paper remarked later in the campaign, " The Americans are

[1] *Constitutionnel*, Sept. 27.
[2] *Ère nouvelle*, July 9.

decidedly intoxicated with their military glory." [1] There
is very little close study of American politics in the radical
papers. Except in the *Réforme*, there are few allusions to
events in the United States. The *Démocratie pacifique* did
give two and a half columns to a reprint of part of Polk's
message of December 7, 1847,[2] but that was exceptional.
In spite of his Icarian colony in Texas and Illinois, Cabet's
paper showed such astonishing ignorance of American politics as to announce that "M. Wuithrop [*sic*] has been elected
president of the republic of the United States in place of
M. Polk." [3]

Slavery is alluded to, when at all, only as a plague-spot
in the American system. The discovery of Californian gold
is reported, and the San Francisco newspaper can no longer
appear for lack of subscribers.[4]

But whether the writer is sympathetic and calls it magnificent progress or envious and calls it egoistic materialism,
the dominant note of all these various comments is wonder
at America's great prosperity. An excellent expression of
this general feeling is given at the very start of the republican era by Cordier, who signs himself "*député du Jura*"
and who was later a member of the National Assembly.
He holds that America is the heir to the power of England.

Indeed, the United States, having neither indirect taxes nor
public debt nor a large regular army, nor colonies, nor navy
de luxe, nor sinecures, nor office-holders for life richly paid,
nor any monopolies nor class divisions, nor germs of intestine
wars, etc.; the United States, disposing of immense forests,
of the finest rivers, of 1500 steamboats, 3000 sailing-vessels,

[1] *Ère nouvelle*, Sept. 6.
[2] *Démocratie pacifique*, Jan. 2.
[3] *Populaire*, Jan. 9.
[4] *Assemblée nationale*, Oct. 12.

in possession already of numerous and large manufactories of stuffs, of steam-factories, of the richest mines of coal, iron, copper, lead, the United States are advancing, almost miraculously, to an extraordinary prosperity, and are entering with advantage into rivalry with the English in all the markets of the globe. . . . The American Union possesses more uncultivated and fertile lands than still more numerous emigrants from Europe could cultivate, a greater surplus of diverse agricultural products than it could consume,[1]

and so on at considerable length and with heightened emphasis on the marvels of the new world.   All of which explains why America was not radical in 1848; she was too busy and had too much room to be discontented with present conditions.

The mention of this deputy suggests that before discussing the speeches in the Assembly, bearing on American solutions, it becomes necessary to classify as far as possible every member of that body who expressed an opinion on the American system.   This classification is undertaken in the next chapter.

[1] Cordier in the *Gazette de France*, Feb. 29.

CHAPTER IV

The Representatives

To classify the members of the Assembly according to party affiliation is not an easy task. It has been pointed out in a previous chapter that there was no strict party system, and that the labels by which men were called indicated rather tendencies of thought than membership in an organization. The " groups " were somewhat more closely bound together and might have been of service for our purpose, had any available lists of their membership remained extant. Under these circumstances it becomes necessary to work out the political cast of mind of the representatives from the facts of their lives, so far as these can be determined, combined with their attitude in the Assembly. For the former purpose, various more or less elaborate directories of members were drawn up at the time, of which Alhoy's *Biographie parlementaire*, Lesaulnier's *Biographie des 900 députés* and an anonymous *Biographie des représentants du peuple*, published by the editors of *Nôtre Histoire*, a weekly magazine, (all three appearing in 1848) are among the best. The *Biographie parlementaire* was compiled by " a society of publicists and men of letters under the direction of Maurice Alhoy"; there were eighteen in the group, each of whom signed his initials to the article for which he was responsible. There is much valuable information in the book, though it is somewhat rhetorical and is inclined to be partisan, in favor of the radicals. The *Biographie des 900 députés* is similarly the work of " a society of literary men and pub-

116 [294

licists under the direction of C. M. Lesaulnier," published June 19. It was apparently Alhoy's main source; some of the sketches in his book are copied verbatim from Lesaulnier, though others differ entirely in their judgments. Generally speaking, the books are written from the same democratic point of view. Some strange discrepancies in dates show the haste with which they were compiled and the caution with which they should be used. The *Biographie des représentants*, issued by *Nôtre Histoire* seems to have been very popular; it went through at least four editions. It is much shorter than the others, with less detail; the sketches are brief and clever, devoting less attention to previous biography, more to a summing-up of the representative's political position. The authoritative compilation to-day is, however, the *Dictionnaire des parlementaires français*, published in 1891, in five volumes, which is a careful study of the members of all the Assemblies from 1789 to 1889, based on many more sources than were available to earlier biographers, whose work was necessarily more journalistic and hurried. J. F. Corkran's *History of the Constituent Assembly* is of interest for its lively portraits of the principal members as they appeared to a keen American observer, but the author is intensely partisan and unfair to all the advanced groups.

The attitude of the representatives toward political questions as they arose in the Assembly may be determined by their votes on a few test issues. Alhoy selects as such issues the Grévy, Leblond, Deville and Goudchaux amendments, and the final vote on the constitution. His record is, however, by no means accurate, and is especially faulty in the vote on the constitution, when compared with the semi-official report in the *Moniteur*. While retaining his test questions, therefore, we shall substitute the record of votes given in the *Moniteur* (often itself corrected in the issue succeeding the report of the vote, by a letter from some member inaccurately reported). Where the *Dictionnaire des parlementaires français* differs, its record is to be preferred, as based on the *procès-verbal* of the Assembly. The unwieldy size of the Assembly is no doubt partly accountable for the frequent errors in the record. To these test questions, suggested by Alhoy, we shall add two others, the Glais-Bizoin and Duvergier de Hauranne amendments, the latter not so much for a party-test, as for convenience in determining the member's attitude on the American example.

The Glais-Bizoin amendment proposed that in Article VIII of the preamble to the constitution, which as reported from the commission August 30, then read in part,

La république doit protéger le citoyen dans sa personne, sa famille, sa religion, sa propriété, son travail, et mettre à la portée de chacun l'instruction indispensable à tous les hommes; elle doit l'assistance aux citoyens nécessiteux, soit en leur procurant du travail dans les limites de ses ressources, soit en donnant, à défaut de la famille, les moyens d'exister à ceux qui sont hors d'état de travailler,

the first clause be allowed to stand down to and including the words "son travail," the remainder being changed to read:

Elle reconnaît le droit de tous les citoyens à l'instruction, le droit à l'assistance par le travail, et à l'assistance dans les formes et aux conditions réglées par les lois.

The point of the amendment was therefore the introduction of the *droit au travail*, which had been recognized only in a very imperfect form by the Provisional Government [1] and had become even more unpopular since the fiasco of the

---

[1] *Vide supra*, p. 38.

national workshops and the June insurrection. The amendment was defeated, September 14, 596 to 187. The final form of the constitution eliminated even the *droit à l'assistance* provided for in the project of August 30 in favor of a still more shadowy *assistance fraternelle* with the dangerous word *droit* quite eliminated.

The Goudchaux amendment proposed that in the second clause of Chap. II, Art. 15, which, referring to taxes, read in the project of August 30,

Chaque citoyen y contribue en raison de ses facultés et de sa fortune,

the words *en raison* be changed to *en proportion*. The reason for this was that the ambiguity of the expression *en raison* was held to leave the way open for the introduction of the progressive tax, a favorite scheme of the radicals for doing away with large fortunes. The amendment ruled out this possibility by incorporating the alternative plan of the moderates, the proportional tax, in the constitution. The amendment was adopted, September 25, 644 to 96.

The Duvergier de Hauranne amendment would change the proposed draft of Chap. IV, Art. 20, from

Le peuple français délégue le pouvoir législatif à une assemblée unique

to

Le peuple français délégue le pouvoir législatif à deux assemblées.

This two-chamber legislature was beaten, 530 to 289, September 27.

The Grévy amendment would amend Art. 41 in Chap. V from

Le peuple français délégue le pouvoir exécutif à un citoyen que reçoit le titre de président de la République

to

L'Assemblée nationale délégue le pouvoir exécutif à un citoyen qui reçoit le titre de président du conseil des ministres

and for the former Arts. 42 to 45, which provided among other things that the president should be named by direct, universal suffrage, with secret ballot and absolute majority of the votes, and that the election should be for four years with a prohibition of re-election until four other years had elapsed,—for these articles would substitute an Art. 42, thus conceived,

Le président du conseil des ministres est nommé par l'Assemblée nationale au scrutin secret et à la majorité absolue des suffrages. Elu pour un temps illimité, il est toujours révocable.

The design was thus to perpetuate the system which then existed, according to which General Cavaignac was merely an executive head, acting during the pleasure of the Assembly. There would be no real executive, as a separate power; the legislature would be supreme. The amendment came to a vote, October 7 and was defeated, 643 to 158.

Immediately afterward, a somewhat similar amendment, proposed by Leblond, was discussed. This would retain the commission's plan of a president, functioning as an independent branch of the government for a fixed term, but instead of having him elected by universal, direct suffrage, it proposed as Art. 43 that

Le président de la République est nommé par l'Assemblée nationale au scrutin secret et à la majorité absolue des suffrages.

Thus the legislature retained a certain superiority by its control over the executive, who, as its creature, could not boast a separate mandate from the people, a very real danger, as subsequent history proved. The Leblond amendment was however defeated, also on October 7, by 602 to 211.

The object of the Deville amendment was to restore to Art. 107 in Chap. IX, which dealt with military service, the words " en personne," and the clause " Le remplacement est interdit," both in the August 30 draft, but later withdrawn by the commission, which instead proposed to refer the decision on the principle they embodied to the organic laws, on account of the angry discussion they had excited. The amendment, by requiring personal service of every Frenchman and forbidding paid substitutes, would provide a national army, in which rich and poor alike would be compelled to serve; the opponents of the amendment wanted a professional army, with the right to hire substitutes. The amendment was rejected, October 21, by 663 to 140.

It will be seen, then, that in general a vote for the Glais-Bizoin, the Grévy, the Leblond and the Deville amendments, and against the Goudchaux and Duvergier de Hauranne amendments would be a radical vote. To remove any doubt on this point, there have been added to the table on pp. 144-146 in which are to be found the votes of all those who mentioned the example of America on any constitutional question, favorably or unfavorably, the names and votes of the leading radicals and conservatives; their attitude on the test questions will be a further aid in determining the political position of the men we are studying.

Certain reservations as to the perfect accuracy of the standards we have chosen, must now be made. The great body of moderate republicans, which controlled the Assembly, furnished the bulk of the majority on all these questions. It was, however, by definition, a center party, neither radical nor conservative in an extreme sense. On the Duvergier de Hauranne amendment, for example, it voted on the radical side, on all the others, it voted with the conservatives. Nor did it ever vote as a unit. Many moderate republicans, particularly of the *républicains du lendemain*, voted with the conservatives on the Duvergier de Hauranne amendment while on the other hand, we find Dupont de l'Eure voting with the radicals on the Deville amendment; F. Arago and Garnier-Pagès, both republicans of the *National* nuance, are on opposite sides on the Leblond amendment. Again, such a pronounced legitimist as De la Rochejacquelein voted with the radicals on the Grévy amendment by the side of Greppo, the socialist. It is obvious, therefore, that no one of these amendments can be taken as a fair test by itself. Party discipline was too loose to control the erratic expression of individual opinions. But it may fairly be said that if in the majority of these seven test votes, a man's voice be given pretty steadily for one side or the other, he can be classified with justice as holding a political attitude in general symapthy with the radical or the conservative position. In many cases, the man's speeches and his previous career will enable us to fix this attitude with greater precision.

For convenience, we shall group the 55 representatives who referred to American example, favorably or unfavorably, into six divisions, three of which, the liberal, radical republican and socialist, express various shades of advanced opinion, while two others, the conservative and legitimist, take the opposite attitude. A few neutral individuals will have to be grouped apart as unclassifiable. Those here called liberals are in general moderate republicans of the *National* stamp, the men who controlled the provisional government and the executive commission and were in majority in the Assembly. The party contained the moderate *républicains de la veille,* as well as some others and took up a left center position. The radicals were that more intransigeant group of *républicains de la veille,* who followed the leadership of Ledru-Rollin and the *Réforme* newspaper.[1] The conservatives were usually *républicains du lendemain* and for the most part ex-Orleanists, often men who had held office under the July Monarchy, though the majority had been in opposition to the Guizot ministry. Some were still Orleanist in sentiment, though most professed republicanism, being practical men. This was the right center party. The extreme groups, socialists and legitimists, require no special elucidation. The socialists had no common program except one of criticism, but each individual leader had a more or less definite scheme of his own; the legitimists on the other hand, were limited to one simple ideal,—the return of Charles X's grandson, the duc de Bordeaux, as Henry V.

In the liberal group, we may fairly place 16 members who alluded to the example of the United States either with approval or disapproval.

M. Barth was the son of a workman who had grown wealthy. He became a Fourierist, but in the Assembly grew more moderate, attaching himself to Cavaignac's fortunes. He voted, however, against the interdiction of the clubs, for the abolition of the death penalty, and against a *cautionnement* for the press. Lesaulnier says that he was light and easily open to influences.

J. B. Brunet was a soldier, chiefly interested in Algerian colonization.

---

[1] It should be remarked that elsewhere in this study we have used the term "radical" in the looser sense to cover all the more advanced groups, rather than in this technical sense, which we have endeavored to distinguish by the term "radical republican." The same caution should be given regarding "conservative," elsewhere employed less specifically.

J. L. E. Cordier, as deputy for many years, had sat on the extreme left, voting against the Pritchard indemnity and for electoral reform. In the Assembly, he occupied a moderate democratic position.

Adolphe Crémieux, one of the party leaders, was a strong Bonapartist in 1815 and always opposed the Restoration. Though an office holder under the July Monarchy, as deputy from 1842 to 1848 he sat with the dynastic opposition. He did, however, at first favor a regency in February, and was said, according to Lesaulnier, to have sat beside the Duchess of Orleans in the Chamber and to have written a little speech for her, which she did not deliver. He managed to change sides quickly enough to become a member of the provisional government, and to hold the portfolio of justice. He was a moderate republican, somewhat vacillating.

P. N. Gerdy, a physician, sat on the left in the Assembly, holding strongly democratic opinions. He did not remain long in politics, and after one session returned to private life.

Jules Grévy, the future president of the Third Republic, was commissioner for the Jura in the early days of 1848 and becoming very popular there, headed the delegation from the Jura in the Assembly. Here he sat on the left and was the author of the celebrated Grévy amendment, previously referred to. Alhoy speaks of his clear and close dialectic.

Alphonse de Lamartine was the principal figure in the first phase of the republic as Cavaignac was in the second and Louis Napoleon in the third. He was still a power in the Assembly, but his glory was on the wane. Born at Mâcon in 1790 of an aristocratic family, he was brought up in a strictly religious, legitimist atmosphere. He hated the Empire and devoted himself to travel and poetry. He married an Englishwoman and during the Restoration held various diplomatic posts in Italy. As a legitimist he opposed the July Monarchy, but he gradually became more and more independent in politics and was finally given up by his old party associates. He traveled in the East, entered the Chamber in 1833, and in 1847 wrote that *Histoire des Girondins,* which flattered the moderate republicans and gave him his prestige at the outbreak of the revolution. Under the republic, he aimed at occupying an absolutely central, nonpartisan position, the friend of all parties. This doubtless accounts for his admiration of Washington, but despite his brilliant oratory, Lamartine was not convincing enough to be permanently successful; men began to suspect his love of dramatic effects and his vanity; despite his undoubtedly pure ideals, he lost popularity and influence.

Lavallée had been a member of the society *Aide-toi, le ciel t'aidera,* Garnier-Pagès being one of his principal friends. According to *Nôtre Histoire,* he had been on the staff of the *National* at one time, and represented its type of politics.

Armand Marrast was born at Saint-Gaudens in 1801. He struggled out of a poverty-stricken home and became a teacher of rhetoric and the humanities, ultimately securing a position in the college of Louis-le-Grand at Paris. While there he took his doctorate at the Sorbonne. In 1827, he made a speech at the tomb of the republican, Manuel, which lost him his academic position. He turned to tutoring and journalism, writing principally for the *Tribune,* the republican paper. After 1830, he vainly sought office and his failure drove him into uncompromising opposition. Imprisoned for his writings, he escaped to England, married a natural daughter of George IV, and after being condemned to death in Spain for a song insulting the queen-regent, returned to Paris and became editor-in-chief of the *National.* He had now learned prudence from experience and his fiery style was refined into a more delicate, mocking wit, sharp rather than profound. Member of the Provisional Government, mayor of Paris from March to July, representative from

Haute-Garonne, president of the Assembly from July 1848 until May, 1849 and reporter of the constitution, he was one of the most important figures in the early republic. Yet his vanity, the ostentatious luxury of his habits and his moderation in politics made him unpopular, especially with the radicals, who regarded him as cynical and selfish and as the real adviser of the government from June to December.

J. B. Payer attached himself to Lamartine, and was *chef de cabinet* when the latter took over the foreign ministry.

Charles Rolland was another follower of Lamartine.[1]

Sarrans had Bonapartist sympathies during the Restoration. It was in his *Nouvelle Minerve* that Cormenin published his famous Timon articles. He was Lafayette's aide-de-camp in July, 1830, but presently turned against the monarchy, about which he wrote several books. He opposed the *cautionnement* in the Assembly and usually voted with the left.

A. M. J. Sénard was made *procureur-général* by the republic. His repression of the election riots at Rouen was not received with favor by the radicals. Elected for the department of Seine-Inférieure, he became president of the

---

[1] There was another Rolland, representing the department of Lot, whose politics are unclassifiable; he voted for the Grévy and Goudchaux projects, against those of Glais-Bizoin, Leblond and Deville, and was absent at the vote on the Duvergier de Hauranne amendment. He was a farmer, a member of the committees on agriculture and on the *Crédit foncier*. One of these two men alluded to the American example in a speech on May 30th, as reporter of the special commission on incompatibilities. The report was discussed at intervals until June 14, when it was adopted, but from first to last the reporter is alluded to only as "the citizen Rolland." It was probably, however, the Rolland mentioned in the text, as Rolland of Lot had other committee designations for which he was peculiarly fitted, and is said to have taken little interest in general politics. The latter's vote on the Grévy amendment shows that he must have had liberal tendencies, though he was obviously not an extremist, and the general classification would be unaffected whichever man is taken.

Assembly. After June, he grew somewhat more conservative. As minister of the interior, he proposed the decree establishing a *cautionnement* or bond, required of all newspapers.

Antony Thouret (incorrectly spelled Tourret in the *Moniteur*) voted with the Cavaignac group.

L. F. Wolowski was a Polish revolutionist who had become a naturalized French citizen in 1834. He practised law, founded the *Revue de législation et de jurisprudence* and finally specialized in economics. He was professor at the Conservatoire des Arts et Métiers; in his writings he opposed Louis Blanc's scheme for organizing labor, but in a somewhat less conservative vein than Chevalier. Under the Provisional Government, he was a member of the Luxembourg Commission and sat in the Assembly for Seine. Here he attached himself to Cavaignac and as member of the committee on labor tried to improve factory conditions for women and children.

Eight others may be classified as radical republicans.

H. G. Didier sat for Algeria in the Assembly, and was member of the committee on the colonies.

Hippolyte Detours, originally a legitimist, became an extreme radical. In the Assembly, he represented Tarn-et-Garonne, sitting on the extreme left, and showed his radicalism by his votes against the *cautionnement*, the interdiction of the clubs, the prosecution of Louis Blanc and Caussidière, the death penalty, imprisonment for debt, and so on. A letter from him to the *Moniteur*, October 10, throws light on the negative vote which some radicals cast on the Leblond amendment the greater number voting in favor of it as the next best thing to the defeated Grévy amendment and from a notion, based on the experience of 1793, that it would be easier to control a Paris Assembly than the country at large. Detours, however, preferred the principle of universal suf-

frage.   He said, " I had supported the Grévy amendment;
I did not want a president of the republic.   Reduced by the
vote of the majority to deciding between choice by the Assembly and choice by the people, I rejected on Saturday the
first of these two modes of election [the Leblond amend-
ment] and without opposing the second to-day [Article 43,
adopted 627-130], I thought I ought to abstain from voting,
in order to remain a complete stranger to the establishment
of a dangerous and anti-republican magistracy."

Deville became somewhat conspicuous by applauding the
rioters who invaded the Assembly on May 15.   He sat on
the extreme left and was the author of the Deville amendment, forbidding the hiring of paid substitutes for military
service.   He wished to declare members of former reign-
ing families and generals ineligible to the presidency and
was interested in other radical measures.

Ferdinand Flocon, born at Paris in 1800, began life as a
teacher, but learned telegraphy and shorthand; his skill
gave him an opening as stenographer for the Parisian press.
His pamphlets against the Jesuits started a career of journalism in service of the opposition.   He became editor of
the *Courrier français* and affiliated with the secret societies.
The year 1848 found him at the head of the *Réforme*, the
organ of Ledru-Rollin's group.   He was a member of the
Provisional Government and when it yielded to the Executive Commission, became minister of agriculture.   As such,
he presented a plan for the organization of the prud'hommes.
The creation of agricultural colonies in France was one of
his pet ideas.   He was, however, not a socialist, and exerted
rather a restraining than an exciting influence on his friend,
Ledru-Rollin.

A. A. Ledru-Rollin, another of the important men of the
early republic, was born at Paris in 1807.   He was a lawyer
of distinction, wrote works of jurisprudence and became

deputy from Mans in 1841. His declaration of principles was so sensational that he was put under sentence of imprisonment for four months, though he escaped on technical grounds. He took part in the Lille banquet, where the toast to the king was excluded. The republic made him member of the Provisional Government and minister of the interior, in which capacity he sent out the commissioners, who so frightened conservative folk. He served on the Executive Commission and as representative for the department of the Seine. Always on the suspect-list as a dangerous revolutionist, he respected property and preferred its extensive subdivision to its abolition. In this vital point, he spoke for the petty bourgeoisie rather than the proletariat. He was a remarkable speaker and would trace his political ancestry back to Robespierre minus the bloodshed, rather than to Babeuf.

A. Martin-Bernard, a famous republican conspirator under the monarchy, became one of Ledru-Rollin's commissioners; his votes were consistently radical.

Félix Pyat, a lawyer, spent most of his days in militant journalism and was the author of several social dramas. Having inherited a million francs, he invested part in the *Revue britannique*, of which he was editor for a while. With Hugo, Balzac, Georges Sand and others, he founded the *Société des gens de lettres*. Like Barbès, he was one of those rich déclassés, whose interest in humanity outweighed personal selfishness. As time went on, he became more and more alienated from his own class, was known as a leading socialist after 1849, spent the last part of his life between prison and exile and in 1871 was an officer of the Commune.

Saint-Gaudens had refused a judgeship in 1832, because of his unwillingness to take the necessary oath of allegiance to the king.

Only two out-and-out socialists are to be included in the list.

Philippe Mathieu, always called Mathieu de la Drôme, from the department he represented in the Assembly, favored state ownership of railroads, and said of socialism that " far from being an enemy, it must purify the sources of property." He opposed the *cautionnement*, imprisonment for debt, and the prosecutions of Blanc and Caussidière.

The other socialist, Pierre Leroux, was a more conspicuous character, though less interested in constitutional questions than Mathieu. He was a workingman turned philosopher. In 1839 he wrote his chief work, *L'Humanité*, whose thesis was the negation of human personality in favor of the absorption of the individual in the whole. This notion of absolute equality was the essence of his socialism, of which he was regarded as the profoundest thinker. His erudition was great, but he had no system, properly speaking; his ideas were large, vague and not well developed. Other more practical spirits borrowed from him, and his authority among radicals was very great, but he accomplished little positive work himself. Alhoy says that he passed his whole life in unfinished undertakings. In the Assembly he contended for the freedom of the press and the perpetuation of the ten-hour law, which was, however, by reactionary legislation, extended to twelve.

The conservative group, most of whom had taken active part in Orleanist parliaments and would have been contented enough with a mere change of ministry in February, numbered 23 members who alluded to American example.

Alcock, a judge and member of the old Chamber, went over to the moderate opposition with Dupont de l'Eure. In the Assembly he usually voted with the right.

J. M. Ambert was a soldier and military journalist; *L'Abeille de la Nouvelle-Orléans* published articles by him on American politics, which he studied on the ground. In the Assembly, he reported the decree creating the *garde mobile*, which did most effective work in helping to repress the June insurrection. His votes were usually with the right, against the banishment of the Orleans family, for the *cautionnement*, and for the interdiction of the clubs.[1]

R. A. Aylies, counsel at the royal court, was elected to the Chamber in 1842, where he ranked in the opposition as a *constitutionnel*. In the Assembly, he sat on the right.

Odilon Barrot, one of the chief men in this party, was born at Villefort in 1791. As a lawyer, he always preferred the more abstract, theoretical elements of his profession. In 1815, he was among the young volunteers who accompanied Louis XVIII to Ghent on his second brief exile. The White Terror alienated him, however, and in 1830, representing the new monarchy, he conducted Charles X to Cherbourg; on his return he was made prefect of the Seine. He sat in the Chamber from 1830 to 1848 and, while a faithful Orleanist, presently found himself on the left as leader of the dynastic opposition. He later allied himself with Thiers, but was one of the prime movers of the banquet campaign. When the Guizot ministry fell, he was named with Thiers to form a new cabinet, but it was already too late. His efforts to establish the Duchess of Orleans as regent failed. In the Assembly he sat for Aisne among the conservatives.

A. A. Billault was an opposition deputy in 1837, but was given charge of the legal affairs of the duc d'Aumale, being important enough to be worth corrupting. In the Assembly, he was a conservative.

Count Louis Combarel de Leyval was a rich land-owner, sitting on the left center during the monarchy, a man of the Barrot sort politically. *Nôtre Histoire's* assertion that nothing but scandals, civil, political and judiciary have been

[1] *Cf. supra*, p. 47 *et seq.*

connected with him, coupled with Lesaulnier's condemnation, shows how much offence he seems to have given to the advanced groups.

F. Dabeaux fought the project to increase the severity of existing laws against meetings, but was considered a conservative and is said to have grown increasingly so, despite his earlier liberal views.

Edmond Drouyn de Luys (or Lhuys) was one of the younger diplomats of the July Monarchy. Elected deputy in 1842, he went over to the dynastic opposition, being classed as a conservative in the Assembly. He was president of the committee of foreign affairs and, as such, reported the message of thanks to the American Congress, though Alhoy remarks that this was a strange choice on the Assembly's part, the member " being still somewhat too saturated with monarchical opinions."

J. A. Dufaure was a seasoned parliamentary veteran, having been a deputy for fourteen years when the Assembly began. He was usually considered a member of the liberal constitutional or third party and was twice vice-president of the Chamber. He was minister of public works under Soult and was regarded as a good administrator. His experience and his compact logic always gave him a hearing. Being very conservative, he opposed the banquets. In the Assembly, he sat for Charente and became Cavaignac's minister of the interior after October 13, 1848. His election to the French Academy under the Empire was considered an Orleanist protest against the imperialists.

Pierre Charles François, Baron Dupin (usually called Charles Dupin) was a mathematician and naval engineer. Deputy from 1827 to 1837, he grew increasingly conservative, defended the clergy, opposed free trade and in 1837 was raised to a peerage. In the upper house, he continued his industrious support of the government. Elected to the

Assembly in June, 1848, he sat there (for Seine-Inférieure) as an extreme conservative.

Prosper-Léon Duvergier de Hauranne was born at Rouen in 1798, of Jansenist stock. A *doctrinnaire*, he was one of the editors of the *Globe* and as deputy (1831-48) lent his support to Casimir-Périer's repressive measures, to Thiers' September laws, to the coalition against the Molé cabinet (believing in pure parliamentary government on the English model). With Guizot and Rossi, he published the *Revue française*, but broke with Guizot after 1840, becoming a follower of Thiers. He was a leader in the banquet campaign. In the Assembly, as a member for Cher, he sat on the right. His parliamentary strategy and finesse were famous. He supported the monarchist majority of the Assembly against Louis Napoleon, and spent the period of the Empire in writing a ten-volume history of parliamentary government in France. He is not to be confounded with J. B. Duvergier, who made the *Collection complète des lois.* Corkran speaks of him as not only well versed in English history, but a close observer of English politics and a personal acquaintance of the leading English statesmen.

Léon Faucher, early on the staff of such conservative papers as the *Temps*, the *Constitutionnel* and the *Courrier français*, later turned to economics, producing in 1845 his *Etudes sur l'Angleterre*. He was a free-trader and an admirer of the English constitution. As deputy from 1846 to '48, he sat with the left center, opposing Guizot, but concerning himself chiefly with fiscal problems. He took part in the banquets and was elected to the Assembly from the Marne. A bitter opponent of socialism, he sat on the right and belonged to the group of the rue de Poitiers. He reported the famous law of May 31, 1850, limiting the suffrage.

A. Jobez, a wealthy factory owner, belonged to the liberal opposition under the monarchy; in the Assembly he usually

voted with the right.   He wrote studies of social economy,
such as a *Préface au Socialisme* in 1848 and *La Démocratie,
c'est l'inconnu* in 1849.

Bertrand Théobald Joseph, baron de Lacrosse, sat in the
dynastic opposition under the July Monarchy, from 1836
to 1848.   His political views were those of Barrot and
Thiers, his interest principally in naval matters and in the
slavery question.   He represented Finistère in the Assembly,
became a secretary, then vice-president, and regularly voted
with the right, thus favoring the *cautionnement*, imprisonment for debt, the death penalty, and the prosecution of
Louis Blanc.

Ferdinand de Lasteyrie, a count, and his cousin Jules de
Lasteyrie, who bore the title of marquis, had sat with the
Barrot party in the dynastic opposition and voted as con-
servatives in the Assembly.

N. H. Levet belonged to a rich, influential family.   He
was affiliated with the rue de Poitiers group, and his conservatism is further guaranteed by Alhoy's assertion that
he " has voted for all rigorous measures " and that " the
unfortunate debtor can hope for nothing from him."

A. J. Lherbette was a deputy from 1831 to 1848, sitting
in the dynastic opposition, like so many other future conservative members of the Assembly of 1848.

François Marrast did not speak on the American example; his vote will, therefore, not here be counted, as we
have definitely confined ourselves to those who did.   His
attitude was so well-known and striking, however, that he
deserves mention.   He was born at Bayonne in 1799, being no relation to his more conspicuous namesake.   He was
in Napoleon's army, on whose defeat he went to aid the
South Americans in their struggle for independence.   He
spent ten years traveling in the western hemisphere.   Alhoy's
account is worth quoting textually in this connection.

He saw several republics of South America establish them-selves, but the anarchy, the disorder, which violent situations and civil wars always necessarily produce, made him prefer sojourning in North America. He established himself in the United States, whose constitution he studied assiduously [*fortement*]. The benefits which it procures to those it rules, and which he enjoyed a long time himself, filled him with ad-miration and gratitude for the work of Washington and of Franklin. So when, several years later, he returned to his natal land, he called himself openly a republican of the Ameri-can school.[1]

Marrast was elected to the Assembly from Landes and placed on the committee of the interior. He voted with the right, for the *cautionnement*, imprisonment for debt, and the death penalty. Alhoy in an instructive passage confirms Marrast's conservatism and his Americanism and at the same time shows what the more radical minds of the time thought about the American system.

He has shown a poor understanding of the French spirit, the popular spirit, in wishing to cut our laws and decrees according to the pattern of the American spirit. Thus he voted for the decree against mob gatherings, without thinking that violence will never be able to accomplish anything against ideas, and that hence if there is a cause impelling men to assemble, if one wants to prevent the meeting, one should remedy the cause and not disperse the meeting by force.

E. F. Morin, baron de Malsabrier, usually voted con-servatively.

Auguste Joseph Christoph Jules, marquis de Mornay was captain of the royal guard under the Restoration. He served as aide to Soult, his father-in-law. Deputy from

---

[1] Alhoy, *op. cit., s. v.* Marrast. Similar testimony is borne by Le-saulnier.

1830 to 1848, he voted with the opposition, but in the Assembly (member for Oise), sided usually with the right.

Felix-Esquirou de Parieu voted for the *cautionnement,* the death-penalty, suppression of the clubs, etc. Finance was his specialty; his works on that subject procured him entrance to the Institute.

Saint-Priest, born 1801, a Toulouse lawyer, was a dynastic opposition deputy from 1842 to 1846. He sat for Lot in the Assembly, on the conservative benches. He was a member of the committee of finances, and belonged to the rue de Poitiers group. He had no connection with the legitimist family of the same name.

Alexis de Tocqueville was born at Verneuil in 1805. Gaining his *licence* in law in 1826, he travelled in Italy and Sicily. As *juge auditeur* at Versailles he made his life-long friendship with Gustave de Beaumont. He opposed the Polignac ministry, but was not sympathetic with the July régime. His travels in America, in the interest of prison reform, and the literary fruits of this journey have been previously considered. He was deputy from 1839 to '48, in the opposition; on January 27, in a speech in the Chamber, he predicted the revolution. Alhoy remarks uneasily, "Despite the just consideration which M. de Tocqueville enjoys, the reproach is made that he has not sufficiently studied American institutions, that he has seen them in a false light and that, in wishing to import them among us, he has not sufficiently considered the difference in manners." He represented Manche in the Assembly, and voted with the right, for the *cautionnement,* imprisonment for debt, and other conservative measures.

Four others may be counted as legitimists.

The abbé Edmond de Cazalès was superior of the Montauban seminary. A royalist, he sat on the right, but was well thought of by his opponents.

Pierre Jouin, born at Rennes in 1818, was a lawyer at the local court of appeals. He is said by the *Dictionnaire des parlementaires français* to have become one of the chiefs of the Rennes democrats, to have been of moderate opinions, very religious, and to have gone toward the left on the election of Louis Napoleon. Lesaulnier says he is a liberal spirit, who has not always believed in a republic, but is no less disposed to do everything to put it on a solid and durable basis, a regular phrase for the *républicains du lendemain*. *Nôtre Histoire* informs us that it is said this young man has more merit than his exterior indicates; he was elected by the legitimists, but there is hope for better things. Alhoy declares it to be uncertain if his tendency is toward democratic constitutions. There is thus some doubt as to Jouin's proper classification, but as all his votes in the Assembly were conservative, it is at least certain that he belongs on the right; his classification as a legitimist or a conservative republican does not affect our conclusions.

Audren de Kerdrel was editor of a legitimist paper at Rennes and sat with that party in the Assembly, representing Ille-et-Vilaine. He belonged to the rue de Poitiers group. He is described as tall, thin and dry like Don Quixote, and as having wealth and ability.

Charles-Forbes, comte de Montalembert, was born at Stanmore, England, in 1810, the son of a French legitimist *émigré* peer of the old noblesse and of a rigid Scotch Presbyterian. Under the influence of Lamennais and Lacordaire, he went into the liberal Catholic movement and co-operated with them in the publication of *L'Avenir*. When the Pope condemned the movement, the men separated, Lamennais preferring to follow his vision of truth, Montalembert and Lacordaire unwilling to leave their Church. Montalembert now devoted himself to a study of the Middle

Ages, and wrote a pious, but unhistorical life of St. Elizabeth of Hungary. He sat in the opposition in the House of Peers from 1835 to 1848, and was said to be the greatest orator of that body. His chief interest was to break down the University monopoly over education in the interest of religious instruction; to accomplish this, he even opened schools himself in defiance of law. In the Assembly, Montalembert sat for Doubs, on the extreme right. He was really more Catholic than legitimist, was member of the committee of cults, and was willing enough to support the republic, if it was sufficiently conservative and better suited to the interests of the Church. In this attitude, Lacordaire sympathized, during the latter's short membership in the Assembly, and in the conduct of his paper, *L'Ere nouvelle*. It was a minority's brave effort to free the Church from past entangling alliances and to set its face toward the future, but it was not wholly successful.

Two men remain unclassifiable.

Amable Dubois, a land-owner, sat in the dynastic opposition during the monarchy, and was much interested in the efforts to do away with child-labor. In the Assembly, he sat on the moderate left (according to the *Dictionnaire des parlementaires français*) as member for Somme. Here he was appointed to the committee of labor. His votes seem to have been conservative, and in 1849 he was counted with the monarchist majority against Louis Napoleon. Dubois seems to have occupied as nearly a central position as possible and it would be unfair to base any conclusions on his political action.

Lubbert was born at Hamburg, Germany, in 1803. He was a sailor from youth. He represented Gironde in the Assembly. His votes were mainly conservative, but the *Dictionnaire des parlementaires français* says that he had liberal opinions, somewhat exalted, and very independent.

Such were the members of the Assembly, who alluded to America in their speeches. Considerations of space forbid extending the list, though the votes of a few leaders, not here included, will be found appended in the table on page 144 *et seq.*

It now becomes necessary to review the eighteen members of the constitutional commission. A. Marrast, Tocqueville, Thouret, Dufaure and Barrot have been already treated as members of the Assembly. The others must now be briefly considered.

L. M. de Lahage, vicomte de Cormenin, was the first president of the commission. He was born at Paris in 1788 of an excellent " family of the robe," held office both under the first Empire and the Restoration and wrote various works on administrative law. He was deputy from 1828 to 1848, sitting on the left. His pamphlets, signed Timon, directed against the extravagance of the civil list, were incisive and powerful. In 1848 he sat for Seine in the Assembly, and is to be ranked with the liberals, voting among other things for the abolition of the death penalty, for the banishment of the Orleans family and against the prosecution of Louis Blanc and Caussidière. He was forced to resign from the commission, having caricatured it in a pamphlet.

G. de Beaumont, born in the department of Sarthe, 1802. was a magistrate under the Restoration, journeyed with Tocqueville to America, writing a novel on the slavery question upon his return. From 1839 to 1848 he was a deputy sitting in the dynastic opposition. In 1848 he was elected for Somme and, like Tocqueville, ranks as a conservative. He voted for the *cautionnement,* but was absent from all of our test votes, representing France at London and Vienna.

Victor Considérant was born in the Jura, 1808, graduated from the Ecole Polytechnique and became captain of engineers in the army. From 1831 he devoted himself exclusively to the Fourierist propaganda, edited successively the *Phalange* and the *Démocratie pacifique*, and was elected as a leading socialist to the Assembly from Loiret. He later attempted a Fourierist colony in Texas, without great success.

A. L. Coquerel, born at Paris in 1795, became a leading Protestant minister in that city. His tendency was more liberal than that of the rest of the consistory, of which he was a member from 1833. He was a moderate republican and sat in the center. His votes were usually conservative, but he is reckoned by some with the liberals of the *National* stripe. It would be difficult to classify him, since he tried not to classify himself.

C. A. Corbon, born at Arbigny in 1808, came from a family of working-people, and as a child worked for a weaver. In Paris he learned wood-carving and became a compositor. In 1848 he founded *L'Atelier*, a liberal Catholic paper conducted by and for workingmen. The policy of the paper and its editor was liberal republicanism. Corbon was elected to the Assembly from Seine.

A. Dornès, born at Lyons, 1799, son of a general, was an intimate friend of A. Marrast and became one of the principal editors of the *National*. He represented Moselle in the Assembly, where he made the motion that created the executive commission. He died in July, 1848, of wounds received in the June insurrection.

André Marie Dupin, called, to distinguish him from Charles Dupin, his younger brother, Dupin ainé, was born at Varzy in Nièvre, 1783. He was a lawyer of great distinction, and had an extremely long parliamentary career, being deputy from 1827 to 1848, representative (for Nièvre) in 1848 and 1849, and afterward senator of the Second Empire. Having been a bonapartist in the last days of the first Napoleon, he was known as a moderate liberal during the Restoration. He became an extremely ardent and very conservative Orleanist and was regarded as the essence and mouthpiece of the bourgeois régime. His sarcastic, powerful language made him one of the efficient supporters of the government, always called on in times of stress. His epigram, *"Chacun chez soi, chacun son droit,"* was held to sum up the spirit of the existing system. He was one of Louis Philippe's most trusted personal counsellors and retained confidential professional relations with the Orléans family even after its fall, with the knowledge and consent of the republic, which he continued to serve as *procureur-général* of the Cour de Cassation. He was eight times president of the old Chamber of Deputies, became one of its famous presiding officers. He was, of course, an extreme conservative during the republic. He was a member both of the French Academy and of the Academy of Moral and Political Sciences. Charles Dupin followed almost exactly the same political evolution in his long parliamentary career as his more famous brother.

F. R. de Lamennais, born at St. Malo, 1782, had already written against the supremacy of the civil over the religious power, when he took orders in 1816. His *Essai sur l'indifférence* made him immensely popular with Rome, where he was offered the cardinal's hat, but declined. His struggle against Gallicanism, however, made him unpopular with the French episcopate, which began to undermine his influence. He founded *L'Avenir* to preach his gospel of religious republicanism and demanded separation of Church and State, administrative decentralization, extension of electoral rights, freedom of association and of the press. His enemies brought about a papal condemnation of his theories in 1832, but while submitting in form, he reaffirmed his principles in the famous *Paroles d'un croyant* (1834).

This brought about his rupture with the Church. He became greatly interested in the working-classes, and in 1837 wrote *Le Livre du peuple*. At the beginning of the republic he founded *Le Peuple constituant*, which endured till the *cautionnement* law compelled its suspension in July. In the Assembly, sitting for Seine, Lamennais worked with the radicals, voting against the *cautionnement* and imprisonment for debt, the prosecution of L. Blanc and Caussidière, the death-penalty, and other conservative measures.

Edouard Martin, known as Martin de Strasbourg, born at Mulhouse in 1801, established himself as a lawyer at Strasburg. He was deputy from 1837 to 1842, sitting with Arago, Dupont de l'Eure and others on the extreme left. After the revolution, he presided over the commission which reorganized the judiciary and was sent to the Assembly from Bas-Rhin; in this body he voted with the liberals, favoring the abolition of the death-penalty, and opposing the interdiction of the clubs, but also opposing the progressive tax and the Grévy amendment. He moved the resolution conferring the executive power on Cavaignac in June, and constantly opposed Louis Napoleon.

Jean-Pierre Pagès, called Pagès de l'Ariège, was born in 1784 at Seix and became a lawyer in Toulouse. Like so many others, he was much in journalism and always a violent opponent of the Restoration government. As deputy from 1831 to 1842 and from 1847 to 1848, he sat on the left, and, elected for Haute-Garonne to the Assembly, voted with the liberals.

A. Tenaille de Vaulabelle, born in 1799 in the department of Yonne, began as a journalist, working on the *National* for a while, and then became an historian. His *Histoire des deux Restorations* (1844) was long the standard authority. In 1848 Lamartine offered him the embassies of London and Berlin, but he refused both. In the Assembly, sitting for Yonne, he voted generally with the liberal republicans. He became minister of public instruction, but only served a short time.

A. F. A. Vivien, born at Paris, 1799, was a lawyer at the Amiens bar. In 1831 he became prefect of police in Paris, served as deputy from 1833 to 1848 and in the council of state, where his administrative abilities were of great value. He sat for the most part in the dynastic opposition, but in the Assembly, a member for Aisne, he voted always with the conservatives. From October to December he was Cavaignac's minister of public works.

Woirhaye was born at Metz in 1798. He practised law in that city, defending the accused in several political trials, and was elected to the Assembly from Moselle. He was a liberal republican, a partisan of Cavaignac.

Having thus sketched the lives and general political attitude of the representatives who alluded to America and of the members of the constitutional commission, it is necessary to show the position taken by these men toward the test-questions selected. As has been explained above, these test-questions serve only as a rough index of general political disposition and must be taken in connection with the biographies of the members to gain a correct view of a member's position.

To aid in understanding the political significance of the various votes, we have added those cast by a few typical leaders of each party. F. Arago, Dupont de l'Eure, A. P. Marie, L. E. Cavaignac and Georges Lafayette (son of Washington's friend) are typical liberals; David d'Angers, the sculptor, A. O. Glais-Bizoin, C. Pelletier and Edgar Quinet will rank as radicals; J. L. Greppo and P. J. Proudhon as socialists; Adolphe Thiers and Charles François, comte de Rémusat, as conservatives; A. P. Berryer and H. A. G. Duverger, marquis de la Rochejacquelein, as legitimists.   Perfect unanimity even among the leaders is not attainable.

Liberals	*Du. de Hau.*	*Grévy*	*Leb.*	*Goud.*	*Dev.*	*Glais-Biz.*	*Const.*
F. Arago	N	Y	Y	Ab	Ab	Ab	Y
Barthe	N	N	N	Y	N	N	Y
Brunet	Y	N	N	Y	Ab	N	Y
Cavaignac	N	Ab	Y	Y	Ab	Ab	Y
Corbon	N	N	N	Y	Y	N	Y
Cordier	Y	N	N	Ab	N	N	Ab
Cormenin	N	Ab	N	Ab	Y	Y	Y
Crémieux	N	N	N	Y	N	Y	Y
Dupont (de l'Eure)	N	N	N	Ab	Y	N	Y
Gerdy	Y	N	N	Y	N	Ab	Y
Grévy	N	Y	Y	Y	Ab	Ab	Y
G. Lafayette	N	N	N	Y	N	N	Y
Lamartine	Ab	N	N	Y	Ab	Ab	Ab
Lavallée	N	N	N	N	Y	N	Y
Marie	N	N	Y	Y	N	Ab	Y
A. Marrast	N	Y	Y	Y	N	N	Y
Martin (de Strasbourg)	N	N	Y	Y	N	N	Y
Pagès (de l'Ariège)	Ab	N	N	Ab	Ab	Ab	Ab
Payer	N	N	N	Y	N	N	Y
C. Rolland	N	N	N	Y	N	Y	Ab
Sarrans	N	Y	Y	Ab	N	Ab	Y
Senard	N	N	Y	Ab	Ab	N	Y
Thouret	N	N	Y	Y	N	N	Y
Vaulabelle	N	N	Y	Y	N	N	Y
Woirhaye	N	N	N	Y	N	N	Y
Wolowski	Y	N	N	Y	N	N	Y
Radicals							
David (d'Angers)	N	Y	Y	Ab	Y	Y	Y
Detours	N	Y	N	Ab	Y	Y	Ab
Deville	N	Y	N	N	Y	Y	N
Didier	N	Y	Y	N	Y	Ab	Y
Flocon	N	N	Y	Y	Y	Y	Ab
Glais-Bizoin	N	Y	Y	Y	N	Y	Y
Lamennais	N	Y	N	N	Y	Y	Ab
Ledru-Rollin	N	Y	N	N	Y	Y	Ab
Martin-Bernard	N	Y	N	N	Y	Y	Ab
Pelletier	N	Y	N	N	Y	Ab	N
Pyat	N	Y	N	N	Y	Y	N
Quinet	N	Y	Y	Y	Y	Y	Y
Saint-Gaudens	N	N	N	Y	Y	Y	Y

Socialists

Greppo	N	Y	Ab	N	Y	Y	N
Leroux	Ab	Ab	Ab	Not given	Y	Not given	N
Mathieu (de la Drôme) ..	N	Y	N	N	Ab	Y	Ab
Proudhon	N	Y	Y	N	Y	Y	N

Conservatives

Alcock	Y	N	N	Y	N	N	Y
Ambert	Y	N	N	Y	N	N	Y
Aylies	Y	N	N	Y	N	N	Y
Barrot	Y	N	N	Y	N	N	Ab
Billault	N	Ab	Ab	Y	Ab	Ab	Y
Combarel de Leyval	Y	N	N	Y	N	N	Y
Dabeaux	N	N	N	Y	N	N	Y
Drouyin de Lhuys.	Y	N	N	Y	N	N	Y
Dufaure	N	N	N	Y	N	N	Y
Dupin ainé	N	N	N	Ab	N	N	Y
Ch. Dupin	Y	N	N	Y	N	N	Y
Duvergier de Hauranne ...	Y	N	N	Y	N	N	Ab
Faucher	Y	N	N	Y	N	N	Y
Jobez	Y	N	N	Y	N	N	Y
Lacrosse	N	N	N	Y	N	N	Y
F. de Lasteyrie	Y	N	N	Y	Y	N	Y
J. de Lasteyrie	Y	N	Ab	Y	N	N	Y
Levet	Y	N	N	Y	N	N	Y
Lherbette	Y	N	N	Y	N	N	Y
F. Marrast	Y	N	N	Y	N	N	Y
Morin	Y	Ab	N	Y	N	N	Ab
Mornay	Y	N	N	Y	N	N	Y
Parieu	N	N	Y	Y	N	N	Y
Rémusat	Y	N	N	Ab	N	N	Y
Saint Priest	Y	N	N	Y	N	N	Y
Thiers	Y	N	N	Y	N	N	Y
Tocqueville	Y	N	N	Ab	N	N	Y
Vivien	Y	N	N	Y	N	N	Y

Legitimists

Berryer	Ab	N	N	Ab	N	N	N
Cazalès	Not given	N	N	Y	N	N	Y
Jouin	Y	N	N	Y	N	N	Y
Kerdrel	Y	N	N	Y	N	N	Y
Montalembert	Y	N	N	Ab	N	N	N
de la Rochejacquelein .	Y	Y	N	Y	N	N	N

Unclassifiable

Coquerel	N	N	N	Y	N	N	Y
Dubois	Ab	N	N	Ab	N	Not given	Ab
Lubbert	Ab	N	N	Ab	N	Ab	N

When it comes to re-classifying these men according to their attitude on the American example, two tests are available, speeches and votes. The latter is the more important test; a man may praise or blame some point of American practice in the only speech in which he happens to allude to the United States, while adopting a directly contrary attitude on the two constitutional issues, in connection with which American example was most strongly urged.

Taking the less accurate test first, however, we find allusions of greater or less length favorable to American example made in the Assembly (the debates in the constitutional commission are not included) by seven liberals, Brunet, Cordier, Gerdy, Lamartine, Lavallée, Sarrans and Senard; five radical republicans, Didier, Flocon, Ledru-Rollin, Pyat and Saint-Gaudens; two socialists, Leroux and Mathieu (de la Drôme); twenty conservatives, Alcock, Ambert, Aylies, Barrot, Combarel de Leyval, Dabeaux, Drouyin de Lhuys, Ch. Dupin, Dufaure, Duvergier de Hauranne, Jobez, Lacrosse, F. de Lasteyrie, J. de Lasteyrie, Levet, Lherbette, Morin, Parieu, Saint-Priest, Tocqueville; four legitimists, Cazalès, Jouin, Kerdrel, Montalembert; one unclassifiable, Lubbert.

Speeches or allusions hostile to the example were made by nine liberals, Barthe, Crémieux, Grévy, Lamartine, A. Marrast, Payer, C. Rolland, Thouret, Wolowski; five radicals, Detours, Deville, Flocon, Martin-Bernard, Pyat; one socialist, Mathieu (de la Drôme); four conservatives, Billault, Faucher, Jobez, Mornay; no legitimists; one unclassifiable, Dubois. Eliminating the five men who spoke on both sides at different times and the two unclassifiables, and grouping together the liberals, radicals and socialists as parties of the Left, and the conservatives and legitimists as parties of the Right, we find the example of the United States favored by 10 members of the Left and 23 of the Right; opposed by 11 of the Left and 3 of the Right. At least 32 other references to American example are not included in the above, as being either not on a constitutional subject or merely descriptive, according neither praise nor blame.

Proceeding now to the other test, it is convenient and fair to use for this purpose the votes on the Duvergier de Hauranne, Grévy, and Leblond amendments. While American example was urged on other clauses of the constitution, as we shall see, it was nowhere more earnestly discussed than in the debates on the legislative and executive branches of the government. The American two-chamber system was cited with great frequency in support of the Duvergier de Hauranne amendment; the American president, chosen as a separate branch of government rather than elected by and subordinate to Congress, was praised by those who opposed the Grévy and Leblond amendments. As the vote of each member on these measures has already been given, it is only needful to point out here that of those who favored American example in their speeches, Sarrans, Senard, Didier, Ledru-Rollin and Parieu voted against it, some on two out of the three votes, some on all. To this list are to be added Flocon, Mathieu (de la Drôme) and Pyat, who spoke on both sides, but voted against the example. Of those who opposed American practice in their speeches on the other hand, Barthe, Crémieux, C. Rolland, Payer, Wolowski, Faucher, Mornay, and Dubois voted for it. To them should be added Lamartine and Jobez, who spoke on both sides but voted for the example. (Lamartine was an admirer of the American spirit, but in most of his speeches opposed the American system, as applicable only to a federal constitution.) Thus modified, the record of those who voted for the American example (using only the members who also spoke on the example as described above) becomes 10 members of the Left and 25 of the Right; those who voted against, 13 of the Left and 2 of the Right. Leroux was absent at the two test votes and cannot be counted. The two unclassifiables voted for the American example.

The complete vote on these two questions has been given on pp. 119-121. It is obvious that the American example triumphed in the votes on the executive and failed in the vote on the legislative. It would be impossible to attempt an analysis of the total vote according to parties, on account of the great size of the Assembly. The statistics here given, however, suffice to show that in general the Left rejected and the Right favored the American example. The liberals, it is true, were nearly evenly divided on the subject, but the more advanced groups tended to oppose American practice decidedly. This will become apparent when the discussion is taken up in detail. To that task it is now time to turn, and a beginning will be made with the discussion in the constitutional commission.

CHAPTER V

The Constitutional Commission

THE account of the proceedings of the commission is to be found in the unpublished *procès-verbal*, preserved in the archives of the Chamber of Deputies. It is in two small volumes, the first of 183 folio pages, containing a report of the sessions from May 19 to June 17 inclusive, and the first draft of the constitution, the second of 75 pages covering the sessions from July 24 to August 17 inclusive.[1] Subsequent meetings are unreported. The reports are all signed by Woirhaye as secretary, though most of them are not in his handwriting; corrections and erasures, however, show that he carefully revised his under-secretary's version. There is no attempt at a stenographic record of the speeches; the most important are given with considerable fullness, the rest briefly summarized. The first volume is much more satisfactory in this respect. The lack of a more detailed report is unfortunate for our purpose; allusions to American example may very easily have gone unnoticed by the secretary. The fact that the summarized report contains as many as it does is perhaps significant.

At the first meeting, May 19, Cormenin, the president, was requested by resolution to draw up a subject plan to guide the commission's work. It is, therefore, not quite fair to say, as some accounts have done, that Cormenin " assumed " the task of drawing up the original draft of the constitution, though he doubtless did interpret his in-

[1] *Cf.* chronological table at end of chap. ii.

structions somewhat liberally, by submitting detailed articles on the chief points as they came under discussion.   But
some one had to take the lead, as there was no further effort
at organization.   At the first meeting, Dornès had suggested
that the commission divide itself into sub-commissions,
each of which should make a preliminary study of some
part of the field, but this idea was not adopted.   While
Barrot, Marrast, Vivien, Dupin, Dufaure and others
took an active part in shaping the constitution, the general
form, because of his initiative, remains Cormenin's.

The subject-plan brought in by the president on May 22
in response to the resolution divided the work into five parts,
declaration of rights, executive, legislative, judiciary and
revision.   Except that the legislative was taken up before
the executive, this general order was maintained.   The
original discussion, lasting from one to four days, on each
subject, the general review of the whole, the conferences
with the delegates of the bureaux and the revision by the
commission bring up each of these heads four times, though
the later debates are extremely summary.   Of the final revision (Oct. 23-31) there is no record.

The earliest allusion to American example occurs in the
debate on the legislative.[1]   Barrot introduced the subject
with a speech in defense of the two-chamber system.   The
dangers of excessive centralization and of the lively French
temperament seemed to call for a balance-wheel, only to be
found in a second chamber.   He referred his colleagues to
historical precedents.   The Convention was the only example of a single chamber [2] and its experience was such that
the constitution of the year III provided for two.

---

[1] *Procès-verbal*, session of May 24.

[2] The text reads, " *Il n'y a point d' autre que la Convention.*"   The
sentence is not given in full, however, which may explain Barrot's apparent omission of the Constituent and Legislative Assemblies.

America, which was favorably circumstanced to make a good constitution, rejected a single assembly [*un pouvoir unique*] and yet there are many differences between America and us.[1] America had before it an entire world, a new world in which it could diffuse its activities. With us, there is hardly any activity except government; by our habits, and education, the government is the center of general activity.

There is here the germ of a grave difficulty, for if the government of a single assembly is not accepted, there will be conflict and then civil war.[2]

The American republic found happy predispositions in its very situation. On the one hand, the supreme power was decentralized and on the other, it found in its English origin traditional habits of respect for law which led it to resist the government.[3] Notwithstanding these checks, which were so many obstacles to the impulse of a single assembly, the legislative authority was divided into two branches which balanced one another.

In France, neither of the natural checks existing, a double chamber was even more imperative. A choice must be made between the system of equilibrium and the system of logical unity.

This was the only speech on the legislative question that day. The following afternoon, the subject was resumed by Marrast.[4] Public opinion and logic alike condemned the two-chamber system. The notion of balance was illusory. In England there are supposed to be three forces, but in reality the aristocracy has absorbed the other two, compelling royalty to do its will and giving only a semblance of

[1] The argument *a fortiori.*

[2] The speaker does not refer to disturbances arising from disappointment at the choice of a dual system, but to the lack of adequate opportunity for legal opposition to the will of a single assembly.

[3] *I. e.*, when embarked on an unlawful course.

[4] *Procès-verbal*, session of May 25.

power to the people. " In America it is the democracy which is everything." In a monarchy, the king may terminate controversies between the two chambers, but who could do it in a republic? These necessary checks to impulsive action must be sought within the single assembly, whether by the English system of several readings or by a council of state to prepare the way for the assembly's debates by a public, preliminary discussion of proposed measures. The single chamber is necessary to maintain national unity.

After a question by Vivien, Tocqueville [2] was recognized. He admitted that the bicameral cause was lost, but felt that the republic must come to it in the end, if it would endure.

We should not insist too much on historical examples, since we ought to try something original, appropriate to our particular situation.

Besides, only one democratic republic has existed in the world; it is that of the United States; it has two chambers. I do not support myself by the constitution of the United States, a veritable work of art, of which we can hardly borrow anything; but by its side, there are in North America 30 republics which are in a position similar to ours, all have two chambers, there is not a single American to whom it ever occurs that one could do otherwise.

Let it not be said that that two-chamber establishment is an English tradition, for the Union commenced by having only one chamber, then a return was made to two.

In Massachusetts, in Pennsylvania, a single chamber was at first established; after 13 years of experiment and a thorough discussion, public judgment returned to the need of two chambers; this example is striking.

There was a mistaken notion in France that the bicameral

[1] Spelled " Toqueville " in the *Procès-verbal.*

system was aristocratic; in our democratic society a single element of aristocracy would mean ruin. " The two chambers must represent, as in America, the same interests and the same classes of the people, in the same manner, by similar means."

The value of a second chamber in a non-aristocratic government is three-fold. It may serve to control the executive in important nominations, treaties of alliance, and so forth, a small body taken from its ranks being chosen for this purpose as an executive council; secondly, it will prevent the dangerous rivalry between the executive and a single chamber; thirdly, it will prevent legislative intemperance and tyranny. The remainder of the speech develops the last thought; several readings for each bill, before the same men, would be of no more value than an appeal argued before the court which pronounced the original judgment.

Coquerel thought the two-chamber system preferable, but impossible for the present because of public opinion. Martin held that public opinion was on the right side, two chambers being a compromise between aristocracy and democracy, containing the danger of revolution. France wants unity. Vivien renewed the argument of checks and balances and did not believe the question prejudged by public opinion, except in the clubs. Martin again insisted that the two-chamber system was unrepublican, supported by those who before February did not want a republic. Considérant, the Fourierist, felt that a second chamber had never been respected in France, because not in harmony with the spirit of the people. A council of state to revise laws (Cormenin interrupted, " No, to prepare laws ") would be necessary as a check to the assembly.

Dufaure admitted that he might be still under the sway of old parliamentary prejudices brought over from the constitutional monarchy, as Martin had charged. He recognized the sovereignty of the people as ultimate in human legislation. That sovereignty is exercised by delegation, however; whether it is better to delegate it to one chamber or two is not a question of logic, but of prudence. The authority conferred upon the executive would influence his decision, but for the present, he must make a choice. He observed that, in the past, public opinion had been so little attached to a second chamber, that the latter was almost useless, a danger rather than an advantage. There was no reason to suppose that it would be more serviceable in future.

The example taken from America is important, but I think that between that people and ours, differences exist which diminish considerably the value of this precedent. Among us, public opinion, the real queen, must needs concentrate on a single point, in the past on the royal power, later on a man, Napoleon, then on a single chamber; I fear that a second chamber may weaken the first and prevent it from resisting the executive power, for I think that this latter will have more authority than we suppose, being the representative of all France and unexposed to the ennuis and dangers excited by monarchies with their long reigns, their regencies, etc.

The check argument seemed to him illusory, as the first chamber will always dominate the second.

Tocqueville, who followed, " re-established the authority of the precedent which may be found in America; there is doubtless a host of institutions there which could not be transported to France, but as for the two chambers, the arguments are the same in the two countries."

Dupin, in a long, and not very cogent speech, reviewed the constitutional history of France since 1791, concluding for a single chamber as simpler and more logical.

Pagès believed the real danger of tyranny to lie in the executive, as shown by the Committee of Public Safety and by Bonaparte; he wished a strong single chamber to resist the executive. " America has sometimes had one chamber, sometimes two, according to its necessities; we too, must act according to the times and the age; I do not know what we shall do in ten years, but meanwhile we can today think only of establishing a single chamber."

Beaumont [1] wanted a strong executive and believed in the double-chamber system but yielded to public opinion.

Barrot said a last word for his cause, after which the vote was taken, the single chamber winning, fourteen to three. The roll-call of the votes in the commission is never given.

It is to be noted that of the fourteen speeches, six referred to the American precedent. Of these Barrot and Tocqueville (speaking twice) favored American example, Marrast and Dufaure opposed it. Pagès, while not unfriendly in his allusion, was against the bicameral system.

Referring to the classification previously given,[2] it will be seen that Barrot, Tocqueville and Dufaure were conservatives, Marrast and Pagès liberals. The American example was, therefore, favored by two conservatives, opposed by one conservative and two liberals.

When the subject is reached in the review of the whole constitution, (June 12-17), the *procès-verbal* dismisses it with the laconic note " Articles 15, 16 adopted." [3]

The matter came up again, when the delegates of the Assembly's fifteen bureaux met with the commission to report their criticisms.[4] A number of these were prominent men, notably Thiers who represented the

[1] Spelled " de Baumont " in the *procès-verbal*.

[2] *Vide supra*, p. 144 *et seq.*

[3] *Ibid.*, June 13. Art. 15 of the first draft reads: " The French people delegates the legislative power to a single assembly." *Ibid.*, " Projet de constitution."

[4] For the discussion in the bureaux, *vide infra*, p. 247 *et seq.*

3rd, Parrieu the 9th, Crémieux the 10th, Duvergier de Hauranne the 14th, and Berryer the 15th. They wanted to have the constitution thrown open to general discussion, leaving the decision on each point to the commission. Cormenin, however, supported by the commission, insisted that the strict terms of the assembly's resolution be followed, according to which each delegate was limited to a presentation of the opinion of his bureau and must not enter into discussion with the commission. This procedure prevailed and the opinion of the bureaux was asked in turn on each article of the constitution. It is plain, however, that in most cases the stronger delegates had been able to swing their bureaux into line with their own views and, where this was not the case, they usually devoted more time to expounding their minority opinion than that of the bureau.

Three of the delegates are reported in the procès-verbal [1] as alluding to American example on the two-chamber question.

Girerd, representing the 1st bureau, which voted for the single chamber 22 to 15, said, "The example of America proves nothing because that people differs from us in customs and in laws."

Chauffour, of the 5th bureau, expounded "a philosophical argument, an historical argument and a mechanical argument" for the single chamber. His historical argument was drawn entirely from French precedents, but, at the end of his remarks, he said: "In speaking of the past, I omitted to say that in the United States, there was at first in the period of the republic's formation, only a single chamber. We can do as America did; if experience proves the necessity of two chambers, we can return to it."

Parrieu reporting the 9th bureau's vote for the single chamber, held that the opposite system merely represented

---

[1] *Procès-verbal*, July 24.

old divisions, specifically the aristocratic and the democratic interest. " The republic of America also commenced by one assembly [*une diète*] and the establishment of two chambers was the result of a compromise between parties." [1]

The subject appears for the last time, when the commission revised the constitution in the light of the bureaux' criticisms. The *procès-verbal's* account is brief. " Art. 20. This is former article 15. A member observes that this article was adopted by a large majority in all the bureaux except one, and that it is therefore useless to return to the grave question which it decides. Adopted." [2]

Allusions in the debate on the executive are less numerous, but cover a wider range. This is perhaps because there was even greater unanimity of opinion on the main issue. On the latter, Cormenin opened the subject by saying that there are three possible systems, (1) the assembly itself exercising the executive power by delegates, (2) three to five consuls or directors, (3) a president or consul. " The commission decides unanimously and without discussion that unity is necessary and indispensable and that the executive power should be entrusted to a single person." The discussion, therefore, centers on the choice, qualifications and powers of the president.

In a previous consideration of possible checks to the power of the assembly, that same day, Beaumont had suggested that " as in America, we might accord the executive power, not a right of *veto,* but permission to suspend the promulgation and execution of the law for a certain length of time, to give the chamber time for reflection."

The matter was not acted on at that time, but was later brought up in exactly the same form and, with no recorded

---

[1] *Procès-verbal,* July 27.

[2] *Ibid.,* Aug. 8.

[3] *Ibid.,* May 27. But *cf.* p. 186, note.

speeches, " it was recognized that in every case there should be, not a *veto,* but a right of observation and of recourse to the chamber better informed." [1]   The brevity of the account here, as elsewhere, leaves much to be desired.

In the discussion of the presidential term of office,[2] three questions were united, length of term, re-election and whether or not the assembly's term should have identical limits.   Cormenin proposed a three-year term for the president and a right to one re-election.   Beaumont opposed re-election, on the ground of its evil influence on the president's first term.   Woirhaye thought it unwise to deprive the nation of a good man's services.

Dufaure brought up the third point: " In America, the legislative and the executive power are generally elected and renewed at the same time.   This rule seems to me very wise; it avoids conflicts which might break out, if the two powers do not have a contemporary origin, if they owe their election to currents of opinion, contrary to one another."

Marrast sustained the opposite opinion, fearing that the complete renewal of all offices at once would throw the government into disorder.

Tocqueville held that this problem and that of re-election aggravated one another.   He did not believe in immediate re-election; Beaumont's point that the president will govern in the interest of a party, was justified.

That inconvenience makes itself felt to a lively degree in America and it is constantly increasing and appearing more mischievous.   But in France, the evil will be greater still.   For in America, the president has little power, he only nominates to an inconsiderable number of offices, but in France, where the executive power will dispose of a great many places and will be able to make many creatures, the excessive influence of the president will be an immense danger.

[1] *Procès-verbal,* June 1.

[2] *Ibid.,* May 27.

On the other hand, a non-reeligible president, being unable to prolong his term and carry out his great designs, might in " the ambition of despair " be inspired with the idea of destroying the constitution.   He preferred to run this accidental passing danger, rather than subject society to the perpetually corrupting influence of a president, employing his power with a view to its prolongation.   He wanted a three-year term for the legislature and four or five for the executive.   Vaulabelle suggested identical terms of two years, Dupin proposed three, Marrast returned to his previous objection.

The commission then voted, twelve to two against immediate re-eligibility.   It is interesting to observe that Tocqueville's rejection of American example in the speech that seemed to sway the vote, if any one speech did, put into the constitution the clause that destroyed the republic.   Terms of three, four and five years being proposed, the commission decided, eight to six, in favor of a four-year term.[1]

The question of an identical legislative term was dropped. The previous decision that the assembly's term should be for three years,[2] remaining in force, automatically defeated the idea.

In the discussions held [3] on ministers of state (whether or not to be necessarily members of the assembly) and on the vice-president (who was to be chosen by the assembly on nomination of the president, for four years, and to act as president of the council of state) no reference to American example can be found; a somewhat remarkable circum-

[1] " The President is to be elected every four years . . . that is to say, the very worst element of mischief in the American Constitution is to be borrowed, without the advantages it carries of a strong Executive." *London Times*, Nov. 7, 1848.

[2] *Procès-verbal*, May 26.

[3] *Ibid.*, May 30.

stance, especially in view of the striking parallel in the vice-presidential office.[1] It was proposed by an unnamed member that the vice-president be chosen by the nation, together with the president, but Cormenin thought this would detract from "the majestic unity" of the latter's election and Vivien added that the vice-president might have more votes than the president, which would be an evil and a cause of enfeeblement for the latter. Was he thinking of Aaron Burr? However tempting speculation is here, there is no direct evidence of American influence.

In the first general review of the whole constitution, several members tried to have the president's election by universal suffrage reconsidered.[2] Considérant proposed that he be chosen by the assembly. Tocqueville wanted the electoral college. He brought out the possible danger of a president chosen by the minority and the inadequacy of the candidature system (*i. e.* nomination by the assembly of several candidates for popular election) as a remedy.

I propose to leave the people the right of election, but to require a majority for election and if there is no majority for one or the other of the candidates to leave the assembly the right to choose among them. Further, as it is desirable that a majority be obtained by one of the candidates and as it is easier to get a majority in proportion as the nominating assembly is less numerous and more intelligent, I would like something analogous to what takes place in America.

There every state names a certain number of delegates, who,

---

[1] But *cf.* Clarigny's article in the *Constitutionnel* for Oct. 11: "We see in the vice-president no other office than that of presiding over the council of state: the importance of these functions is far from being in accord with his title: we think that the constitutional commission has here an unhappy fancy for imitation: of the American constitution, it has kept only the names and the external forms, it has carefully rejected the spirit."

[2] *Ibid.*, June 15.

to avoid intrigues, plots and violence, do not meet together. There are as many electoral colleges as states. Each of these states meets the same day to name the President.

In France it would not be necessary to have as many electoral colleges as there are departments, that would be too many; we might take the districts of the courts of appeal.

Marrast and Coquerel returned to the assembly-election plan, Dupin opposed it, Dornès seconded Tocqueville's majority requirement, with assembly-choice if no majority, but opposed the electoral college, Barrot indicated assembly-election as his first choice, the electoral college as his second, Martin spoke for universal suffrage, Beaumont agreed with Dornès, Vivien wanted a two-thirds majority, Marrast thought that practically difficult, Dufaure assented to Dornès' proposition.

The votes followed. Election by the assembly received only two votes, the candidature system four, the electoral college four; the majority requirement as proposed by Tocqueville and Dornès passed by a large vote.

The final reference to American example on the executive was made during the conferences with the bureaux' delegates by Thiers, representing the 3rd bureau. He wanted the president elected for three years and reeligible once. " In free states like America and England, it is not a man who prevails, it is an idea represented by a few men, that idea must be given the time necessary to become known and its policy tested." Pitt stood for opposition to the French Revolution, Peel was also " the expression of an arrested thought," that is why they were kept in power.

In the succeeding revision, however, the old article was maintained without discussion.

Omitting the last-mentioned, Thiers not being a member of the commission, four references to United States practice are found in the commission's debates on the executive. All of these are favorable. Those who made them, Beaumont, Dufaure, Tocqueville (twice) were all conservatives.

A few scattering allusions are to be found in the debates on the judiciary.

Barrot brought out the dilemma in the matter of appointment: either the people elect the judges, in which case their ignorance and passions may lead to bad selections, or the executive power names them, which gives him a dangerous authority. His solution was a strict separation between those who decide the facts (the jury) and those who apply the law to the facts (the judge), in civil as well as in criminal jurisprudence. (The original plan had been to confine the jury to the latter field). " The tardiness of English and American procedure may be avoided and most of the difficulties which judicial organization offers solved, by the introduction of the jury into civil matters." [1]

It was decided, after further discussion, that the extension of the jury to civil matters should be left to legislation.

The next question was the choice of judges of the peace, whether by election or appointment, on which there was some controversy. Coquerel, the pastor of the Oratoire, opposed election. " He cites as analogy what takes place in Switzerland and in America where pastors are elected; the choices are generally bad and those elected do not have the authority necessary for the proper exercise of their ministry." [2] The question was, however, decided against him.

When the Court of Cassation, the highest regular court, was reached, the question lay between election by the assembly and appointment by the president.

Beaumont spoke for the latter. " In America, it is the president or the governor who nominates, after having con-

---

[1] *Procès-verbal*, June 5.

[2] *Ibid.*, June 6.

sulted the senate, this example should be followed." [1]   The
majority, however, thought otherwise.

In this debate, Barrot spoke of the power of the court
mentioned, "the power to pronounce in an abstract and dogmatic manner on the meaning of the law, which approaches
the legislative power especially." During the very last
session of the commission, this matter was brought up again
by an unnamed member, who said that " Experience has
proved that considerable embarrassments often arise from
the fact that the courts, considering a law as contrary to the
constitution, do not know whether they ought to apply it.
It would be proper to foresee this case and to say how the
difficulty may be regulated." [2]   A discussion arose, in which
Dufaure and Tocqueville took part. The commission decided that it would be very difficult to establish proper rules
for this case and that it would be best for the constitution
to be silent on the subject. One would give a good deal to
know what Dufaure and Tocqueville said (*the procès-verbal*
is mute on this point) and whether the practice of the American Supreme Court was mentioned.

Cormenin's two remaining heads, the preamble with its
declaration of rights and the matter of revision, brought
forth no remarks on America, so far as the source indicates.

Enough material is thus extant to justify the conclusion
that on several important subjects, American example was
brought to the attention of the constitutional commission,
usually by the more conservative of its members. A more
satisfactory, because a more complete view of the extent of
American influence is afforded by the debates in the Assembly.

[1] *Procès-verbal,* June 6.

[2] *Ibid.,* Aug. 17.

CHAPTER VI

THE ASSEMBLY DEBATES

It will be remembered that the constitution did not come fairly before the Assembly for discussion until after it was reported from the commission on August 30.   Prior to that time, American example was mentioned in the Assembly on various questions of general legislation, but only twice on a constitutional point.   May 11,[1] Senard proposed the separate and prior settlement of the executive branch by the commission about to be appointed, that this section of the constitution, being decided as soon as possible, the government might receive a strong, permanent head at once. In his speech, he remarked, " In all the constitutions without exception, in that of '91, in that of '93, in our constitutions or rather in our charters of 1814 and of 1830, in the constitution of the United States of America, the executive power is considered separately;" the proposition was opposed, on the ground that it would be unwise to put part of the new scheme into operation without the counterpoised balances, and was defeated.   May 30, Rolland, reporting from committee a bill on the vexed question of incompatibility between the functions of representative and of other public office, denied the applicability of constitutional precedents drawn from aristocratic England or federated America.

Aside from these two cases, there are no other instances

---

[1] The reports of these debates are to be found in the *Compte-rendu* of the Assembly or in the succeeding issues of the *Moniteur*.

until the debates on the constitution began, September 4.
The chapters which suggested the greatest amount of interest in America were those on the preamble, the legislative
and the executive branches and these must be considered in
order.

Before the constitution was taken up seriously and fought
out article by article, opportunity was given for a general
discussion on the whole project before the Assembly. On
the first day of this discussion, Sept. 4, Jobez objected to
the preamble.

Why this declaration? Is it not an anachronism, a plagia-
rism from another epoch? When the Americans wrote their
famous manifesto, they were separating from their mother-
country, and appealing to the judgment of the world. When
our fathers in 1789 proclaimed the rights of men, they did it
in face of the chains they had broken; at sight of that Bastille,
which they had conquered, they turned their backs on the past
and marched toward the future. But we, what need have we
to repeat these principles incarnated in our nature?

The general discussion was ended September 5 and detailed consideration began, the preamble coming first. This
part of the constitution was especially dear to the advanced
men and odious to the conservatives. It was too reminis-
cent of the great Revolution and held too many dangerous
possibilities. Radical ideas could slip in more easily
under the guise of " rights of man " than of cold constitutional provisions, but, once in, might furnish the occasion of
annoying demands for their conversion into undesirable
legislation. It was a delicate task to oppose the preamble,
however, without appearing to break completely with the
rosy illusions of February, which the conservatives were
not yet quite ready openly to do. A good example of nice
balance along this line is shown in Levet's speech on Sep-

tember 6. He holds that the essential features of the preamble have been incorporated into Chapter II of the constitution. As for the remainder, they are brilliant, but not
always possible of realization. The *droit au travail* for
instance, even as modified by the commission, can amount
to little unless the resources of the state are immensely increased, perhaps by a progressive tax or some other anti-
property, communistic legislation. Better be less dogmatic
and promise no more than one can realize.

It is very wrong, according to me, to justify the necessity
of absolute principles and of declarations of rights adopted
in a constitution by the example of our preceding constitutions, for, and that has already been told you, it is too true
that the brilliant preambles, those pompous theories which
decorate the frontispiece of our constitutions, have not prevented them from having only an ephemeral duration, while
we see the constitution of the United States, which, whatever
has been said of it, contains nothing similar, nothing which
resembles these general and dogmatic principles, shining in all
its vigor, although its existence goes back several years before
our first revolution. Those who made that constitution, the
Franklins and the Washingtons, knew as well as French legislators, that principles of universal morality must dominate
all positive laws. But they understood the danger that there
was in copying such principles into a constitution, which must
be, before all, a practical work, and which, so to speak, is only
the putting into action of results attained by experience and
theory. Thus, the sole concession made to the ardent and
systematic spirits who expected to see a declaration of rights
and duties in the constitution, the sole concession is the amendments which you may see at the end of the constitution of the
United States, amendments in which you remark nothing that
resembles the dogmatic and absolute principles which figure
in the frontispiece of our constitutions; amendments which
contain only purely legislative dispositions on the liberty of

the press and individual liberty; amendments in a word, which present nothing similar to what you are desired to adopt.

An important speech by Crémieux favoring a preamble, was next opposed by Cazalès, on the ground that it was more prudent to confine the work of the Assembly to laws than to venture into philosophy. He would call their attention to the lessons of history, pointing out to those who say, " We are not English, we are not Americans," the fact that there are certain general rules which have proved their universal validity. He then shows briefly that the English have always opposed general maxims in favor of immediate, definite, clearly applicable truths.

I arrive at an example more important for us, it is that of the Americans. Here there are more points of contact, more analogies. The constitution of the Americans is more modern; it is perfectly republican, no one will deny that. Assuredly if there is a country where there is liberty, that individual liberty which was just being discussed, it is certainly America. I appeal to all those who have visited that country or who know it by the writings to which it has given occasion. If I look at the American constitution, what do I see there? No declaration, no aphorisms, no political maxims, simply rules; declarations, without doubt, but declarations of positive things. I do not wish to fatigue the attention of the Assembly by historical details; yet this is a considerable example—a republican constitution, perfectly republican, made by a people which has very republican manners, which has lasted for sixty years, and which has to its account a long duration, and a very great prosperity. Now I come to the French constitutions.

A moment later he remarked, "A republican constitution, the example of America proves it to us, may exist without a declaration of rights," to which response was made by one of his own party, " a voice at the right," evidently recalling the amendments, " That is a mistake.   There are twelve preambles! "

Lamartine then delivered one of his brilliant speeches which swept the auditors off their feet by stately rhetoric rather than by close logic.   He defended the preamble on the ground that if it were not inserted, a future generation might pervert the constitution to false interpretations for lack of knowledge as to just what the ideals of 1848 really were.   He felt that it was not enough to cite the bare letter of the American constitution.   " Did the American Congress of which mention was also made, without recalling that admirable germ of declarations and rights which Franklin wrote at the very side of the code of its constitutions, hesitate? " [1]

The following day, Detours offered an amendment designed to separate the " anterior and superior rights " from the constitution, that they might not be subject to revision, holding that their insertion in that document did not guarantee their inviolability.   M. Cazalès might feel that the English and American constitutions could guarantee all rights sufficiently without a preliminary declaration.   Their case was different.

Gentlemen, the English constitution is a compromise between three equal, sovereign and independent powers, each treating for itself. . . . It is the same in the United States, where the thirteen states which negotiated, treated one with another, in such fashion that nothing can be changed in the constitution, without unanimous consent of all the states, outside of the cases stipulated for the majority.[2]

[1] Referring perhaps to the Declaration of Independence, translated into French by Franklin's efforts. *Cf.* H. E. Bourne, "Am. Const. Precedents in the National Assembly," *Am. Hist. Review*, vol. 8, p. 467.

[2] The speaker is apparently confusing the rule of the Articles of Confederation with that of the constitution.

Detours' amendment was lost, but the preamble passed with modifications.

The curious elasticity of American example in this matter of the preamble is striking. Friends and foes of the scheme used it with equal fluency in support of their case, the former by enlarging their view to include the amendments or the Declaration of Independence, the latter by confining themselves strictly to the body of the constitution itself.

The first reference to the United States in the discussion on the legislative branch of the government, was made in A. Marrast's report, presented together with the text of the constitution after revision, August 30.[1] The report concludes for a single chamber. If two chambers are created, either they will agree, in which case the double vote is superfluous, or they will disagree, which will bring strife and anarchy into the system of government. Each chamber may attract partisans to its point of view, and thus the contest spreads discord throughout the state. Two chambers furthermore enfeeble the legislature's power of resistance against executive usurpations; " When one has the Ancients on his side, he makes the Five Hundred jump out the windows." What arguments are there to support the other opinion?

We are given only two motives: one is serious, the other is not. The latter is the example of England and of the United States. We might easily show that two chambers in England represent two different interests, sometimes contrary, which exist in the parliament, because they exist in the country. We might show that in the United States, sovereignty divides and subdivides itself, that it is partial, local, formed of independent groups, and that it reproduces itself in the government

[1] *Moniteur*, Aug. 31.

as it is in its origin. We will make a single reply which will dispense with every other. We are in France, we constitute the French republic, we are acting in a country, which has its own manners, its personal character; we do not have to clothe it either à l'américaine or à l'anglaise. Full of respect for other nationalities, full of admiration for the great and lasting things they have done, we would abdicate, if we copied them. A reason, emigrating from London or from Washington, is bad by the very fact that it comes from there. To transplant a political organization to a foreign soil, is to will that it shall develop no roots. The foreign argument would prove, then, rather against than for; let us be moderate, it proves nothing.

The other, more serious counter-argument, is the possibility that a single chamber may be swept off its feet and act prematurely. This he thinks sufficiently guarded against by the provision requiring three readings of every measure at ten-day intervals, by a council of state, to prepare and develop proposed measures and by the executive's right to require a new discussion of any ill-advised legislation.

The matter next came up on September 4, when Jobez defended the bicameral system in the same speech in which he referred to the preamble. He held that a possible contest between the two chambers would be no more of a danger than the tyranny of a single popular chamber, and that those who continually asserted the unity of the nation forgot that this unity veiled two interests, inherent in human nature, the interest of continuity and the interest of progress. Experience pronounces for two chambers. " Pennsylvania, after having decreed a single chamber, returned to the creation of a senate."

The following day, Alcock made a very long speech, in the course of which he accepted the single chamber, but to guard against the dangers of its tyranny, proposed a strong executive, elected by universal vote. This power he would further buttress by giving it the function of appointing all public officials, even members of the Court of Cassation (the highest court in the land) and of the council of state. " Instead of trying to diminish the old prerogatives of governmental power, we should try to extend them. The Americans have strongly felt that necessity, the Romans thought like them; with them, the power of their magistrates was of short duration, but it was almost absolute." The executive should not vote in the legislature, but he should have the right to demand a new deliberation. " The United States, with the eminently practical sense which distinguishes them, although they have two chambers, require, in case of conflict with the president, a majority of two-thirds of the votes in favor of the law which he rejects."

The serious discussion of the matter did not commence, however, until September 25, when article 20 of the project (" the French people delegates the legislative power to a single assembly ") came up in the detailed discussion.

Duvergier de Hauranne now offered his two-chamber amendment. He opened his extremely long speech against the single chamber by a preliminary remark that prior to February, the bicameral system seemed to be a definitely accepted principle of political science. He spoke not only of constitutional monarchists, but also of republicans. They had said to him that he must not think them so infantile as to forget the lessons of experience and to recommence the errors of the past. They recognized that absolute unity of the directing power was incompatible with liberty. " What we want is not the republic of the Convention, it is an American republic, with an elective president in place of an hereditary king, with a House of Representatives and a Senate which mutually limit one another." This system, they added, has all the advantages without any of the inconveniences of the constitutional monarchy. Such was their language. It seemed to him a most astonishing thing that suddenly, these universally admitted ideas seemed to the commission outworn prejudices, unworthy serious consideration. He recognized two sources only, whence a just determination could be derived, experience and logic. Not so, the commission. " In the eyes of the former president of the commission, 'the supporters of two chambers have, to demonstrate these two sources, exhausted history, dogmatics, aesthetics and pathetics. They have crossed the seas; they have rummaged the parchments of Albion and dissected the Americas.' " The speaker then quoted Marrast's phrase that a reason from London or Washington, is bad from the mere fact that it comes from there.

Thus to reasoning, they oppose the instinct of the masses, and nationality to experience; that, it must be confessed, is to disembarrass oneself easily, quickly of all serious discussion. . . . I understand, further, the rejection of England's example; it would be easy to demonstrate that the origin of the division of legislative power in England is not what is supposed and that the *raison d'être* of the two chambers is not because they correspond to different interests. But, finally, England is a monarchical country, an aristocratic country; it is rejected, nothing simpler. But, I ask you, is it not strange that the example of the American republic, that example so often cited by republicans, should become today, because it bothers them, the object of their sarcasms and their disdain? (Cries of " Good! "). Is it not strange that we are hardly permitted to recall modestly that in America, not only the federal republic, the great republic, but each of the little republics of which the Union is composed has thought it necessary, indispensable, to divide the legislative power? Is it not strange that the authority of the only great modern state which has flourished, increased, prospered under the republican form, should be thus brushed aside or despised? As for me, with due respect to the former president of the commission and to its honorable reporter, I think that this authority is very considerable, and I take the liberty to avail myself of it before the National Assembly. It is furthermore totally false that it was a pure imitation of England which drew America after it; on the contrary, at the start, the federal constitution was unitary, several of the local constitutions were unitary; it is experience which brought all the good minds in that country to the duality with which we are concerned. So much for England and America.

The remainder of his argument was taken up with political reasoning, the necessity of checks and balances to protect the minority rights, the dangers of too great simplicity, nothing being simpler than despotism, the danger of conflict between an all-powerful chamber and an equally powerful executive (either have no president, or else divide your legislature), and the necessity to provide for a more mature deliberation, the various provisions in the bill to that end seeming to him insufficient. To the dilemma, either two chambers are useless (being in accord) or breed anarchy (being in disaccord) he opposed the alternative: if the chambers are in accord, the law, having passed a double test, will have greater authority; if in disaccord, that is in itself proof that the national will is not yet clear, and that the question requires further discussion. The council of state seemed to him absurd, a mere permanent commission of the Assembly, which would be free to follow or reject its advice at will. He then put forward his counter-plan, two chambers, distinguished by age, number and length of term, but to avoid any suspicion of aristocracy, both elected by universal suffrage (though personally he would have preferred a difference here as well). The two chambers were to sit and vote together if at loggerheads on any subject. He concluded his long, but very clear speech by an admission that he had neither desired nor foreseen a republic, but now that it had come, the important thing was to found it solidly, setting up bulwarks of order and moderation.

The next speaker, Thouret, less able and less distinguished, was, however, a member of the commission, and, as such, defended its plan. This speaker regarded the single chamber as the best feasible substitute for direct popular government, the whole people meeting in one body, which would be the ideal exercise of sovereignty. The remainder of his speech was a repetition of Marrast's points and an endeavor to refute Duvergier de Hauranne's arguments.

Is it necessary to stop at another series of reasonings which I will call the sophistry of comparisons; for God knows what degree of intensity the malady of comparison has reached among our modern publicists! Formerly they used to compare France to all monarchical countries to prove that it ought not to have a republic; today they compare it to all republican countries to prove that it ought to construct a bad one.

If I wished, I might reply by a final refusal to accept it, and say that no comparison is possible here below; because in nature as in languages there are no synonyms. Comparison has always seemed to me the ambush laid for good sense by paradox. However, it is in such good company, in such good taste, at the present time, to speak of America à propos of liberty and of England à propos of everything, that one must make a little concession to the taste of the period, but I do not guarantee the correctness of my pronunciation!

After showing (humorously) why he would not borrow from woman-ruled England, he continued,

But America! Oh, America, I more than esteem her, I love her, because that sublime slave, having become mistress, produced two great men, of whom one would like to possess something more than a shadow; two great men who live in the heart of the two republics, separated by the ocean, reunited by history! But though France and America are united in their love of popular sovereignty, must they be united in the exercise of that sovereignty, composed of interests, always different and sometimes opposed? America is too much studied in perspective, on maps and in magazines. The magazine increases objects, the map diminishes them, and neither of the two glasses of this double historic telescope, at the service of our sedentary publicists, succeeds in showing them the truth in its just proportions.

Believe me, learned travellers in Bibliothèques Nationales, leave America her instincts—what shall I say?—her necessity of federalism, which lay upon her a law to unite, on the most diverse points, interests as varied and as numerous as her once primitive lakes, her once virgin forests, and her half-conquered rivers where crocodiles are pursued by steamboats. Let us leave America the unity of her patriotism struggling against the division of her soil, and let us give France the right she has conquered to express directly that will which has overturned three great dynasties, which has made three great revolutions, and which will not content itself with three great words.

Lherbette next took up the cudgels in favor of two chambers. He considered this the most important point of the constitution. He regarded it as false reasoning to hold that because popular opinion favored a single chamber, the Assembly must so enact. Furthermore, the best minds favored a dual system, nor was the opinion of the masses unshakable. " The two-chamber system is adopted in England and in the United States; it was recently still existing in France." Marrast's point, that a precedent from London or Washington should be *ipso facto* rejected, he considered not well taken. There was no reason why another country's institutions should not be adopted, if desirable.

They add that this English and American institution of two

chambers should be rejected because of differences in the situations; for it has for origin in England, it is pretended, the aristocratic principle; in the United States, servile imitation of the mother-country and federalism; in France, the constitutional monarchy and the same spirit of imitation. In these assertions, there is no exactitude. No, in England, it is not only the aristocratic principle which established the two chambers. No, that guarantee was not in the United States and in France the fruit of servile imitation; for the United States and France commenced by putting in practice the opposite system. It was after fifteen years' experience in the United States, after several years' in France, that the system of a single chamber was abandoned and so completely abandoned in America, in the several states as in the Union, that the opposite system, that of the duality of chambers, has there passed into an axiom not even discussed any longer. No, it is not the principle of constitutional monarchy nor that of aristocracy which serves for base of the double chamber; for it exists in the United States, where neither constitutional monarchy nor aristocracy have been met with. Neither is it federalism; for the two chambers exist in England and have existed in France, where there has never been federalism. What has caused its admission, is the wish to give the different real forces of the country a real representation, to organize a better mode of deliberations and to safeguard the independence and the existence of the different powers.

Unity of sovereignty does not involve a single chamber; if division of delegated authority were inconsistent with that of unity, all power would have logically to be entrusted to a single individual. Three vital principles must be respected in all free governments: political rights for the people (else no guarantee of liberty), the influence of intellectual superiority and experience in public councils (else no guarantee of wisdom), an executive of force and independence (else no guarantee of tranquillity). Of these

three, the commission omits the two latter.   A single chamber will of necessity be large, but it is a well-known fact that
the larger a chamber is, the more it is swayed by passion
and the less by reason.   The commission's various readings
will constitute no barrier to hasty legislation, because a
majority, under the empire of passion, may sweep them
away by declaring the proposed law " urgent."   Under the
monarchy, complicated legislation, such as the civil code and
the military code, were always referred to the Chamber of
Peers, because its membership, hereditary or appointed by
government, had special qualifications for such work; a
Chamber of Representatives can never be more than a political chamber.   Aristocratic governments have always had
more continuity in policy; England owes it to its House of
Lords, Austria to its Aulic Council, Russia to its Councils.
Rome owed its perseverance to the senate.   A second chamber with a longer term and only renewed partially is needed
for this purpose; it is required also to guard minority rights
and to prevent a struggle between the sole chamber and the
executive.   " Some one asks who will decide between them,
if they are divided?   A method is adopted in several countries, in the state of New York, for example, and I think
that it is proposed to you in several amendments; it is a
joint vote in grave and exceptional cases of dissidence."
The commission's council of state is an admission of all
these arguments; named by the Assembly itself and with
meager prerogatives, it will be no real check.   This revolution differed from that of 1789 by being directed against a
man who had played false, while its predecessor was intended to overturn a whole governmental system.   In view
of this, let us preserve the best features of the past.   Let us
reverse the mistake which in a former day concentrated the
legislature into one body and divided the executive; by such
reversal, we shall have wisdom in the laws, forceful rapidity
in their execution.

These were the main lines of Lherbette's careful argument. It is impossible to give an outline of all the speeches here, but these will show the general trend of the argument on the question.

Marcel Barthe, the next speaker, favoring a single chamber, made a passing reference to American federalism. France, in the time of which M. Lherbette spoke, was divided into a multitude of little provinces, each with its own laws and customs; " France was then, to some extent, like the United States, composed of adjoining states," now, however, the country is completely unified. Later, he reverted to the possible collision between two chambers, both the offspring of universal suffrage, to which he thought Duvergier de Hauranne's proposed remedy inadequate. " In America, in a calm country of easy manners, in a city but little agitated, such disagreement might have no consequences; but in France, at Paris, in the midst of an intelligent, passionate, mobile population, such antagonism would be very dangerous, as is well understood."

Another speech was made the same day by Charles Dupin, upholding the bicameral scheme in the interest of the defence of the present social order. The objection had been raised that one of the two chambers might favor communism, while a single chamber would always have a majority against it. Such, however, had not been the case with reference to the theories of Babeuf and Saint Simon.

If socialism, if communism could root themselves anywhere, would it not be in America, in the absolutely levelling republics founded by the William Penns? Would it not be there that antagonism between the two legislative chambers would have to be born? If antagonism were possible on such a subject, would it not have taken rise at least in one of these twenty-seven republics, from New Orleans to New York, and from Pennsylvania to the Rocky Mountains? Well, never for three-quarters of a century, never in the twenty-three states has there appeared the insensate antagonism with which people wished to frighten us, to turn our eyes from the real danger, internal peace compromised and soon disappearing in the absence of a counter-weight, the incessant revolution returned to the order of the day and France forever deprived of that security so necessary if a revived agriculture, industry and commerce are to lift themselves from the ruins which they owe to only six months of a state of revolution, and which are already immense.

On the 27th, the discussion was concluded. Two important speeches were made on that day, one for the single chamber system by Lamartine, the other by Odilon Barrot for the two chambers. Lamartine admitted that his decision was purely opportunistic; were the republic firmly established, he would perhaps favor the dual system. Nothing is absolute in politics. England's dual system was due to aristocracy, America's to federalism. The latter point he developed at some length. America's bicameral legislature, thus considered, represents a defect in democratic unity, a sort of anarchy from which the nation has not yet evolved.

And if, turning your attention now from a nation which has so few essential points of contact, so little analogy, so little conformity of origin and of nature with the French nation, to your own situation . . . you ask yourselves, do you demand that a French chamber should imitate that constitution, adapted to another people? Should it represent federal elements which no longer exist among us? You will answer, a thousand times no! You would be imitating a defect! You would be copying a vice! You would be introducing a federal imperfection in France's unity of representation.

The new democracy would view with alarm the restoration

of an aristocratic institution. The safety of the republic against plots from left or right demanded the concentration of its strength in one chamber. Folly, to amuse ourselves with historic, theoretic, geographic considerations, variable with periods and people, while realities confront us. Russia would be at the Rhine, Italy devoured from the north, anti-social factions twenty times on the barricades, attacking the very roots of society, the family, property, the state, while your laboriously balanced legislative bodies tried to agree on a plan to save the fatherland, society and civilization. The bicameral system was justified in the past, because there was a strong sovereign ruler in the center. To-day the Assembly is sovereign. No president will be strong enough to settle a conflict between two chambers, unless he has the right to dissolve the Assembly. Again, how shall the electors determine who should sit in the upper, who in the lower chamber? Wealth, profession, chance, age are equally unsatisfactory. The lower house would lose all authority and majesty, if because of their superior age, " you should say to Franklin, to Royer-Collard, ' Get you gone into the other chamber, I exile you to the Luxembourg.' " In so critical a time, when the political horizon of Europe is covered with clouds, a national dictatorship is necessary. If you do not confide that dictatorship to a single assembly, it must needs be confided to a man. But there are two names in history, which should forever prevent a French assembly from confiding the dictatorship of its republic, its revolution, to a man. These names are the name of Monk in England, and in France, the name of Bonaparte.

Odilon Barrot followed Lamartine, as the last speaker for the dual system. The field was now cleared for the leaders, and in Barrot, the chief man of the conservatives answers the chief man of the liberals. Barrot's speech was somewhat less rhetorical than Lamartine's. The latter was a remarkable extemporiser; he closed his speech with the statement that he had mounted the tribune almost undecided as to his vote, or at least as to the analysis of the reasons for his choice, and that he had been questioning himself aloud rather than communicating fixed convictions, but that as he descended, he hesitated no more to vote for a single assembly.   Odilon Barrot, learned in constitutional law, was much more ponderous than Lamartine; as Corkran says, " not a man of ready judgment." [1]   He was, however, quick enough to see and to seize the opening given him by Lamartine in that speaker's figure of a dictatorship.   It is well, said Barrot, that the veil has at last been pulled aside. The question could not have been better stated; it is whether you prefer to continue a dictatorship under constitutional forms, thus continuing the revolution, or to found a normal, permanent government.   The single chamber necessarily involves a subordinate executive; it will be all-powerful. There is no real danger confronting France, either externally or internally; the organization of a dictatorship would rather tend to provoke trouble, being a notice to the country that the revolution has not yet given way to a settled state of peace.   It is natural for a democracy sprung from revolution to want to concentrate its power.   But unless it provides a counter-weight, by dividing its power, facts will reassert their empire over theories and bring intestine convulsions to pass, which will force the division, or destroy the state.

We are told that it is obsolete, it is a reminiscence of aristocratic power, or it is borrowed or rather plagiarized at the expense of England and of America; you are not in the same circumstances: there aristocracy, here a federal power.   You are right, circumstances are not the same; you will not divide

[1] *Op. cit.,* p. 65.

your legislative power on the same conditions as England or the federal power of the United States of America. It is true; your second chamber or your moderating power will have another principle of authority than the high chamber in England or the senate in America. The upper chamber in England, in its wealth, in its origin, in its traditions, in its real pride and in its patriotism; the United States in the federal principle, these, it is true, are the forces which come to the assistance of the moderating power, which aid it to function efficiently; you have not those forces; I will not ask you to create them. Does it result that, because your moderating authority will not find that force which it finds accidentally either in America, or in England, that no moderating authority is needed? But I will draw an opposite conclusion.

Democracy, thus left more powerful than elsewhere, is in even greater need of balancing, moderating agencies. The presidency and the council of state are both inadequate in this respect. Construct a constitution according to the laws of experience and society, and do not prepare for yourselves eternal regrets.

Dupin *aîné*, as representing the majority of the commission, made a final argument in favor of its conclusions. While repudiating Lamartine's notion of a dictatorship (the division of powers was sufficient to obviate that) yet they considered it necessary to have one chamber in view of the danger still to be apprehended from the reds.

The vote, being taken after this speech, resulted in the defeat of the amendment.

When the vote on the constitution took place, November 4, one of the negative votes was cast by A. Lubbert. He explained his vote in a letter to the *Moniteur*, dated Paris, November 4, and published the next day, in which he said: "I voted against the adoption of the new constitution. I think the stability, the prosperity of the republic dependent upon the establishment of two chambers, on the pattern of the United States." He thought also that in case of dissidence, the president should have the right to consult the country, and the Assembly to recall the president. Stability seemed to him to require subordination of authority.

Several other references to American example in relation to various legislative problems, outside of the two-chamber question, were also made. On September 28, Art. 21 was before the Assembly, fixing the membership of the forthcoming single legislative chamber at 750, including representatives from Algeria and the colonies. An amendment was offered by Point, proposing a sliding scale, giving one member for every 60,000 of population; each fraction above 30,000 to have one representative, any fraction below not to count; Algeria and the colonies to be regulated by a special law. This would, for the present, give an Assembly of 586, which would be more efficient than a larger number. The article was further inconsistent with Art. 23, providing that the election shall be based on population.

The amendment was opposed by Dufaure, in the name of the commission, who showed that 750 had been taken as a fair number, by comparison with the 745 fixed by the National Assembly of 1791 when the nation had 25,000,000 population (in 1848 it had 35,400,000), and with the 668 of the English House of Commons, representing a population of 26,000,000. He recalled the old Chamber of Deputies with its 450 members and maintained that the disorder was quite as great as in the present Assembly. The article was not inconsistent with Art. 23, whose object was merely to fix population as the base instead of territory or property. Furthermore, the number 750 was in fact based on population.

What we did there was done in all the constitutions of the

United States of America. A beginning was made by fixing the number of representatives on the basis of the population, which was feeble. It was found that in many states the population gave one representative for 30,000 souls. The population has increased there in the proportions which you know, which have been considerable for several states, to such an extent that there are states where now, the number of representatives remaining fixed, one representative is named by 123,000 souls where in the beginning it was by 30,000. I do not conclude from that that the number will always be fixed; when the constitution is revised, the increase which has taken place in the population will be seen.

The constant tinkering of the number each year would be attended with much confusion.

Neither speaker took note of the decennial revision required by the American constitution, which Point might have used as sanctioning his principle of a sliding scale and Dufaure in opposition to an annual revision. The amendment was defeated and the commission's article passed.

By October 4, Art. 36 had been reached, providing that each representative should receive a salary, which he may not renounce. Morin (de la Drôme) opposed the article in these terms.

I encounter this provision in the general constitution of the United States; I encounter it in the constitutions of the several states of the American Union. I confess that I should be strongly surprised to find it one day written in that of the nation which was once and which will be always, I hope, the chivalrous nation.

He continued that either Art. 36 provided for poor men, unusually numerous at that time, who could not otherwise afford to hold office (in which case it was allowable, but should be a matter of law, not constitution), or it was intended to proclaim a great democratic principle, (which it failed to do). " If you want to inscribe a great democratic principle, follow the example of America. In America, in the United States, not only legislative, but municipal functions are paid. If you want to set forth the principle, proclaim it loudly; . . . say that all offices will be salaried, those of mayor, of adjunct, of municipal councils, of general councils; without that, gentlemen, you are inconsistent."

Dufaure, the commission's usual spokesman, defended the article. It was not a temporary expedient, but a constitutional principle necessary to prevent the eligibility of all the citizens, already recognized, from being a farce.

And the honorable M. Morin was wrong again when he said, that after searching well he had been able to find a salary given to legislators only in the American constitutions. If he had sought a little better, he would have found that the members of the Constituent Assembly had a salary; that those of the Legislative Assembly had one and that the principle of salary, as we write it, is written in plain words in the constitution of the year III. It is not only then in the American constitutions, but among us that this has been written.

The article was then adopted.

A few moments later, Art. 39 came up, providing for three readings of every bill with ten-day intervals between. To this, Saint-Priest objected that this delay of a month, designed to prevent undue haste, would have a contrary effect, by increasing " votes of urgency," the special danger of one-chamber assemblies. " In the United States, and permit me to cite the American republic, this delay is only three days. The Constituent Assembly established a delay of eight days." · Even that proved too long and almost all laws were declared urgent. He considered five days long

enough between each of the three readings. This change
was accepted by the commission, and with this modification
the article was passed.

The debate on the executive was somewhat more varied.
The appeal to or from American example was made not only
on the advisability of having a president, (which was never
very seriously opposed), but even more on the method of his
election and the extent of his power.   It is a little curious
that there should be so much more talk about the excellences
of the American senate than those of the American president, though the adoption of the presidency by France is
usually accredited to American example [1] and the former
was not imitated.   It will be seen that the English example,
almost constantly coupled with the American in the discussion on the legislature, now drops out of sight.

The first mention of the American executive was made
by Mathieu (de la Drôme) as early as September 11, in the
development of his *droit au travail* amendment to Article
VIII of the preamble.   He accused the statesmen of the
past of showing interest in the manufacturers only and
neglecting agricultural interests, because the manufacturers
sat in the Chamber of Deputies and their votes were needed.
He proposed a system of land credits to repopulate the
country districts.

There would be another thing to do, but I am convinced
that you would not accept it, and yet I am convinced that this
thing would be one of the best articles of your constitution:
it would be to write in your constitution that the chief of the

---

[1] *Cf.* Ch. Seignobos, *Histoire Politique de l'Europe Contemporaine*, p.
151 "...the executive [delegated] to a citizen named president of the
republic, for four years, probably in imitation of the United States,
with the right to choose his ministers. . . . It was the American mechanism transported from a federal government without army and without
bureaucracy (*fonctionnaires*) into a centralized government provided
with an irresistible army and a bureaucracy accustomed to dominate."

executive power could never choose a minister on these benches. That is what takes place in America. You know that in the United States, the president cannot take a minister from the parliament; if it is not so with us, France will continue to assist at these oratorical struggles, at these word-tournies which intoxicate the people, instead of giving them bread.

The question of the executive was brought definitely before the Assembly on October 5, when Chapter VIII of the constitution was reached. Articles 41-45 inclusive were at first thrown open for general discussion. Felix Pyat started the debate by declaring that he opposed having a president at all. In his view, the political system of the country should follow man's physical constitution; a single legislative chamber, corresponding to man's brain, a subordinate executive to carry out its will, corresponding to man's arm. Absolute monarchies have one sovereign, the king; constitutional monarchies two, the king and the people; the republic one, the people. It must be represented by one dominant legislative chamber. A president, elected by universal vote, would be a great peril; he might easily claim to represent the people more truly than the whole legislature, composed of members elected by relative majorities, while he was chosen by an absolute majority. The responsibility of the president is badly defined; the whole office is a mistake.

The partisans of presidents quote to us, like the partisans of two chambers, the example of the United States. Citizens, that example again turns against them. What is the republic of the United States? The word indicates it: a federal republic, girondine (excuse the word), an aggregation of different states or bodies, a nation of alluvial accretions (*d'alluvions et d'attérissement*), composed successively of heterogeneous parts, without solidarity with one another. A hoop was necessary to hold together all these staves, ready to disjoin and separate. A single executive power was necessary, precisely because the legislative power was divided, because there were two great national chambers and as many little chambers as states. The danger for America is dissolution; the federal republic has felt the need of unity.

France, however, is the nation of unity par excellence; a president would over-emphasize that tendency, so that the republic would be subject to the danger of becoming a monarchy. " The danger in France is in the opposite direction from that in the United States. In the United States, it is in the dispersion of the provinces, and a president was necessary; in France, it is in concentration; only an Assembly is necessary." Pyat concluded by expressing his desire for a simple president of council, the object of the subsequent Grévy amendment.

Tocqueville next addressed the Assembly. He held that the principle of division of powers, already accepted by that body, would be destroyed if the executive were practically absorbed by the legislative. He further felt that the dangers of executive power had been grossly exaggerated; without popular election, they would be nothing.

" In the legislative sphere, the president, as the constitutional project establishes him, can do nothing; he has neither the absolute veto of the constitutional king nor the suspensive veto of the president of the United States." The council of state, so far from limiting the Assembly's power, furnishes it (being named by the Assembly) an opening to share in the execution of laws, the naming of public officials, the judgment of accused statesmen. Even more, the council of ministers gives the Assembly a chance to control the executive. There are two constitutional systems in this matter; one makes the executive irresponsible, but as in fact he can do nothing without his ministers, who are chosen from the Assembly, the latter's influence on the government remains very great; that is the system of constitutional monarchy.   There is a second system; in this the executive is directly responsible, but at the same time has no need of the assistance of any of his ministers in order to act; his ministers are chosen by him outside the Assembly.

That is the system, which has been practised up to the present in all the republics, which have not confounded the powers; it is to be found not only in the United States, but in France, in the constitution of the year III.   The chiefs of the executive power were indeed responsible, but they could act freely; the United States constitution presents the same character.

By the new constitution, however, an unheard-of hybrid scheme has been created; the president is declared responsible, yet at his side is placed an equally responsible council of ministers, without which he can do nothing and which may reduce him to powerlessness; thus the National Assembly remains the supreme power despite M. Pyat's fears. Were it not for the election of the president by universal vote, it would be as absolute as the Convention.   It will not mean the Terror, but it will mean tyranny and corruption. This Assembly has no right to name the president, nor has any Assembly whose duration will not be equal to his own, i. e. four years.   Through the bureaux you have already pronounced for universal suffrage; that in fact is the central feature of the republic; you cannot defraud France of it now, just because certain members now fear that a name hostile to the republic may be the choice of the people. The Assembly is the sole force that has worked for stability in these late troubled times; the reason is, that its strength is drawn from universal suffrage.   The danger of France's throwing itself into the arms of the first phantom whose name is a guarantee of strength, is due to the fear of social revolution; the remedy for that real danger is, however, not legislative tyranny, but such complete reprobation of that type of revolution, that you will stand at the head of the orderly majority. Then when confidence is restored, you have nothing to fear from a popular presidential election.

Parieu, the following speaker, opposed universal suffrage, but from another point of view than Pyat. Though a conservative, Parieu too feared the possibilities of too strong an executive. Conservative and radical alike drew back at the menace of Bonapartism, which had already begun to cast its shadow over the land. It is curious to see him supporting the American example in a cause directly opposite from Tocqueville's; the latter admired its executive's independence of the legislative; the former praised its system of indirect election as opposed to a direct, universal vote. Where Pyat favored the Grévy plan, Parieu supported in this speech the system proposed in the Leblond amendment. "There was much talk of history in the two-chamber question, and especially about America," he said.

Indeed, the republic was such a sudden thing with us, to employ the expression of the minister of finance, so little expected, that it was natural that France and those who represented her should cast their eyes over the widest possible horizon, that they should question the history of all the republics, and that with some timidity perhaps, some humility for the lessons of experience, they should question all the republics, all the great republics, for the lessons of their past and of history. America was much, even exclusively talked about (*on a beaucoup parlé, uniquement même parlé de l'Amérique*), à propos of the two chambers. Permit me to cite her à propos of the question we are discussing here, not especially from the point of view of the president's nomination by the legislative body, but from the point of view of a question which is at the bottom of the other, that of the direct or indirect election of the president.

America was in a very different situation from ours, it was completely republican; it had not the least reminiscence of monarchy, not the least discord on the subject of the form of its government. The monarchy! It could only recall for her the enemy, whom she had driven away after such long combats. America was republican, entirely republican, and further, there could not be for the election of its first president, of him who should be the founder of that republic, an instant of indecision and hesitation; it had a man who had conducted it at once to liberty and to victory, a man of whom one said in 1787 at the moment of his election, what one said at his death, those three words which were his funeral oration, the most beautiful which can be pronounced over a citizen's tomb, to wit: that he was first in peace, first in war and first in the hearts of his countrymen. Those words, which were pronounced at his tomb, were in every mouth in 1787, and thus the president of the American republic was named, so to speak, the day when the republic was founded. However the Americans did not think that it was direct universal suffrage which should normally preside at the nomination of the republic's president; they looked further, and it was by indirect election, summoning men placed at high points of view, discerning the political necessities of the country, necessities often so delicate,—it was by indirect election that they organized the naming of the republic's president.

There, gentlemen, is what we are taught by the past of the only republic whose history it has been thought proper to interrogate in this gathering. Were it necessary to search elsewhere, I would ask of you, (but they would be examples too restricted to be compared with the one I have just cited and even to be compared with our situation), I would ask of you permission to invoke the example of the little modern European republics.

He then quoted Switzerland, whose executive power is chosen by the legislative, and Holland where the States

General more than once chose the *stathouder*. Turning
from history to logic, he criticized that feature of the constitution, which in case of no absolute majority, provided
a reballot by the Assembly, among the five leading candidates; the Assembly might elect the last of the five and
that by a slight majority.

I think the idea was to imitate America, for I find all there
repeated. It is the same number; it is also among the five
candidates who have obtained the most votes, that in America
the legislative bodies of Congress may choose in default of
absolute majority. But there is an immense difference. In
America, the electors charged with choosing the president are
the same in point of numbers as the members of the representation [in Congress]. Then I understand it, when there is
no majority among the electors, that another assembly equal
in numbers should proceed to an election and settle the first
one; here are scores of votes compensated by scores of votes.
But to settle millions of votes perhaps with a few votes of
the National Assembly when one has commenced by denying
the National Assembly the right of choosing the president of
the republic, this is to do an inconsequential thing, something
which can never be sustained.

This plan seemed to him to combine the evils of the two
systems, popular and Assembly election. " Gentlemen, I permitted myself to say a word concerning the situation of the
country, and I made a comparison just now without wishing
it in speaking of America. Well, is our position the same
as that of America?" He proceeded to show that America
of the past century was very differently situated from
France, a people of royalist traditions, where royalist sympathies in some parts still exist. An appeal to the suffrages of a divided nation was full of danger.

What is the executive power which it is sought to make for

us? Is it a kind of constitutional king, having a veto, having his part in the legislative branch, able like the American president, to say to the legislative body: You are the majority, but that is not enough; you must deliberate anew, and make your decision by a two-thirds majority; that is to say, that my voice alone is worth a sixth of the national representation?

No, the proposed executive had only the right to ask the Assembly to vote once more. " Well, he who has only the right to say that, who must execute the law, and perhaps obey a thought contrary to his own conviction, he is not a semi-constitutional-king-president, like the one in America. No, he is a first magistrate of a democracy, a chief who executes and does not deliberate." And it is to such an officer that you would give an independent source! For a president of the American type who has to be strong enough to balance a majority of Congress and compel its submission to his veto, such a popular backing might be important, but it is folly here. He would go so far as to say that if the president is to be elected by universal vote, his powers should be increased; to refuse him the power which is the natural consequence of what he represents is to threaten disaster. If, however, the executive is made too strong, his responsibility becomes a myth. An antagonism without issue arises between executive and legislative. In the old days, the dissolution of the chamber provided a way out. Now, that is forbidden. Nor can the president resign and contest the matter at the polls, for he cannot again be a candidate. The only sensible way is to have the president chosen by the Assembly. There is no foundation for the idea that this violates the principle of division of powers. That division is one of functions, not of the nomination of individuals. There must always be links between the powers. The naming of the supreme court by the Assembly does not violate the principle, for the latter never expects to interfere with its decisions. So here, Tocqueville's objection of corruption (that the president will seek to influence the Assembly which elects him) will only hold under the system of re-elections, which has been banished from your constitution. " But re-election by the country entails also all those evils which M. de Tocqueville has so well described in America, where the president, as he admits I think, has in view, in all his acts, in his whole administration, only the goal of his re-election." The objection that election of the executive by the Assembly is to reproduce the Convention is an error; the Convention did not create a definite executive with a fixed term; it kept all the authority to itself. It is well to have a strong executive, but if you make him too strong, it will be impossible to limit his term of office; he will dominate the legislative and arrange the question of re-eligibility to suit himself. The remainder of this long, but important speech was taken up with a demonstration of the dangers of a too strong executive, the impossibility of fettering him by rules, as the coup d'état against the constitution of the year III proved, and with a defence of his system against the charge of legislative usurpation. He closed with a clever adaptation of Tocqueville's statement that the Assembly had recently been the one stable thing in France; as such, he said, dare to think and plan wisely for France, do not abdicate your powers in a sort of scepticism, saying that the country will do what it pleases. A curious echo of that very scepticism was found in Lamartine's famous speech the next day, which turned the scale against M. Parieu's system.

The next important discussion of the subject was by Jules Grévy, offering his amendment,[1] at the following ses-

---

[1] *Vide supra*, p. 119 *et seq.*

sion, October 6. The point of difference between his system and legislative choice of a president, as desired by Parieu, was that Grévy merely wished to make the present Cavaignac régime permanent. Instead of having a president elected irrevocably for a fixed term, he would have the choice made for an indefinite period, always subject to recall. After refuting the objections that the Assembly had no authority to deprive the people of the right of directly choosing the president, and that the principle of separation of powers was endangered (to which two points, he replied much as his predecessors had done), he turned to criticism of the commission's plan. The proposed president, having the disposal of the army, the nomination to civil and military positions and the tremendous force of a popular election, will be really more powerful than the late king. Bonaparte based his throne on the elections of the year X. And you say you are founding a democratic republic! How else would you go about restoring a monarchy? The temporary term of office is no barrier; an ambitious man will brush it aside. Suppose this ambitious man has known how to make himself popular, suppose him a victorious general or a scion of one of the families who have ruled France and has not expressly renounced his pretended rights, suppose an economic crisis, can you answer for it that this ambitious man will not overturn the republic? Despotism has destroyed every republic of the past, yet you take no steps to avert that danger. The Assembly's choice among the first five, if there is no absolute popular majority, is a delusion; either it will always choose the candidate with the highest popular vote, in which case it is a formality, or it will choose another and thus a less popular man, entailing probable civil discords or even strife. What has led the commission to its ill-starred conception? Historical precedents? No

French constitution has provided for direct, popular election. The examples of neighboring republics?

There is not one of them, not a single one in which the executive power is delegated directly by the people. In the United States, which is incessantly proposed to us as a model, the president of the republic is not named directly by the people; he is named by an indirect method, by a delegation, more or less complicated according to circumstances. Thus this pretended principle of direct election would be a novelty in history, a novelty in the world.

Constitutional principles? Not the doctrine of popular sovereignty, for the judicial power is a constant example of indirect delegation and this Assembly of divided delegation; direct, undivided delegation is therefore not necessary. The system of checks and balances, perhaps. He would boldly assert his belief that in that doctrine the publicists of the eighteenth century and their modern successors made the greatest political error of the times. They found in England a state in process of transition, no longer an absolute monarchy and not yet a republic; they found a royalty, aristocracy and democracy dividing the sovereignty and hence the government; their error was to suppose that an equilibrium was thus formed, guaranteeing a stable government; omitting the past and the future, they failed to see that the popular element was established only at the expense of the two others, that it was slowly, but unceasingly pushing its conquest and that an obscure struggle was going on, which would inevitably result in the triumph of the democratic element over the two others. The same struggle in France was shorter and more terrible, because here it was between the people and royalty over the corpse of aristocracy. Aristocracy perished here in 1789 and every subsequent effort to galvanize it and build a second chamber out of it, has been a failure. Instead of equilibrium, history shows on every page the antagonisms and conflicts organized under that lying name, the inevitable result of the juxtaposition of independent powers. The so-called system of balance is correct for a period of transition; all one can do is to give each of the contending forces a part of the ground. But when monarchy and aristocracy, defeated, leave democracy mistress of the battle-field, it is an absurd anachronism to divide the field according to the old forms, thus splitting democratic unity and recurring to inevitable antagonisms. You felt this when you decided for a single chamber, thus setting aside the upper house, which represents aristocracy, an element now dead in France. Why then should you maintain the other power, the royal power, when there is no longer royalty? You had to choose between two systems, that of the past which divides sovereignty into three branches and that of the future, which unifies it. You have already pronounced against the first, by cutting out one of the branches; to hesitate now, and retain the two others, would be to establish a mutilated, bastard government, aggravating the dangers of the old system by increasing the antagonism and giving it no issue. To be consistent, you must go on to the acceptance of my amendment. Election of a president for a fixed term by the Assembly, though much less dangerous than choosing him by popular vote, is to be rejected as still creating two antagonistic powers. The only forceful government is one in which Assembly and president are united; June proves that. Parieu has successfully dispelled the fear of a dictatorship by a Convention. You have been happy enough to find the best government, be wise enough to keep it.

This beautiful example of French logic in its most uncompromising clarity, was followed by Jules de Lasteyrie's defence of the older theory of government. Division of

powers alone confers responsibility, without which despotism is inevitable.   It is more than bold to treat these great
constitutional truths held by all humanity with such supreme
disdain.   It is an error to identify the separation of governmental powers with the elements of society, represented by
democracy, aristocracy and royalty.   The distinction between the various systems calling for election of the executive by the legislative is over-subtle; one and all they violate the foundation-rule of sound government and decree
a permanent revolution.   You are planning to give the Assembly the naming of the council of state, the court of
cassation and the president; what a chance for corruption!
The reason why there is now such opposition to popular
election of the president, is because the state of the country has changed in the last few months; it is feared that the
country will not choose rightly.   But if you do not trust
the country, you are not republicans; that is the very spirit
of monarchy.   If you engage the Assembly in a struggle
against the country's will, then indeed comes disaster.   It is
then desirable to have the country elect the president.   But
to avoid the objections to that system, the backing of the
successful candidate by millions of votes and the difficulty
of the masses' distinguishing between good and poor candidates, why not let the country elect indirectly?   " There is
an argument for this opinion, *mon Dieu*, I know it! "   To
which " a voice " replied, "An American argument."   The
speaker resuming,

You have said it.   Truly, I do not understand why this should
not be an excellent argument.   This system has been practised
for exactly sixty years in America, and by a singular abuse
of argumentative subtleties, the honorable M. Parieu yesterday even supported himself by the example of the United
States.   In that country where, however, there is no adminis-

trative centralization, where the president disposes of so few positions, there is such a fear of corruption, which as Monsieur the Federalist Hamilton says, is the vice destructive of free governments,—the corruption which the executive power might exercise is so much feared, that all the representatives, all the public functionaries, all the persons having political or administrative relations with the president, are excluded from the right to belong to the nominating electors! And it is thus that for sixty years, the United States have progressed, increased, prospered.

Thus the conservatives made clever use of the republican example, even posing as the supporters of republicanism against tyranny, and as more democratic than the professed democrats. Neither side was perfectly sincere in its arguments, though the real truth was more than once hinted at. The fact was that the men of the Left opposed election by universal suffrage, because they were convinced that the country at large did not have sufficiently republican sentiments; the men of the Right favored it for precisely the same reason. They were willing enough to adopt a democratic method to produce an anti-democratic result, thus hoisting the enemy with his own petard. Both sides were ready to sacrifice consistency of principle to secure a political victory. Perhaps they were right, for at this critical juncture, the very constitutional framework of the country depended on holding the reins of political power, as events soon showed. The election of Louis Napoleon carried with it the inevitability of Empire.

Leblond now offered his amendment, designed as a middle-ground, he said, between the Grévy scheme, which would make the president a puppet at the Assembly's mercy, intriguing constantly to keep his place, and the popular suffrage scheme, creating a popular king, as dangerously strong as the other would be dangerously weak.

He was succeeded by Lamartine, whose speech was one of the most famous he ever made and carried the day for the commission's plan. The speaker first discussed briefly the question of whether a president should be chosen at all and summarized the alternate tyranny and feebleness of the committee-executive, whose irresponsibility is its undoing. Incidentally he rejected the phrase "division of powers," inapplicable to unitary France with its unitary Assembly expressing the national sovereignty; in its place he would prefer to say "distinction of functions." He now took up the question of how the president should be elected. He had heard, with the liveliest interest, M. Parieu going over, page by page, the lessons of history and politics on this matter. These considerations were not new to him. He, too, had studied the systems of the United States, the American republics, Venice, Genoa, even the conclaves of the Catholic republic and the French constitutions of the past. He had tried to understand the motives of all these combinations. He declared frankly that he found nothing applicable to the present French situation in any of them. M. Parieu cited yesterday the examples of the United States, Switzerland and Holland in favor of indirect election, but these are inapplicable.

The United States name at two degrees, [*i. e.* by indirect election] Holland named at two degrees, Switzerland named at two degrees, why? Because these three countries are federated states; because before the federal unit, which is the only one represented in the nomination of the supreme power which corresponds to the entire federation, before these federal unities cast their vote to consecrate the presidential right of the chief of the republic, they must come to an understanding with themselves; because in a word, they do not represent an individual will, but the will of each member of the federation. Here is the secret of these three methods;

these republics have or had peculiarly powerful natures; the United States had made alliance with the ocean, Switzerland with the mountains, Holland with the marshes; a strong power was less necessary to them. But, gentlemen, it does not escape you that France has nothing, has had nothing, will have nothing comparable, in its social and national constitution, to these federations which are without end cited to us as examples, without having understood their nature and their necessity.

Leaving these secondary, scientific considerations to plunge into the merits of the controversy, one thing is certain; power, in republics, lies in popularity. At present it is in this Assembly. But should it gradually leave the Assembly and the executive whom it has chosen, the power of the government would crumble in all its parts. Opposition to the system of popular election finds one of its motives in the fear that the fallen dynasties will seek to return to power by means of the popular vote. For the two royalist families, this is a foolish fear; it would be beneath their dignity to make such an effort. As for the third dynasty, which perhaps you have in your mind, the representatives of France have already decided to respect the avowals of that family and to restore them their rights of citizenship. The fear which preoccupies the Assembly's thought, that a posthumous fanaticism will lead a great military nation to confer dangerous honors on the heirs of a great name, he neither confessed nor denied to be well-founded. He could not read the future, but he did respect the honesty of the republican avowals made here by that family. And as for the factions of that party, they would be foiled in their hopes; " to arrive at an eighteenth brumaire in our time, two things are necessary; long years of terror behind and Marengos, victories before!" The dangers of a counter-system presented as an ideal come after years of political discontent;

the present peril is rather that of a certain lukewarmness, a loss of the initial February enthusiasm, due to misrepresentation of the republic on the part of its enemies and excessive radicalism on the part of its friends. In such a situation, to take away the people's share in its own sovereignty, to restore its old exile, endured for thirty-six years under past constitutional governments, is surely a poor way to restore enthusiasm for the republic. Rather let the people choose its own head, its personification and its chief. The Assembly remains the supreme and indivisible representative of sovereignty; the president has no share in its power, he is only a function of government. The deliberate vote of each citizen is the very sacrament of authority. The right of primogeniture is only the right of the first comer, the right of conquest defiles the people with its brutal violence; divine right is but the priest's blessing on royal races; the sacred right of popular vote is the stripping off of the people's sovereignty by its own volition to clothe a government, if possible more collective, universal and popular than itself. Election by the few votes an Assembly has to cast suggests always the possibility of favoritism and selfish purpose, not to use the word, corruption. " One poisons a glass of water, not a river; an Assembly is suspect, a nation is incorruptible as the ocean." The objection that the executive would be too strong, if popularly elected, is absurd; " would to God the infant republic were born with all its energy, like the god in the ancient fable which strangled the serpents in his cradle; " the executive's strength would be merely that of the country itself. To put the vote in the hands of each citizen is to give him the right and duty of defending the republic against whomsoever might attack it.

The great orator concluded his speech with that famous fatalistic peroration, which swept the Assembly off its feet.

I know well that there are grave dangers in both systems; that there are moments of aberration in multitudes; that there are names which draw the crowd as the mirage draws herds of cattle, as the red rag attracts unreasoning animals. I know it, I dread it more than anyone, for perhaps no citizen has put more of his soul, his life, his sweat, his responsibility and his memory in the republic's success! Should it become established, I have won my human gage against destiny! Should it fail, either in anarchy or in a reminiscence of despotism, my name, my responsibility, my memory fail with it and are forever repudiated by my contemporaries! Well, despite that redoubtable personal responsibility in the dangers our problematic institutions may run, although the republic's dangers are my dangers, and its loss my ostracism and my eternal grief, should I survive, I do not hesitate to pronounce in favor of what seems to you most dangerous, the election of the president by the people. Yes, even though the people should choose him whom my perhaps badly enlightened foresight dreads to see it choose, no matter: the die is cast! Let God and the people pronounce! Something must be left to Providence! He is the light of those who, like us, cannot read the shadows of the future! Let us invoke Him, let us pray Him to enlighten the people and let us submit ourselves to His decree. Perhaps we may perish at the task? No, surely, and yet it would be beautiful to die initiating one's country into liberty.

Well, if the people deceives itself, if it allows itself to be blinded by the dazzling reflection of its own past glory; if it withdraws from its own sovereignty after the first step, as though frightened by the grandeur of the edifice we have opened to it in its republic, and by the difficulties of its institutions; if it wants to abdicate its safety, its dignity, its liberty into the hands of an imperial memory; if it says, take me back to the paths of the old monarchy; if it disavows us and disavows itself, well, so much the worse for the people! It will not be we, but they who shall have lacked perseverance and courage! I repeat it, we may perish at the task by their fault, but the ruin of the republic will not be imputed to us! Yes, whatever happens, it will be beautiful through history to have attempted the republic! The republic as we have proclaimed, conceived, outlined it for four months, the republic of enthusiasm, of moderation, of fraternity, of peace, of protection to society, to property, to religion, to the family, the republic of Washington!

A dream, if you will! But it will have been a beautiful dream for France and for the human race! But that dream, let us not forget, was the act of the people of February during its first months! We will restore it! But, finally, should this people abandon itself; should it gamble with the fruit of its own blood, spent so generously for the republic in February and in June; should it say that fatal word, should it wish to desert the victorious cause of liberty and human progress to run after some meteor that would burn its hands—let it so speak! But we, citizens, let us at least not speak for it in advance! Should that misfortune arrive; let us rather speak the word of the vanquished at Pharsala; the victorious cause pleased the gods, but the lost cause pleased Cato! And let this protest against the error or the feebleness of this people be its accusation before itself, and our absolution before posterity!

After that extraordinary speech, in which one is uncertain whether to marvel most at the eloquence, the clairvoyance, the frankness or the obstinacy, nothing remained to be said. Two insignificant speeches were made the following day, and then the Assembly, with eyes that had been opened to the danger ahead, but with the exalted fanaticism, which a poet had kindled in its heart, deliberately took the step which was to destroy it.

The next allusion to the American executive was made in the short debate on the Leblond amendment which took place before the vote on that plan, but after the Grévy amendment had been defeated.

Flocon, speaking for the amendment, disclaimed Lamartine's pessimism, but disclaimed also his fatalistic willingness to stake all on chance; a danger should be guarded against. He would have the president's rôle less splendid, more useful than his opponent. He did not comprehend Lamartine's statement that the Assembly alone would remain sovereign; if named by the people, surely the president would have equal claim to sovereignty. An Assembly sufficiently republican to vote one chamber, must now carry out the consequences of that vote.

M. de Lasteyrie spoke to you yesterday, and if I am not mistaken, he will make of it the object of a proposition, the president's election at two degrees, in the American fashion. I ask of M. de Lasteyrie, if he will find here in France the elements of that election. Is it a question, in America, of making the people vote, gathered in its electoral assemblies, or on the public square, to make it vote for a candidate who will have more or less votes, through these united electors? Not at all. The Americans have taken more precautions; and they have made skillful use of what you, happily for yourselves, do not possess, I mean the federation. In the American election, each state names two candidates; it takes one from itself and one from outside. Do you not admire the mechanism which brings it about that, outside of personal relations or local influences, must of necessity emerge the name which best sums up the general opinion? But what have you like that here and can you think of it for an instant? Have you not decided that the republic was one and indivisible? . . . You see in what complete anarchy of ideas you are going to cast yourself if you would apply to our country institutions that are not made for it.

This speech is typical of the inaccurate knowledge of the American system revealed by the radical wing, no account being taken of its modification in practice by party development.

Martin (de Strasbourg) then defended the same cause in the name of the minority of the commission. As "a republican by birth" he opposed the "English school" which for the past eighteen years had stood in France for the principle of checks and balances. No legislator, no writer, however, had even dared suggest that the executive should be chosen as was the legislative and with the same authority. "You have no example of it, either in America, in our constitution of the year III, or in that of 1791."

He was followed by Dufaure, representing the majority of the commission. He showed that a consistent desire for absolute unity would have entailed a vote for the Grévy plan; there was just as much duality in character and attributes of office in the Leblond plan as in that of the commission. "So, do not reproach us, when you are really establishing a power which has the same character as ours, do not reproach us with belonging to some English or American school; I do not know that the system which we propose to adopt has ever been put into practice either in England or in America."

Shortly after, the vote was taken on the Leblond amendment, which was defeated.

On the 9th, another amendment was proposed, which had for its object the adoption of indirect election and was confessedly influenced by the American system. It was offered in the names of Mortimer Ternaux (an ultra-conservative historian) and Lacrosse and read as follows:

The president is elected by secret ballot, by electoral assemblies gathered at the chief towns of the departments and composed of cantonal delegates, in the proportion of one delegate to 2000 inhabitants. The cantonal delegates are named in the form determined by art. 30 of the present constitution. They shall receive no imperative mandate. They shall receive the same pay as jurors.

Lacrosse in developing his plan asserted his belief in universal suffrage as the base of presidential power, but felt that a more deliberate, careful choice would be made by the indirect system.

Let us only search the example and experience of free states, if there may not exist wise precautions which, introduced into our constitution, would give it a new force by setting aside candidates and names too little known, and names perhaps too dazzling.

While the average man can choose an acceptable representative from his neighbors of distinction, it is a much more difficult task to pick out one of presidential calibre.

I permit myself to call " a prejudice " that antipathy which is manifested against a system to which the United States of America owe for sixty years so magnificent a development. It is in vain that in the solemn discussions which have filled the last week, an effort has been made to repel in advance all assimilation between the executive power of our republic and the power which presides over the action of the American government. The internal administration of the states of the Union is doubtless outside the attributions of the president of the United States. But the federal system changes in no way the essence of the executive power. Each of the separate states possesses its constitution, its legislature and its administrative personnel independently of the central government; that is known and did not perhaps require the developments which we have heard. They have not been exempt from mistakes; further, it has not been denied that the action of the executive power sitting at Washington is superior to all local authorities. The executive power encounters certain obstacles born of that organization of a great federal state. In our republic, which we have wished one and indivisible, the action of the executive power will have analogies, even an identity, which can escape none of you; the identity exists at least in the resistance to its action. The president of the United States disposes alone of the land and naval forces. In concert with a senate composed of about fifty members, he treats with foreign powers, but it is by means of an indirect system that America has acquired these illustrious chiefs of executive power, who by their disinterestedness, by their personal abnegation, have given the world the most majestic example of public virtues; it is also to this mode of indirect election that are due other magistrates who have great pages in the history of their country. When the flag of the United States saw itself outraged by jealous England to. assure its own maritime omnipotence, it was then that the United States had to commence the struggle, gloriously sustained and ended by them in 1814. Those negotiations which have extended the arms of America to the Pacific Ocean, the diplomatic conquest of Oregon, were made thanks to the skill of a president, chosen by indirect election. The conquest of Mexico, these extensions of territory subject to the arms of the Union, probable seed of enfeeblement, but at present a subject of enthusiasm in the United States, these sucesses are due also to a magistrate chosen by indirect election. And this indirect election is condensed further than what has been proposed to you; the number of electors hardly equals that of the members of our future legislative assemblies. So restricted a number is far from giving the authority which the president of the French republic would receive here from indirect election. The second degree electors are six or seven hundred: we shall propose to you eighteen thousand.

Payer next took the floor to oppose the amendment, on the ground that it merely repeated the notion of choice by the Assembly, already discarded. He thought also that minority rights were less secure, being less able to register themselves in a vote; the electors, named by a majority, would merely represent that majority. He rather adroitly turned Lacrosse's presidential calibre argument against him by declaring that a man not well-known to all France was certainly not big enough to be president.

The honorable M. Lacrosse said to you: What we propose is practised in America: the president is named by indirect vote. Yes, assuredly; but the representatives are also named by indirect vote; all the citizens are not electors; a property qualification is exacted and if one once admits the rule of exceptions, it makes small difference, according to my opinion, whether one extends it more or less. Besides, has this system produced in the United States the excellent results just enumerated? Either I am much mistaken, or it seems to me that often in the history of the republic, I have read that the best candidate has not always been named. The country, divided into two camps, rejected the man who would enter neither one nor the other, whatever his other merits. To obtain that sovereign magistracy, the presidency, it was necessary to join a party, and in consequence to have for himself, at least in relation to his chiefs, less independence when he was raised to power.

Ternaux had a final word, recalling Pyat's original fear of too strong an executive, which he had shared.

The amendment thereupon came to a vote and was defeated. Valette had offered a similar one, which he now withdrew. It is curious that in the whole debate on the executive and particularly in this final phase, no one seems to have recognized the complete nullification of the electoral college idea in American constitutional practice. Payer's speech comes nearest to an appreciation of it, but does not really grasp the situation. One would have supposed that some supporter of universal suffrage would have made telling use of the American example as it worked itself out in this regard. If this indicates anything beyond carelessness, it would point toward a better knowledge of the written American constitution than of living American constitu-

tional history.   Other amendments were proposed, one calling for election by the Assembly from a list of ten candidates chosen by universal suffrage, another for a universal
vote, but requiring a two-thirds majority in order to elect,
another requiring an absolute majority of all registered citizens (not merely of votes cast), but all were defeated without general discussion, and Art. 43 of the commission plan
then adopted.

After Art. 44 had been disposed of, return was made to
Art. 42, which had been temporarily passed over.   An
amendment was proposed by Deville, "the presidency shall
never be conferred upon any general officer," which was
received with much hilarity and general disorder.   Deville,
with some difficulty, essayed to explain his idea.   He held it
to be one of the principal lessons of history, written on each
of its pages.   (Several members) "And Washington!"
The speaker ignored this interruption.   He recalled the
history of England, France, Sardinia, Naples, Spain, the
southern part of North America and all South America to
support his thesis of the danger of military ambition, and
then passed to a defence of the *république rouge* against
what he called the *république blanche*.   The amendment was
then voted on and defeated.   A long debate on the proposed
ineligibility of members of families which had reigned in
France was followed by the adoption of Art. 42 and a discussion of Art. 45, fixing the term of office at four years.

This, Kerdrel would amend to provide for a right to re-
election at the expiration of the president's term, a second
re-election to be permitted only after four years had elapsed.
He began his exposition by an admission that all present
knew the republic theoretically.

We have all without exception, lessons to take, instruction
to demand from those who have practised the republic with

success and with glory. Let your eyes turn toward America, toward the United States. There the republic is not a simple thought, a pure theory; it is a glorious practical reality; it is a fact. Well, in the United States you know the president is re-eligible. In law, he is so indefinitely; in fact, he is so once after the expiration of his functions.

This "anomaly which has its sublimity" he explained as a result of practical experience, left to usage rather than law to avoid the danger of writing into the constitution any limitation of "their most sacred political right, the liberty of suffrage."

We had thought at first, the honorable M. de Montalembert and I, that we could imitate the United States so completely that we could pass in complete silence the right of re-election. Others have thought otherwise; . . . have seen behind our amendment a sort of cloud, all charged with monarchy.

The objections to immediate re-eligibility are all set forth, he continued, in the very remarkable book of M. de Tocqueville. They are, the president's governing with an eye to his re-election rather than for the good of the country, the greater danger of corruption, the growth of his office into a disguised constitutional kingship. The true remedy to the corruption-danger, which is not denied, is a system of decentralization. But aside from that, a president who could not be re-elected at all until four years passed, would be even more likely to use corruption; knowing that his time was short, he would try to leave memories of his administration in the minds of those whom he could corrupt and would try to be popular at all costs and to make his successor unpopular. The Assembly, which had been growing restless, began to clamor for the vote, to the speaker's despair. "What, you are between an article of the commission and an article of the American constitution and you do not reflect! Construct a democracy like that of the

United States, and then you can say that you are satisfied."
The speaker next took up the objection of a disguised kingship; his eight-year maximum limit to re-elections, he declared, would remove that peril.   But he foresaw a very real
danger if no re-election were permitted and an ambitious
president in control of the army found it impossible to prolong his term by legal means.   The Assembly was unwilling to listen further to this Cassandra prophecy, and after
cutting the speech short, defeated the amendment, then
passing Art. 45.

On the 12th, Mathieu (de la Drôme) presented an additional article, calling for the suspension of the president by
a two-thirds vote of the Assembly.   This was, however, opposed by the commission on the ground that it was the
Grévy amendment in disguise, and defeated.

Art. 46 was then passed (" He watches over and assures
the execution of the laws ").   The presiding officer then
read an amendment by Saint-Priest, offered in connection
with Art. 49 (" He presents every year, by message, an exposé of the general state of the republic's affairs "), but
which he thought more appropriate at this point.   The
amendment read, " He presents bills to the National Assembly through his ministers, who explain the reasons for
them and defend them in discussion."   Saint-Priest's defence of his plan opened with the statement, " This Art.
49 is taken from the American constitutions, but those constitutions preserve the strictest silence regarding the president's initiative and this silence is the denial of the right."
In republics, he continued, the president does not have the
initiative, which belongs exclusively to members of parliament, and if ministers exercise it, it is not as such, but as
members of parliament.   He did not argue against this conception and in favor of the executive's right to initiate legislation in his own name, as to which he assumed all present

were agreed.   His point was that for the sake of clarity, the right should be inserted in the constitution and not left to assumption.   " Further, please notice that the government's article would apply as well in the American republic, and even in the English government, as in your republic."

Vivien in the name of the commission, suggested that Art. 72 contained the necessary authorization, but was willing to allow the old Art. 46 to become the second paragraph of a new Art. 46, the first paragraph to read " He has the right to present bills to the National Assembly through his ministers;" that portion of Saint-Priest's amendment which referred to the exposition and defence of these government measures by the ministers on the floor of the Assembly, he rejected.   Saint-Priest agreed to the change and the amendment, thus modified, was adopted.

Arts. 47-51 inclusive were voted at once, with slight verbal changes.   A discussion arose over Art. 52, on the president's right of pardon, the chief point being whether or not the council of state should first give its opinion, as the commission required.   This was opposed both by the conservative Dabeaux and the liberal Crémieux, but was maintained.

When Art. 59 was reached Dabeaux proposed that the salary, fixed by the commission at 600,000 francs a year, be left undetermined, except that it must be settled before the president's election and the figure mentioned be made a minimum.   " What I propose exists in the United States " he said, meaning as he later showed, that " in the United States, the salary, by a wise provision, is not fixed in the constitution, the legislative chambers must determine its amount at each nomination of the president." [1]   He quoted

---

[1] *L'Ère nouvelle* of Oct. 13, quoting this speech, which it wrongly ascribes to Saint-Priest, remarked: " The United States have the privilege of furnishing examples to all, both for and against."

Hayti and Santo Domingo as instances of the meagreness of the proposed salary. The amendment was not seconded and finally the commission's text was adopted.

The remainder of the debate on the executive presents small interest. There was at least one other allusion to the relations between the executive and legislative branches in America, before November 4.

On October 18, Art. 100 was under discussion, providing that the Assembly should have the option of sending an accused minister before the high court of justice, the ordinary civil tribunals or the council of state. Combarel de Leyval vigorously opposed mention of the council of state, which he considered a mere tool of the Assembly and a clever way for that body to rid itself of its political enemies.

There is in America, whence this institution has been imported, something which is not similar, but analogous: it is sufficient to remark the difference which separates us from the customs of Oregon and the laws of that country, for you to judge the proposed innovation. What happens in America? The House of Representatives may send before the Senate, by virtue of an old English or rather Saxon law, all the public functionaries and ministers. But who names the Senate? Is it the House of Representatives? Is the Senate the emanation of the House of Representatives? No, it has been brought out in this discussion, the Senate is made by a special mode of election. Then it is understandable that the Senate may have the character of judges, since it is completely independent, both by origin, by sentiment and by absence of passion, from the House of Representatives, which accuses. Here on the contrary what do you do? You send before the council of state which you have named, the ministers who have displeased you. Did one ever see such a judicial enormity? Notice especially this capital difference. You have created in the constitution the council of ministers; in consequence, you have created a struggle in the Assembly; you have created, if not parties, at least groups, fractions which dispute the power. In creating these elements of strife, you have created adversaries to the ruling opinion. Do things happen so in America? In the United States, no member of the legislature is admitted to form part of the executive power. It is evident that the House of Representatives has no interest in accusing, nor the Senate in condemning. Here, on the contrary, there is an enormous interest in ridding oneself of an ancient adversary; there is motive for a party to rid itself from public life for five years, of a man who may have superiority of talent or have won a distinguished popularity or a personal influence in the National Assembly.

This opinion prevailed and the offending words were removed from the constitution.

Aside from these three constitutional questions of first importance, the question of a preamble, of the legislative and the executive (the American doctrine of the authority of the Supreme Court to determine the constitutionality of legislation does not seem to have been discussed at all), there were two other debates in which appeal was made several times to our example. Though not on strictly constitutional issues, they are included for the sake of completeness.

The first of these was on government purchase of railroads. On the 17th of May, Duclerc, then minister of finance, presented a government bill, having as object, the authorization of the state to purchase the railroads. The bill was preceded by an interesting and very modern report,[1] which called attention to the growth of fluid capital during the Restoration and its increasing political power, the government having corrupted its supporters by the organization of financial companies, the danger of tying up gov-

[1] *Moniteur*, May 19.

ernment money in private enterprises, the danger of private railroads with their foreign employés in time of war, the power of railroads over commercial enterprise through mani- pulation of freight charges, which the most ingenious rate regulation cannot correct, the danger of these great powers becoming stronger than the state, the bad financial condi- tion and unpopularity of the railroads. The report then points out the advantages of government ownership engag- ing the state in a great enterprise, which will show its strength by reviving industry and thus settling the danger- ous labor-problem, by reducing rates to the general advant- age of the public and by checking the excesses of speculation. It shows that no attack is made on the principle of property, the roads being paid for at full value and that both public and commercial credit will be improved by the transaction. It mentions the railroads which should be acquired, and others whose purchase should be optional, and then goes into a long discussion of the proper basis of valuation, finally deciding that the original cost, the present value and probable expectation of the roads should all be taken into account and that the fairest measure for all three was the average market value of the stock on the Paris Bourse for the six months which preceded the February Revolution. The financial crisis had been so acute and all values had so shrunk since that time, that it would not be fair to the roads to take a later date. The value thus fixed (which would amount to 518,052,690 fr.), he would proceed to exchange railroad stock for five per cent government *rentes*, using the same six months' average to determine their market value. The rolling stock would not be an extra charge, its value being included in that of the shares; the financial obli- gations of the roads would, however, have to be taken over by the government. These amounted to 90,698,750 fr. In buying the roads, the state assumes the obligation of putting them all in complete operation (many were still unfinished). But the state was already heavily obligated in the matter, to the amount of about one-third the total necessary expenditure; if it assumed the rest, the total would amount to 955,000,000 francs, spread out over a series of years. To the report was appended a bill, authorizing the various projects above recommended.

The bill was referred to the committee of finance, which rendered its report through Bineau, June 6.[1] The report decided that the state had no right to purchase the roads, according to previous agreements with them, until 1852. The undoubted right of expropriation could only be exercised under imperious necessity, which did not exist, the companies protested that the suggested scheme of purchase was unjust and finally the state of the treasury did not warrant the operation.

The matter came up before the Assembly, June 22. The first speaker was Morin, who opposed the purchase. He recalled the fact that in 1838, the monarchy had requested of the legislature, funds wherewith to endow France with this new mode of communication; it was the chambers which refused. "But England, North America were already honey-combed with lines of iron; Belgium, Germany even distanced us in the accomplishment of that vast enterprise. Was it necessary, in such a race, to let oneself be distanced by European civilization? No. It was then that appeal was made to the great financial companies."

Cordier, another speaker in the same debate, took a similar stand. Pointing to the huge public debt which would be loaded on the country, he showed that England, though heavily indebted, has an enormous commerce and the labor of 150,000,000 subjects, counting the colonies, while happier still,

[1] *Moniteur*, June 9.

the United States have no debts, the rural districts are free from taxes and prosperity is so rapid, that in a short period, they are destined to succeed England.

It would be highly imprudent to bring the Bank of France into the financial operations of the proposed purchase. "Let us recall that it required all the heroic energy of President Jackson to deliver the republic from the fatal domination of the principal bank of the United States." He would permit those who developed industry to profit by it to the utmost.

It is to such perpetual corporations (*associations à perpétuité*) freed from governmental arbitrariness that England owes, in the mother-country and in the colonies, enterprises without number, a complete network of railroads and canals, 1000 steamboats and the conquest of the Indies. It is by such perpetual corporations that North America, born in our time, having at the commencement of the century, neither engineers, nor capital, nor factories, nor extended territory, has built canals, railroads, telegraphs 5000 leagues long, and has conquered a surface as large as Europe; yet its annual budget is only 125 millions a year, or 6 fr. per inhabitant.

Instead of this whole scheme, he recommends other measures to restore prosperity, after which the workers will receive "no longer 8 fr. a week as an alms in the national workshops, but from 4 fr. to 10 fr. a day as in the United States and in England."

Mathieu (de la Drôme) next spoke for government purchase. He brought out the corruption that grew up in connection with the railroads under the old régime, when the 130 to 150 stockholders who sat in the Chamber of Deputies placed the interest of the companies above that of the state, secured state loans whose interest was not payable until after the stockholders received a four per cent dividend and

passed other astonishing legislation.   He then defended
the right and utility of the proposed transaction.

Monsieur the minister of finances had said: the existence
of great financial companies is incompatible with our republican institutions.   And everybody has hastened to oppose to
this assertion, the example of the United States. That is what
the honorable M. Cordier did, an instant ago.   There is here a
preliminary remark to be made: the United States form a federated republic, while we intend to form a military republic.
If some of the states of the Union were in a position to build
railroads on their own territory, most of the states would not
have been capable of satisfying the necessary expenditure.
Hence the necessity was felt, the absolute necessity, of con-
ceding these enterprises to companies.   But in all the con-
tracts, great care was taken to embody the right of purchase
in favor of the states.   From another point of view, there
would also be several observations to make on the pretended
comparison which it is attempted to establish between France
and the United States.   The United States have not, like us,
an immense stretch of frontiers to guard: they are not ex-
posed to sudden invasions, which, with the railroads that cover
Germany today, might be quick as lightning against us.   Add
that the United States have fertile lands, a virgin soil which
provides abundantly for all their needs, while we are too often
obliged to look for a portion of our subsistence in foreign lands.

The speaker held that it was ridiculous to invoke the principle of association,[1] in which he firmly believed, in the in-

---

[1] This very just criticism should be constantly kept in mind in connection with the ambiguous use of the word "association." It is used
for anything from Louis Blanc's syndicalist coöperative unions to the
most ultra-capitalistic combination.   Great confusion of thought arose
and both individualists and socialists are found praising "the principle
of association" and meaning entirely different things by it.   It seems
best, therefore, to translate the word uniformly by its English equivalent and thus make more comprehensible the resulting misunderstand-
ings.

terest of the workers, but which should consist in a union of labor and capital, having properly nothing in common with the creation of great combinations of capitalists.   His chief reasons for desiring government ownership were the greater facility of provisioning France in case of famine and the transportation of troops in time of war.   He concluded with a technical analysis of the financial elements in the situation.

Montalembert opposed the plan, confining himself to the political and social side of the question.   From his economic standpoint of laissez-faire individualism, he held the " spirit of association " to be the fittest formula of the liberal spirit and showed how in 1838, the chief republicans had so regarded it.   To the minister's thesis that great corporations (*associations*) and even the spirit of association could only exist with monarchical and aristocratic institutions, he opposed the example of Russia, which was applying to its public works the principle supported by the minister in the name of democracy.

But it[the minister's thesis] is refuted especially by that example which the honorable and eloquent gentleman who has just spoken seemed to make of so little account, the example of the United States.   He has told you that that country had no frontiers to defend.   It has, however, and immense ones, both on the side of the north against England, and on the side of the south.   But, before all, permit me to cite it to you as the model of republics, as the sole republic which has yet succeeded in the modern world, in being at once solid, durable and flourishing.   Well, in that country you know, everything is given up to association, everything flourishes, everything is made fertile by association; not only public works, but also instruction, charitable establishments, establishments of public aid, all the branches of political and civil fruitfulness in the country.

Association, which has made America one of the greatest

powers of the world, is neither an English nor an American, but a liberal principle.

Let us learn to recognize it, the struggle is not between aristocracy or royalty on one side and democracy on the other; the struggle is between the spirit of monopoly and the spirit of liberty, between exaggerated centralization and the free development of individual forces, the free development of the spirit of association.

He proceeded to develop the advantages of individualism in the best vein of the Manchester school. The state should not interfere, where individuals can act as well or better; it is the protector, not the perpetual tutor; the state should, where possible, make those who profit by public works, pay for them; it should not enter into competition with citizens and crush them by superior force or arbitrarily suppress their enterprises; it should not extend the monopolies it possesses by confiscating an industry as soon as it proves profitable; its operation is costlier than that of private citizens; the ultimate goal of this plan is to make the state the entrepreneur of every industry and thus to destroy the liberty of capital and of labor; an insupportable weight of industrial centralization would be added to the burden of administrative centralization, now resting on the shoulders of the state; this would be a retrograde step, going back to the time when labor was a royal right, which had to be held from the state, the time when there were great alienations of the public domain. Politically, there are two sorts of progress, one towards what is called unity, but which is really towards despotism, where the state does everything, and of which Egypt is a type; the other towards liberty, where the state is as restrained in its action as possible, where the citizens do everything for themselves that they can; that is the true progress, the kind which exists in the United States. Of these two, the system toward which this law tends is not that of the United States. And yet for him, the system of the latter represented real emancipation, the coming of a people out of tutelage into its self-directing manhood. A citizen's dignity is greatest when the number of public officials is as small as possible. Private interest is the greatest motive of human effort. Great republics have risen in history from commercial association; Holland, Venice, the United States, the English East India Company are examples. The spirit of association is the greatest barrier to political despotism; the principle of unity leads, on the contrary, directly to it. You must hold to your contract with the roads or violate property rights; you have surrendered the right of purchase for the present, and there is no necessity to expropriate. The proposed bargain is unfair. The only real danger which the republic has to fear, is the terror it inspires among property-holders. The peasant esteems political theories highly, but even dearer to him is his little patrimony, the free possession of the field he received from his fathers and wants to leave to his children. Beware lest the Revolution of 1848 become linked in his mind with its destruction.

The discussion was resumed on the 23rd, but the great June insurrection had now begun and it was very difficult for the Assembly to consider calmly anything else. A short speech by Guérin in favor of the purchase was followed by a longer one by Jobez, who declared himself in favor of the execution of public works by the state, but opposed to the present plan before the Assembly. The general question has nothing to do with monarchy or republicanism; " it is the state, in fact, which executes all the great public works in Belgium or in Russia; it is, on the contrary, the companies which have honeycombed republican America with canals and railroads." In his mind, the real motive behind the present plan, however, was the government's need of money and its consequent desire to get it from the roads, in spite of all previous engagements with the companies.

The next speaker, Laurent (de l'Ardèche) was in the midst of his remarks in favor of the purchase, when he was interrupted by the entrance of General Cavaignac with news of the battle. That ended all thought of the railroads for the day. The subject was not resumed until July 3, when the new cabinet withdrew it from further consideration as a practical project, without, however, condemning the principle.

A lesser discussion took place on the acquisition by the state of the railroad from Paris to Lyons, which was further complicated by the need of urgent relief-works for the unemployed. In this debate on August 16, Wolowski, who opposed the larger plan, expressed himself in favor of the smaller, as an interesting experiment in government ownership, and as devoid of some of the previously raised objections, this being a purchase, freely agreed to, and in no sense an expropriation. Behind this particular road lay the colony of Africa, whose immense destiny was still obscure, " and which is perhaps for France what the vast possessions of the west are for the United States, the means of solving peacefully most of the great problems which torment our epoch." After complicated financial safeguards had been added in the interest of the stockholders, the bill was passed.

Another subject on which American example was quoted a number of times was the liberty of the press. The question was on a government bill of July 11, proposing a bond of 24,000 fr. to be deposited in cash at the treasury by the owners of every metropolitan journal appearing more than twice a week, 18,000 fr. for a semi-weekly issue, 12,000 fr. for a weekly, 6000 for a monthly; dailies published in other departments than Seine, Seine-et-Oise and Seine-et-Marne in towns of 50,000 inhabitants and upwards, to pay 6000 fr., 3600 in smaller towns and half of these respective sums for papers appearing less frequently. The bill was presented by Senard as minister of the interior and was defended by him as far milder than the law under the late monarchy, whose maximum was 100,000 fr. The bill was the result of the alarm occasioned by the June insurrection and was part of the restrictive measures taken in consequence. The matter came before the Assembly, August 7.

Sarrans, the fifth who spoke to the measure, admitting that certain papers had exceeded their privileges and should be repressed, opposed the general scheme of the government, as a falling away from the principles of February and an instrument of prevention rather than (as was claimed) one of repression. Without attempting to summarize his speech attention must be called to a passage in which he declared,

Mon Dieu! England was mentioned to you a short time ago,[1] the United States should have been brought up as well: an authority on these grave press-questions exists which you all know and respect: it is the treatise of M. Chassam, published in 1837. Its influence too was cast in favor of fiscal hindrances to be opposed to the press; but do you know what argument it used? It said: " In the United States, in a country where democracy is said to reign, no bond is necessary, no fiscal hindrances, no prevention of any sort: but they are still necessary in a monarchical country like France, where equality is daily obliged to bow before political necessities." That is what a monarchical writer said in 1837; but today in 1848, are you still at such a pass, I ask, that equality must give way before the necessities of royalist politics? I do not think so.

---

[1] By Thouret, pointing out that though giving no bond, English papers were under an equivalent repression through fines, damage suits and the like.

Sarrans was succeeded by Félix Pyat, who of course, also opposed the *cautionnement*. "In 1848," he cried, "the French republic, the democratic republic as it is called, would be less free, I do not say than the federal republic of America, but than the old English monarchy or the humble Belgian royalty!"

August 8, Laurent (de'Ardèche), speaking against the measure, drew a distinction between "journalists of the school of Franklin" and "those of the school of Marat and *Père Duchesne.*"

The general discussion was then closed and the project taken up by articles. To Art. 1, which asserted the principle and fixed the various amounts payable, a counter-project was presented by the minority of the commission as an amendment. It provided for registration of the name, profession and address of the editor-in-chief prior to the publication of any journal, signature of articles by the author responsible, retention of manuscripts by the printer for a fixed period and their surrender to the courts by him on demand, prosecution of the editor for anonymous articles, deprivation of his civic rights for five years of any author hiding under the name of another, suppression of any journal condemned three times for omission of signature, and several minor regulations. If conforming to these requirements every Frenchman had the right to publish his opinions freely in the press.

Duprat began the defence of the amendment, Berville, the reporter of the original decree, assailed it. Ledru-Rollin then spoke for the amendment.

The 24,000 fr. of the decree was not enough to deter the rich, but too much to expect of the poor, he said. The signature provision was not only feasible, but would be a real safeguard; men thought twice of what they wrote, if they had to sign it. The chief objection seems to be its novelty. But everything is new here, including the present government. Switzerland has no *cautionnement*, but its laws are so strict that calumnies there are few.

Have you then never read the history of America? You speak to me of England! What have I to do with England? She is aristocratic. As for England, you mistake, you said that there was no *cautionnement*, there is one; the laws of 1819, of 1832 require a bond of £200 sterling. . . . Further, England is aristocratic. I speak to you of America; she apparently has her growth (*sa grandeur*), and I think that we can consult her. In America, the bond is unknown. There, liberty is absolute and yet authority is also great. Means have been found to conciliate the two principles and no recourse has been had to the bond, and from the start, there has been no trifling with words as here; no one has said: Let us make a temporary law, in imitation of England, with which we have just broken. Let us commence the republic by an act which leaves out the sacred principle of liberty. No, no, that was not said in America; on the morrow of the rupture with England, and when a law of *cautionnement* and a stamp act were agitated, it was declared that even at the cost of a break with the mother-country (*pour rompre avec la métropole*), there should be neither bond nor stamp, and that it was not with old expedients (*avec du vieux*), in enlightened America, (*au grand soleil de l'Amérique*) that a young, vigorous and invincible republic could be founded. In America then, in that great country which surely has its value as an example, no stamp, no *cautionnement*, absolute liberty. . . . Yes, yes, you wished to give us a lesson; we want no *cautionnement*, hence we are men of disorder and of anarchy. Well, let me in my turn present to you the precepts of America's great statesmen, who understand their republic (*se connaissent en république*). Do you know what they want for the press? The opposite of what is asked of you. And I address this to those among you who, like me, find that the press is too great a power when the republic exists. Do you know what they do? They multiply newspapers; and the secret of their statesmen, of a president from whose mouth I had the honor to hear it, is to decentralize the press, instead of centralizing, fortifying it; it is that the press should not be a collective power, a crenellated citadel from which one may fire mysteriously, but that it should be, on the contrary, an individual protest. Those are the maxims of a veritable statesman; that man was no agitator; for, it must be said, he had governed his country with glory, and all those who in that country attain public office (*aux affaires*), have the same idea. Let journals be published and multiplied, that they may neutralize one another, and that in the middle of that ocean of indecisive, tumultuous, but floating polemic, something stable, immovable, should rise: the love of order, love of liberty, love of country. Well, in acting thus, the statesmen of Switzerland, the statesmen of America, are consistent with the principles of liberty and at the same time they are skilful. Skill and logic are almost always the same thing. Thus they conciliate the great principles: respect for liberty, safeguard for authority.

Ledru-Rollin spoke for the liberty of the press, though it had called him a thief and a libertine. " I could not reply to these attacks; but with Franklin, the master of them all, I said to myself: 'If these are vices with which they reproach me, their censure will correct me; if they are slanders, perhaps one day history, in its turn, will correct them."

Senard, as minister of the interior, then returned to the defence of the government project.

Just now, gentlemen, citation was made to you of the words of statesmen before whom I bow, and the example of Switzerland and of America was set forth at length; but it was forgotten, and that is perhaps the key to the enigma which holds us in suspense, that the freedom of the press is without danger, when the press only is and only wants to be a simple instrument of discussion, in the midst of a free country; then indeed, every fear is vain, every precaution, every repression even, useless.

The discussion was resumed on the 9th by Léon Faucher, who now made a second speech for the bill. In the course of it, he said:

Gentlemen, we are not desired to explain the example of England, for it was not we who cited it, and there is an effort to make use of the example of the United States. Permit me a few words in this connection. The republic, gentlemen, has its doctrinaires, like the monarchy. The monarchy had recommended to the faithful, the imitation of England; it sought to construct among us, what cannot be constructed, an aristocracy; it was mistaken, in time and in place. The doctrinaires of the republic commit a mistake of the same nature; they recommend to us the imitation of the United States. They forget that the United States are a federation, they forget that if there is a country where the federal government cannot establish itself, that if there is a country where the government is strongly centralized, that if there is a country whose work for centuries has been the tendency toward unity, that country is France. I say, gentlemen, that if one wishes to take account of the difference in places and nations, the example of the United States will prove nothing for us. A few words on what happens in the United States. Yes, in the American Union, the press enjoys a liberty without limits, a liberty which is for me no liberty; for I know no serious liberty, which does not have its limits, and what has none is license, in my eyes.

The United States, then, enjoy that liberty which is recommended to us. What is the result? In the first place, the press in the United States is not a political press; it is a local press, a press of advertisements, it is a press which discusses affairs but little, preferring to attack persons; it is a press which, too often, uses and abuses defamation. Do you know what is the counter-balance of that limitless influence? I will tell you. The counter-balance is in the customs. It happens that if by chance a paper, this time doing a praiseworthy act, wishes to preach the abolition of slavery, the enraged mob demolishes the presses; it happens that a polemic between papers ends too often, in what? In a rifle duel. It happens that a person attacked in a paper executes justice himself, and in what manner, gentlemen? By a knife-thrust or by a pistol-shot. In a word, gentlemen, the counter-balance of that boundless liberty is, in the Western states, principally what is called *lynch law,* that is to say, the custom of doing justice oneself, that is to say the absence of all law, that is to say the return to a savage state. This is what I am not ambitious to bring to my country.

This vicious attack on American journalism in the '40s seems to have put a quietus on any possible inclination to quote it as an example, for throughout the remainder of the rather long debate, it was never referred to again. Five other speeches were heard, most of them briefly, before the minority amendment was defeated; the government measure was then passed, substantially in its original form.

The United States was also quoted a number of times in connection with the encouragement of agriculture. Toupet des Vignes, Sept. 19, set forth the failure of communistic colonies in America as an argument against giving state aid to similar enterprises in Algeria. Amable Dubois, Sept. 23, opposed an elaborate scheme for agricultural instruction, reviewing the situation in Belgium, England, Normandy, Switzerland, Germany and America, in some of which countries there were no such schools and in others they were of doubtful value. In America there were private schools; " the state does not mix in the matter at all," but American agriculture owed more to the lessons of Belgium and England. De Tillancourt interrupted with the assertion that America had five state schools for agriculture, but his correction was unheeded. Flocon thought that the Swiss, American and German schools had been of such service that it was only a question of transporting their lessons into France. The project was carried, Oct. 2, 3.[1]

A few speeches might be classified as remarks on the American spirit of individualism.

Thus, on Aug. 1, Cordier, speaking against a financial measure of the government (adversely reported by the committee of finance), which proposed a tax on mortgage-secured loans and which was feared by the conservatives as a start toward an income-tax, ridiculed its supposed necessity, the Assembly having in the space of a month authorized an issue of *rentes* and two loans from the Banque de France, amounting in all to 950 million francs, " A sum equal to eight times the annual budget of the republic of the United States, which has an area six times greater than France and a prosperity ten times more rapid, because of its freedom from all taxes on agricultural properties." By a close vote, the principle of the project was carried the following day, but on the 4th an amendment being made which displeased the finance minister, he withdrew the whole proposition.

On Sept. 12, Mathieu de la Drôme's proposal to insert the *droit au travail* in Art. VIII of the preamble was under discussion; Tocqueville, opposing the amendment, made a vigorous attack on socialism. Its adherents, he said, pretend it to be the legitimate development of democracy. For himself, he refused to traverse the garden of Greek roots, searching for the true etymology of the word "democracy," as was done by certain colleagues yesterday.

I shall seek democracy where I have seen it, living, active,

---

[1] *Cf.* also the annex to the original government report of July 17, which dealt with agricultural instruction in several countries, a number of American private schools being described, with emphasis on their practical, individualistic character. This annex is not printed in connection with the rest of the report in the *Moniteur* of July 22; it is, however, to be found in the *Compte-rendu*, vol. 3, p. 322 *et seq.*

triumphant, in the only country in the world where it exists, where it has been able to found, up to the present in the modern world, something great and durable, in America. There you will see a people, where all conditions are more equal than they are even among you, where the social state, the manners, the laws, everything is democratic, where everything comes from and returns to the people, and where, however, every individual enjoys an independence more entire, a liberty greater than at any other time or in any other country of the earth, a land essentially democratic, I repeat, the only democracy which exists today in the world, the only truly democratic republics which are known in history are in [*sic*] these republics. Not only have the theories of socialists not gained control of the public mind, but they have played so small a rôle in the discussions and in the affairs of that great nation, that they have not even had the right to say that they were feared there. Democratic America is today that country in all the world where democracy is practised most completely (*le plus souverainement*), and it is also the one where the socialist doctrines which you pretend accord so well with democracy, have the least circulation, the country in the whole universe where the men who support these doctrines would certainly have the least advantage in presenting themselves. For my part, I confess I should not see a very great inconvenience in their going to America; but in their own interest, I do not advise them to do it.

It was no doubt with a clear perception of this very fact that, on the 14th, Martin-Bernard, speaking for the amendment and principally for the idea of " association," and exhorting his hearers not to attempt to put society back in the old rut by juggling with words whose sense disappeared with 200-franc electors, continued:

Nor speak to us further about America. That country, as everybody knows, is in political, philosophical and territorial conditions, which compel it to be what it is. We are France, oldest daughter of civilization, who will know well how to accomplish her task. Especially make us no tirades for effect, about liberty, when we demand bread, an honorable bread for the people, for we might prove to you that we more than you are men of the ideal; we might tell you that we have spent long years in dungeons, with one sole sentiment in our hearts, our faith, our spiritual faith in the triumph of human liberty.

Two men alluded to American financial difficulties (to say nothing of Cordier's speech, referred to on p. 230.

Léon Faucher in a report of the finance committee, Aug. 29,[1] on a paper-money project, adverted to troubles produced by that agency in Russia and Austria. " It was the same in the United States, in 1837, before the suspension of specie payments. The banks of the Union, by disorganized issues, had made the exchange of their notes for specie, the redemption on presentation, so difficult, that these notes, in certain states, lost up to 50% of their value." [2]

Thiers, the same day, remarked that the most honorable men sometimes commit execrable errors. Paper may legitimately serve for money, when it is bank-paper; it does so in France, England and America. It may be very gradually introduced as legal tender, where there is no silver, as in Russia and several northern countries. But suddenly to create two or three billions of paper in a time of financial stress is an execrable error. Even bank-notes are dangerous; England and America are the proof. In England they had risen to several billions; Peel, in reducing this bank-paper (which is not true paper money) to 900 millions, rendered a great service to his country. " In America they did not have this prudence, and America has been subject to terrifying crises, solely because the bank-note had been abused, which, however, is always placed under the

[1] *Moniteur*, Sept. 2.

[2] Faucher made a similar reference to American paper-money, Oct. 11.

guarantee of conversion into gold or silver." Thiers later alluded also to the "numerous examples of accidental insufficiency of specie" in England and America, as the result of a too great issue of bank-notes.

There were a number of miscellaneous allusions to America, which should also be mentioned.

June 15, Pierre Leroux, speaking on the plan of a union between France and Algeria, which he favored, held that the subject had been treated too much from the military point of view, rather than from the present advanced state of civilization in France, which should be extended to the colony. One of the preceding speakers had been too much occupied with admiration of the ancient Romans.

Yet there are modern colonies which he should have examined, for great colonies have been founded since the Romans. I see the whole of America arising from the revolution against England, and I do not at all know that there was not given to Penn, bearing civilization to the United States and founding the Union, and to his descendants, the right of being at the most advanced point of civilization at that epoch.

In any case, France should extend the widest liberties to the new colony, not place it under outworn institutions. To M. Dupin, who praised Roman colonization, he would oppose "the manner in which the English, bearing Protestantism to America, colonized the United States. I see that it is religion which colonized that great new world called the Union; it is religion which founded it. And for colonization, you would bring us worn-out ideas, from one of the oldest and remotest periods of inequality!"

Later, referring to the troubles of the Lyons silkworks, dependent on America, England, Germany and France, especially on the two former, he said: "America, every time it has placed considerable orders, has failed [a fait faillite]. Several times fifty millions have been lost on

American orders by the Lyons works, with the result that the Lyons works have no faith in America."

On the 17th, the same speaker used the United States and Prussia as illustrations of the principle of Malthus, according to which, he said, the population doubles every twenty-five years. The misery produced by social conditions prevents it in France.

July 12, Drouyn de Lhuys, in the name of the committee on foreign affairs made a report on the situation on the Rio de la Plata, in course of which he referred to the American protest against the Anglo-French blockade of Buenos Ayres.

July 28, Emile Leroux in the name of the committee of justice [1] reported on a government project revising the jury-system. Having shown that jurors must be free from government influence, he pointed out that they should also be selected with some reference to ability and character, describing the English law to that end and continuing: " In the United States, where the democratic principle dominates legislation, the jury law also requires conditions of property and capacity, and the jury is chosen by the special council of the town." He therefore would modify the government plan, which provided no property qualification, and thus " has not followed the example of England and the United States," by adding a special list annually selected, from which panel the jury should be drawn by lot. This arrangement was carried.

July 29, Ambert reported adversely from his committee a government bill appropriating 9,600,000 fr. for the Paris *garde mobile;* the committee would reduce this figure to 5,500,000, by decreasing the number of men in each company, and leaving out a whole battalion. The core of his

---

[1] *Moniteur*, Aug. 1.

argument was that the closer a people approaches democracy, the simpler should be its military organization.

Look at the two extremes in the scale, Russia and the United States. In Russia, you have extremely complicated corps: the imperial guard, the regular Cossacks, the irregular Cossacks: it is an offensive army in the hands of the authorities. In the United States, you have an extremely simple army: you have only the militia and a small army. The army is always employed against foreign enemies, in Florida, in Texas, against the Mexicans, but, in the interior, you have only the militia. And what is the militia? It is the shield on the people's heart; it is the people's guarantee against the authorities [*le pouvoir*]. I do not wish to tell you, however, to imitate the United States completely, to suppress the standing army in order to make a militia. But I ask you to accept the principle, the principle which brings it about that the Americans have been willing to put arms in the hands of their brothers, of their friends and not to leave to the authorities the choice of their army.

The plan of the committee was adopted.

August 17, Saint Priest made a report[1] on the subject of postal reform, in which he mentioned that England, Austria, Prussia, Switzerland, Spain and the United States had all lowered their postal rates.

On the 24th, Bastiat, speaking of this measure, told of reforms in England and Austria and of how " in the United States the government is expending enormous sums to save money to those who want to correspond."

August 25, Ledru-Rollin, defending himself against the accusations of the committee of inquiry concerning the events of May and June, said:

We respect property, but on the condition that . . . it becomes multiplied to infinity and in so saying, we represent the

[1] *Moniteur*, Aug. 19.

great thought of the Convention. You know perfectly well that it wanted the dissemination of property; it was right, for every republic (and I reply here to certain socialist ideas), whether in antiquity, or in the Middle Ages, has perished by concentration of property. At the present moment, that magnificent, that gigantic country, America, is decidedly alarmed by the concentration of property. (Expressions of dissent). It would be hard for me, you understand, to reply to interruptions which I do not comprehend; I have said and I repeat, and I cannot be denied by those who are well-informed. that at the present moment, in North America, property is suffering from its own concentration, and that they are asking, not the agrarian law, but the distribution of lands belonging to the state; they are crying from one pole to the other of that country: "Land is liberty."

August 16, a report[1] was made by the committee on legislation, through its chairman, Hippolyte Durand, calling for the restoration of imprisonment for debt. In it the sentence occurs: "In Switzerland, in the United States, imprisonment for debt is authorized."

Sept. 1, Wolowski started the debate against the proposed decree.

It is in vain that the report invokes the memory of Athens and of Rome, and even of the republic of the United States. . . . In the French republic, there will be no recognition of slavery. . . . As for the United States, we know it only too well, they still maintain in a part of their territory, the slavery of a part of the inhabitants; that is an example which we must repudiate. Let us then also repudiate imprisonment for debt, which is only maintained in certain states of the American Union.

The decree was, however, passed.

Sept. 18, the discussion being on Art. 7 of the constitution, Lavallée proposed an amendment, thus conceived:

[1] *Moniteur*, Aug. 20.

No one may be forced to contribute to the expenses of any cult. The republic gives financial support to none.

He said in part, speaking for his amendment:

The American republic has not supported any cult; are churches then less prosperous than with us? Has religion disappeared in the United States? Quite the reverse. Every religion finds in voluntary gifts large supplies for the expense of the cult. There, each builds his church, his seminary and the religious establishments, already numerous, increase daily. A state salary is therefore not essential to the existence of religion. On the contrary, as I have already said, it can only compromise its dignity and independence, without which it has only a quite precarious moral existence.

Sept. 20, Pierre Leroux spoke to his amendment, "the printing-press [*imprimerie*] shall be subject to no monopoly." He declared that no monopoly of the sort existed in any free country, neither in England, Switzerland, Belgium nor the United States.

Oct. 19, chapter VII of the constitution, which dealt with internal administration, was the subject of debate. Jouin was given the floor to defend an amendment by Béchard, in the interest of administrative decentralization and local self-government. Duprat, the preceding speaker, had quoted Tocqueville. Jouin did likewise, to this effect:

"If it should ever come to founding a democratic republic, like that of the United States, in a country where the power of one person had already established administrative centralization and caused it to pass into the customs as into the laws, I do not fear to say it, in such a republic, despotism would become more intolerable than in any of the absolute monarchies of Europe; one would have to go to Asia to find anything to compare with it." This is how M. de Tocqueville expresses himself in his magnificent work on "Democracy in America." He has studied democracy in the country where it reigns, in the country where liberty is best understood, where one sees in some sort, liberty and nothing but liberty. Well, in studying the manners and politics of America, he had his eye also on France.

The speaker went on to say that Tocqueville foresaw the February Revolution and dreaded the tyrannical administrative centralization that would be likely to follow. Cormenin, a friend of centralization, had announced that its force was such that the artisan class, whenever it wanted to unite, could impose any form of government it pleased on France, even though the agricultural class was five or six times more numerous. The testimony of these two eminent men on centralization terrified him. Later he pointed out how foolish were the fears of some, that with local self-government, the roads, the churches, the town halls would all go to rack and ruin.

I beg, gentlemen, those among you who are frightened at the idea of that administrative decentralization, to which we are unfortunately so unaccustomed since the empire, I beg them to cast their eyes on what is going on in the country where liberty reigns, in America. There, gentlemen, the community life is as free as possible; let those among you who do not know the mechanism of those institutions read the remarkable pages which M. de Tocqueville has written, pages from which were extracted the lines that the honorable M. Pascal Duprat read to you just now from the tribune; let them read what M. de Tocqueville has written on town liberties (*les libertés communales*) in the state (*sic*) of New England; let them examine town liberty in the state of Massachusetts, in that state where since 1774, since (*sic*) a republican such as the world rarely sees, Samuel Adams, founded the principles of a truly liberal constitution, a constitution which has not ceased to rule since 1774. Well, since 1774, there too reigns perfect town liberty. In almost all these states, I think one might say in all the states of the two Americas, reigns the most entire, most complete, most absolute town liberty. Has that liberty compromised the general interests of the Union? Have the great or local roads suffered from it? Have communications become impossible? Has nothing more great and fine been done in that country? Are there then no railroads in America, are there then no long-distance roads (*voies de grande communication*)? Then villages have not been seen there becoming in a short time cities of the first rank? Then they are not advancing there in the ways of progress and civilization? What! In that country where liberty is so great, where one enjoys so many liberties, the general interests are sacrificed? No, gentlemen, you know perfectly that if liberty rules in that great and glorious republic, order rules there as well, and that general interests are carefully conserved there.

With this speech, the record of allusions to America prior to the adoption of the constitution on Nov. 4, comes to an end. Were the limit of the inquiry prolonged after the constitution-making period to the final adjournment of the Assembly, May 26, 1849, the list would be considerably increased. At least thirty further references were made, the majority of no great value, to be sure, but some showing continued interest in the American constitution, notably a debate on Feb. 28, 1849, on the principle of representation, when the American compromise on three-fifths of noncitizens was food for argument and Algeria was compared to a territory of the United States.

The focal points of American influence and the party alignment on them have, however, been sufficiently illustrated by the foregoing complete account of the period up to Nov. 4. Before commenting on the facts thus presented, it is important to study the trend of public opinion outside the Assembly. This is most easily done through the newspapers and reviews, and will be the task of the following chapter.

CHAPTER VII

Contemporary Comment

THE periodical literature of 1848 is useful to our study in two ways. It reflects what the popular mind was thinking about, and the trend of its opinions; secondly, it shows what influences were at work on the mind of the Assembly. The press in those days was a great political power. In the period before 1848 journals were comparatively few and were usually published by some prominent political leader or in the interest of some political group. In the absence of opportunity for wide self-expression at the polls or in parliament, due to the restricted franchise, party organs came to have undue importance in public life.

It has been shown how the provisional government was the result of deliberations in the back-rooms of two newspapers. In spite of the institution of universal suffrage and a free press in February, with the resulting flood of cheap, ephemeral papers, the tradition persisted to some degree, particularly when, after June, police laws again fettered the liberty of publication and the weaker papers were eliminated. Granted the great political influence of the press, its effect on the mind of the Assembly becomes significant, when it is observed that not only did a number of papers publish special articles on American constitutional practice, but that these articles were in some cases apparently timed to coincide with the Assembly's discussion of a particular point.

For an intelligent appreciation of the meaning of this

press comment, a preliminary classification of the newspapers is necessary.[1]

Beginning at the extreme right, five papers represented
the legitimist party in 1848.   The *Gazette de France*,
founded in the 17th century, was the old organ of the ultras
during the Restoration.   In 1848 it advocated a hereditary
president, but the spirit and real purpose remained royalist.
The paper was suspended Aug. 24, but its policy was continued under the name of *Le Peuple français* and later
L'Etoile de la France until the *Gazette* resumed publication,
Oct. 25.   *L'Union monarchique* started in 1847 as a fusion
of the famous *Quotidienne* with two other royalist organs.
L'Assemblée nationale was published from March 1 to June
25, when it was suspended, reappearing Aug. 7.   *L'Assemblée constituante* was founded by a group of seceders from
L'Assemblée nationale with similar political views; it was
short-lived and unimportant.   *L'Opinion publique* was a
boldly legitimist paper, started in May, 1848.

Five papers represented conservative republicanism, four
of which at least were ex-Orleanist and retained a large
measure of sympathy for the fallen cause.   The *Journal des
débats* had been the semi-official organ of the late monarchy.
It was a dignified paper of the highest type, and of great
prestige.   Lamartine says it supported every government in
turn as the necessary expression of the most essential and
permanent interests of society and that the fullness and
impartiality of its parliamentary debates, its foreign cor-
respondence, its accurate and complete news service made it
the manual of every court and diplomatic office in Europe.[2]

---

[1] *Cf.* E. Hatin, *Bibl. hist. et crit. de la presse périod. franç.*; the same
author's *Hist. polit. et lit. de la presse en France*, vol. 8; H. Izambard,
La Presse parisienne.   Most of the information here given is, however,
derived from a study of the newspaper files themselves.

[2] Lamartine, *Hist. of the Revol. of 1848*, bk. i, secs. xi, xii.

Always solidly conservative, it had supported Guizot to the end. The *Constitutionnel* had been the great royalist opposition organ during the Restoration; under the July monarchy and in 1848, it represented the opinions of Thiers. It had at one time an immense circulation among the bourgeois class, but had somewhat lost in influence since the height of its power in 1830. The *Siècle*, which appealed to the rural working-class, is said to have occupied a position in the July monarchy, analogous to that of the *Constitutionnel* under the Restoration,[1] with the difference that the former was friendly to the ruling dynasty of its day, which the latter had not been. Both were thus Orleanist papers, the *Siècle* representing the constitutional opposition opinions of Odilon Barrot. The *Courrier français,*[2] like the *Constitutionnel*, was a Thiers paper. The *Patrie* was less important, but was likewise of conservative tendencies.

Of the moderate republican stripe, that of the dominant party in the government, which we have called the liberal party, three papers may be cited. Most important was the *National*, the semi-official mouthpiece of the government, supporter of General Cavaignac. There was also the *Bien public,*[3] representing the Lamartine interest and the *Journal* (July 28–Nov. 1), a less important Cavaignac paper.

Three may be classed as radical, the *Réforme*, organ of Ledru-Rollin and Flocon, the *Peuple constituant*, Lamennais' paper, which was forced to suspend in July for lack of money wherewith to pay the required bond, and the comic *Charivari*, which finally supported Cavaignac.

Eight belong to the extreme left wing, seven of them definitely socialist. The *Représentant du peuple*, Proud-

---

[1] Hatin, *Hist. . . . de la presse*, vol. 8, p. 590.

[2] No file preserved in Bibl. Nat., Paris.

[3] File in Bibl. Nat. begins May 24.

hon's organ, lasted from April 1 to August 24 with intermissions; it was succeeded by the *Peuple,* which ran from Sept. 1 to June 13, 1849. Its standpoint was anarchist. The *Ami du peuple* was Raspail's bi-weekly, published from Feb. 27 to May 14. The *Vraie république* (Mar. 26–June 24, Aug. 8-21) was edited by Thoré with the collaboration of Pierre Leroux, George Sand, Barbès and others; it believed in state socialism. The *Démocratie pacifique* represented the Fourierist views of Victor Considérant. The *Populaire* was the organ of Cabet's communism. The *République* represented Blanqui's interests; it occupied a moderate socialist position. The *Atelier,* a workman's paper of the Christian socialist type, edited by Corbon, preached voluntary association. *Père Duchêne,* a violent, coarse sheet with very large circulation, was said to have been one of the prime agents of the June insurrection. It represented the club interests rather than any reasoned theory of socialism. Its career was run from April to August, but it was suspended at the end of June and published only five numbers in August.

These were the chief socialist organs. Two other working-class papers were published in the Bonapartist interest: *Napoléon républicain* (only six issues, all during June) and *Le Petit caporal* (June–Dec., with a suspension during July).

Of much greater importance and stability were three personal organs, whose politics are hard to classify: Émile Girardin's *Presse,* a brilliant eclectic paper, usually friendly to the Molé right-center position in the July monarchy, but really a clever free lance at all times; Victor Hugo's *Evénement,* begun Aug. 1 with the motto " Vigorous hatred for anarchy, tender and profound love of the people;" A. Dumas' *Liberté* (Mar. 1-June 26, Aug. 7-Sept. 2, Nov. 8-Dec. 31). The *Presse* and the *Liberté* were on the whole of conservative republican politics; the *Evénement* had no party interests, but grew friendlier to the socialists in time.

Two others were devoted to the interests of the Roman Catholic Church: the *Univers*, edited by Louis Veuillot, of moderate republican tendency (in the next decade becoming ultramontane), and the *Ère nouvelle*, Lacordaire's more liberal enterprise, endeavoring to show a community of interest between the Church and the republic.

The official mouthpiece of the government was, as always, the *Moniteur universel*, colorless and heavy but (theoretically, at least) accurate.

A few reviews may be mentioned, the important bi-weekly *Revue des deux mondes* (of Guizot sympathies under the monarchy, afterward conservative republican), the quarterly *Revue de législation et de jurisprudence*, also conservative republican, the bi-monthly *Revue britannique*, Dumas' *Mois*, and the weekly *Revue nationale* of the *Atelier* nuance.

The foregoing list makes no pretence of being exhaustive, but it contains all the important papers and is believed to be representative of all schools of political thought.

References to America made in the press fall naturally into three categories: news reports, editorials and special articles. It will be convenient to add to these an account of the book and pamphlet literature dealing with the subject, so far as this has not been already treated.

It is best to take the news reports first. A significant light is cast on the Orleanist attitude toward America by contrasting two articles in the *Chronique de la quinzaine* of the *Revue des deux mondes*, just before and just after the February revolution.

In the former occurs the passage:

There are instructive lessons in the latest news received from the United States. The government of the Union is often presented to us as the type of free and constitutional governments; it is well to see which of the two systems, that of the monarchy or that of the republic, offers in fact the most guarantees.[1]

The article reports a vote by the Senate to the effect that the President had begun the Mexican war needlessly and unconstitutionally. In England or France such a vote would entail either an appeal to the country or a change of ministry; the royal power being irresponsible, no collision was possible between it and the elective power. The President of the United States was really an unremovable prime minister, who could continue a war opposed by the legislature, with volunteers if necessary.

In the very next *Chronique*, the work of republican organization in France is discussed; the national representation must be organized on large bases, making it the real expression of all interests and rights, industry as well as property, capital as well as labor. " For that necessary work, neither the studies and attempts of our fathers, nor the great experiment, of which we have had the spectacle in another hemisphere for more than half a century, will be lost." [2] Within a fortnight America had ceased to be a menace to monarchy and had become a bulwark against socialism. This number contains also an account of Mr. Rush's recognition of the new republic, with the statement that these are not new sympathies and that while the minister recognized the republic without instructions, he found them " in the traditions and memories left by the most illustrious citizens of America." [3]

Early references in radical papers were equally friendly.[4]

---

[1] *Revue des deux mondes*, Feb. 14.

[2] *Ibid.*, Feb. 29.

[3] *Cf.* ch. iii for other newspaper accounts of American recognition.

[4] *Vide supra*, pp. 80, n., 110.

Another note was, however, increasingly sounded. Proudhon's paper, *Le Représentant du peuple*, describing the presentation of the American minister's credentials and Lamartine's speech in reply, commented:

That is as vague as possible. M. Lamartine, further, is not ignorant that the republic of the United States is a federal government, containing two chambers, and accommodating itself to slavery. Assuredly, what we want is not [to be found] there. For the rest, all the political systems in the world are powerless to solve the questions raised by the February Revolution. Let us more than ever keep from imitating the old errors of the past. The social edifice cracks in every part. If we do not want to be crushed—instead of whitewashing it, let us busy ourselves in constructing it.[1]

Despatches from Germany indicate interest in America on the part of republicans there. A despatch from Hesse-Darmstadt gives the substance of a manifesto by the republicans of Germany to the new parliament, supporting their governmental theory by the example of the American republic, " which has remained calm in the midst of the greatest commotions." [2] The United States federal system should be established, with a national assembly and a responsible governing committee, according to the views of the radical democratic party at Frankfort.[3] A despatch from Cologne tells of riots at Berlin and comments: "Certain individuals still want a United States republic, but they forget the recent events which drenched Paris in blood." [4]

The London letter of the *Revue britannique*, speaking of the opening of the London season, reminded the writer that

---

[1] *Le Représentant du peuple*, Apr. 29.

[2] *Le Peuple constituant*, Mar. 28.

[3] *L'Ère nouvelle*, June 9.

[4] *L'Union*, July 4.

he was addressing republican readers, who no longer had king, queen, court or nobility, but were enjoying at the cost of some disorder " all the pleasures of the classic republics and those of the republic of the United States." [1]

Of much greater importance is the report of the bureaux' discussions of the first draft of the constitution, which fills a lacuna left by official records. The *Journal des débats* gave a good summary of the speeches, day by day. In its first article it stated that discussions had begun in the 4th, 5th and 6th bureaux. The first chapter, on popular sovereignty, was approved almost without opposition, especially the article on the separation of powers. The section concerning the legislature, on the contrary, was long discussed. " Many members, notably MM. Ch. Dupin, Belhard, Bonjean, Laussedat,[2] Roux-Lavergne, spoke in favor of the bicameral system, supporting themselves by the examples of the United States, England and of France itself." Pagès de l'Ariège and Edgar Quinet opposed them. " M. de Montalembert, who belongs to the 4th bureau, gave a remarkable opinion on the necessity of having two chambers." M. de Montalembert said that no republic had ever amounted to anything, had even survived, without a second chamber.

In this connection, the example of the United States is of incomparable authority. At first governed by a single assembly, that great republic promptly recognized that its duration and its prosperity required the creation of two legislative bodies. One sees there not only the Senate of the United States, which may be regarded as the fruit of the federal principle that does not exist in France; but also and more particularly the Senators of the thirty republics which compose the federation. These thirty states, all unitary like

---

[1] Letter dated May 23. *Revue britannique*, vol. 15, p. 208.

[2] Error corrected in next issue; this deputy favored one chamber; Laussat defended the dual system.

France, all democratic, and where the slightest germ of a political patriciate has never appeared, differ among themselves in their various constitutions, but all these constitutions, without a single exception, proclaim the necessity of two assemblies. France could not, without inexcusable temerity, quit the path where all these glorious and upright [honnête] republics have preceded her, and into which all truly politic minds have striven to make her enter.[1]

Three days later, the story is resumed.

One of the gravest questions raised in the Assembly bureaux concerning the projected constitution is to know whether there should be one or two chambers. The defenders of the two-chamber system appealed especially to the example of the United States, which commenced by forming a single assembly, and did not delay recognizing the necessity of a second chamber.

A single chamber would be tyrannical or servile, it was felt. Those who defended the dual system were Victor Hugo, Isambert, Jules de Lasteyrie, Raimbault, Demésanges, Pigeon, Oscar Lafayette, Abraham Dubois and Etienne.

The partisans of a single assembly tried to repel the example drawn from the United States, because those states form a federal republic. The principle of the French republic, they said, being unity, the two chambers would be in constant conflict and would offer a usurper the double means of oppressing one by the other. In this sense spoke MM. Marrast, Crémieux, Babaud-Laribière, Havier, Donatien Marquis, Regnard, Gaudin, Barthe, G. Sarrat, Fleury, Conti, Grévy, Brunet and others. M. Thiers spoke in favor of two chambers.

Cormenin, in contrast to his political friends, General Lafayette and Armand Carrel, had defended the single chamber

---

[1] *Journal des débats*, July 4.

in 1830 and continued this policy with vigor. A résumé of his opinion and those of Thiers and Tocqueville was then given.

Thiers said among other things:

You see how many services the Senate renders in the United States, and how it is esteemed for its reputation of wisdom. What faults it has anticipated! What imprudent decisions it has delayed or prevented! For example, the danger of the United States is in the spirit of enterprise, for they are large enough to have no need of making conquests, and a conquering general might make a rude assault on their constitution. What restrains that spirit? It is the Senate, the Senate alone.

Later he came to the question of its election. Fortune, circumstances, political relationships carry men to different destinies in every republic, even in the United States, " in the midst of the most democratic society on earth." The electors will naturally decide whether a candidate is fitter for the Assembly or for the Senate, the men of action or the men of counsel. There are so many ways to make a difference in the method of election, that the difficulty is purely imaginary.

What! In that country of the whole universe where the greatest, the most extraordinary equality reigns, in the United States, a way has been found to elect a Senate of remarkable wisdom, and it could not be done in France, where the level of equality has exerted far less pressure [*a beaucoup moins broyé*] on every existence! It is an objection with no foundation. Ah! I wish that the North Americans could hear us and reply to us from the other side of the Atlantic. I have the honor to count several friends among the eminent citizens of the United States. All those who are at this moment in Europe have strongly advised me to tell you and to tell you with the greatest warmth, that in adopting the unicameral system, you would be committing the gravest of faults. They express ardent hopes for the success in France of those republican institutions which they have had the honor of inaugurating on a large scale in modern times. In the ardor of their good wishes for us, they earnestly desire you to adopt that bicameral system, to which they returned after hard experiences.

Cormenin in the course of his remarks expressed the view,

that it is unnecessary to quote eternally the example of the United States of America, an English colony which reproduced quasi-mechanically the usages and forms of the mother-country; that America is essentially federal, while we are essentially unitary; that to distinguish the Senate from the House of Representatives it was necessary to attribute to the American Senate governmental functions which we would not tolerate in France.

Tocqueville asked if the bicameral system did in fact of necessity lead to aristocracy. Nothing was easier to disprove.

If there is a country in the world exempt from aristocracy, it is assuredly North America. There aristocracy has not been destroyed, it has never existed. The manners, ideas, laws, spirit, heart, all are democratic. Yet the Americans have established two chambers in the midst of each of their thirty republics. Have they made of one an aristocratic body and of the other the representative of democracy? No, without doubt. In most of these republics, the two chambers differ only in the number of the members who compose them; they are elected in the same manner, composed of those equally eligible, named for the same time. Might the American democracies have been led, unknown to themselves, toward that system by imitation of aristocratic England, their mother-country? Another error, for several of them began by having a single assembly; the experiment ended in making them renounce it.[1]

[1] *Journal des débats,* July 7.

The *Constitutionnel* also published an analysis of Thiers' speech, commending its wisdom and patriotism and noting the deep impression it made on the bureau. "The experience of all history and the contemporary experience of the United States added to the authority of M. Thiers' counsels." [1]

Three days later it reproduced Cormenin's arguments, refuting them point by point. (a) That two chambers with the same origin, electors, authority and subjects of discussion were incomprehensible. But special attributes might be given to one of the chambers, as in the United States; special conditions of origin and eligibility required, and in any case a double discussion would be useful. (b) That a second chamber is purely aristocratic, of English origin. But while the House of Lords has in fact served that purpose in England, a second chamber may represent something quite different; "there is no aristocracy in the United States, and a second chamber exists not only in the representation of the Union, but in the representations of the individual states." (c) That second chambers are repugnant to the genius of equality, to direct and universal suffrage, and to the French spirit of unity, which recognizes two chambers in parliament no more than it would two nations in France. "The example of the United States is there to reply. There are two chambers, which does not prevent the existence of complete equality, and it is a fact that two nations do not exist there within the nation." (d) That the example of the United States should not be eternally quoted, an English colony, reproducing quasi-mechanically the forms of the mother country. "The United States have to so slight an extent mechanically reproduced the example of England, that they commenced by establishing a single chamber and that experience alone brought

---

[1] *Constitutionnel*, July 7.

them later to the two-chamber system." (e) That America is essentially federal, while we are essentially unitary. "The individual states of the Union are unitary, and they almost all have two chambers." (f) That to distinguish the two houses, the American Senate was given governmental functions, intolerable in France. But he does not say why they would not be tolerated here. (g) That one need not be a great prophet to foretell that the Assembly will defeat the two-chamber system by a large majority, for these reasons and for still better ones. But if the chamber does so, it will be for other reasons than those of M. de Cormenin.[1]

The *Union* likewise gave long accounts of Thiers' and Cormenin's speeches, with the comment:

The partisans of the two-chamber system, the bicamerists, did not fail to cite the example of the United States, but it seems to us that they did not draw all the advantage that they should from the attributes of the American Senate. These governmental functions of which M. Cormenin spoke too disdainfully in our opinion, are, however, exercised with immense usefulness for the regularity of action of the central power in foreign affairs and for the good of the general policy of the Union. That is a side of the question which remains almost untouched and to which it will be necessary to call public attention.[2]

The *Siècle* reported Odilon Barrot's opinion, expressed in the 9th bureau. He thought that the commission would have decided for the dual system, had it not been for present circumstances. Since the experience of France, the United States, England and even Switzerland had all proved favorable to the dual system, care was necessary to foresee the difficulties which might hamper the future progress of the republic.[3]

[1] *Constitutionnel*, July 10.   [2] *Union*, July 8.
[3] *Siècle*, July 8.

The deliberations of the 14th bureau also received comment by the press. In this bureau the two-chamber system won, 26-10. The *Journal des débats* gives the speeches of Victor Hugo, de Rémusat and Léon Faucher. M. de Rémusat said that he had lived with members of the original Constituent Assembly, who felt that the single chamber was one of its greatest errors, and if he might quote the explanation of an authority particularly precious to him, General Lafayette attributed the pernicious mistake (as he also regarded it) to the influence on the one hand of Rousseau's doctrines in the Social Contract, and on the other hand of the school of Turgot, who had borrowed the idea from Franklin, at first followed in this respect by America, then abandoned by her. Later the Convention, after its terrible experience, put two chambers in the constitution of the year III. Ever since, this idea, professed by Daunou and his friends, had been sustained by the chiefs of the liberal school.

The most striking example in the direction of two chambers is that of the United States. How refrain from citing it? It is the glorious and unique example of the existence of a republic in a great country. But it is replied in objection that the United States are a federation. The argument might be employed on the opposite side. The federal government, having few attributes, not having to legislate on those internal questions which are especially exciting to opinion, might more than another dispense with those guarantees, those dispositions, necessary to shield the government from hasty impulses. Nothing of the sort, however. Everyone knows how great a rôle the Senate plays in the federal power, and every state reproduces faithfully the duality of the center in each local legislature. Shall one say, again, that the two chambers are an aristocratic affair? But there is not an atom of aristocracy in the American constitution; it is pure democracy, it is at once the ideal and the reality of democracy.

M. Léon Faucher arose to confute the idea that to establish a dual system involved a necessary antagonism between the chambers. There is only one element to be represented in every country. In England the government is aristocratic and the two chambers represent only aristocracy. "In the United States, democracy is equally alive in the two assemblies which form the American Congress." In France there is no thought of having one democratic and one aristocratic chamber. "It is the Senate which has made the force of the United States, which has given them a policy, which has made them rivals of England and of Russia." [1]

It is to be observed that the reports come solely from conservative papers, and that the only defender of the single chamber quoted is Cormenin, though his opinion was that of a very large majority in the bureaux.

The discussion concerning the executive power received scant record in the press. The only account of the use of American example is in a speech by Léon Faucher. Thiers, Berryer, de Rémusat are mentioned as having spoken for the direct, universal method of election, as did the majority in the bureaux. Faucher defended election by the Assembly, though he was a conservative and later voted against the Grévy and Leblond amendments. He said that the other method would be safe only if the two-chamber system had been adopted. Again, it should be remarked that in the United States, notwithstanding the existence of the two chambers of Congress, the naming of the first magistrate, being left to electors, springs from indirect suffrage. Yet even that modified system of popular choice would be dangerous in France.

[1] *Journal des débats*, July 9. These two speeches also reported in *Le Siècle*, July 10.

Let us not seek to imitate the United States completely; we are in a different situation. The American Union was founded by descendants of Penn. Even before having conquered their independence, the Americans had the habit of governing themselves; the exercise of the suffrage was popular among them; they applied it to everything, to the government, to interests, to beliefs. That people, truly republican, might elect its chief; yet it does so only in an indirect way. But with us, the representative system has not thrust its roots so deeply. The French people has hardly left the mould of monarchy. . . . If you summon the whole people to choose the president of the republic, it will choose under the name of president the equivalent of a king; it will perhaps found a new dynasty. It will allow itself to be seduced by the power of the sword or by the éclat of an historic name. It will do what it did under the Consulate and the Empire; it will choose, not among illustrious legislators, but among the pretenders.[1]

It is a curious fact that Faucher became one of Louis Napoleon's ministers.

The only other report of the bureaux' proceedings in which allusion was made to America has no connection with the constitutional plan. After the June riots, a bill was brought in to regulate the clubs very strictly, and was duly referred to the bureaux. In the 1st bureau's discussion, F. de Corcelles said that he discovered and considered it a misfortune that French clubs were not organized as in America, where a club is an association for some special object, as the abolition of slavery; the members are agreed on the purpose and can attain it with greater ease. In France, where affairs in general are discussed, passions are more easily aroused. He proposed assigning each club a special object.

To this Xavier Durrieu replied that the preceding speaker

[1] *Journal des débats*, July 16.

confused liberty of association with liberty of discussion; the latter alone concerned them. The fact that American clubs were only associations proved merely that American society was not in a state to practise publicly liberty of discussion. It was well known that when different opinions arose in an American club, the discussion degenerated into a violent quarrel, ending in a fight. Not the laws, but the manners, forbid clubs there. Thank Heaven, France had not reached that point! [1]

When the constitution was read to the Assembly for the second time, the *Univers* published an editorial criticism, in which it was noted that the new president was to have 600,000 francs, though in America the salary was only 125,000. "Every constitution has, so to speak, left its mark on the present plan; the United States have lent us their president; it is the only combination that we have not yet tried." Local self-government and indirect election limited the executive's power in America, however, while the new French constitution made him a sort of king.[2]

In September the *Bien public* published a eulogy of Lamartine, delivered by Mr. Winthrop, Speaker of the House, at the dedication of the Washington Monument.[3]

The report that the "intelligent American democracy" had appointed an ambassador to the Holy See was greeted by the *Univers* as a "great and solemn spectacle," and comment made on Catholic liberty in America as contrasted with the tactlessness and bad faith of England.[4]

The report of the customs administration for the fiscal

[1] *Opinion publique*, July 16.

[2] *Univers*, Aug. 30. Same ideas repeated, Oct. 6. "If authority were centralized in the United States as in France, that country would still be in search of order and liberty."

[3] *Bien public*, Sept. 6.

[4] *Univers*, Sept. 6.

year of 1847-8 received this comment: " The United States
continue to occupy the first place in the order of our commercial relations. Between them and us, the worth of 222,-
000,000 was exchanged in 1847. England comes next with
189,000,000." The figures include imports and exports
combined. In imports, the United States led with 110,000,-
000, Belgium being second; in exports, the United States
were first with 112,000,000, England second.[1]

Finally, President Polk's last message was published in
full by the same paper, occupying a page and a half of its
issue, with the comment: " Since a government has been
cut for us on the model of the United States, and we too
are destined to have our annual message, we engage our
president and his ministers to read attentively what we publish today." Then follows a eulogy of Polk, who, though
unknown when chance bore him to the head of affairs, had
conducted the most complicated matters with extraordinary
tact, energy and success.

Those men are not rare in the United States, which proves
why each administration marks its passage through the conduct of affairs by new progress. One would seek vainly in
that country where facts and good sense occupy the place
which we give here to phrases and discussions, a government
which has not added something to the glory, the power and
the well-being of the Union. Which proves, be it said in passing, that the republicans who have governed us since February 24, were not raised in the same school.

The message impressed the writer by the brevity of its gen-
eralities as compared with the fullness of the portion devoted to business and also the emphasis on non-intervention
in the domestic affairs of other nations.

[1] *Presse*, Oct. 5.

What touches us closest perhaps in the message of Mr. Polk, is the comparison which he makes between Europe shaken by revolutions and whose credit, industry and commerce are killed by civil war, and the Uni+ed States where public and private credit make new progress. The situation was so prosperous and the interests of the country so well guarded, that to continue the war against Mexico, the Minister of Finance (*sic*) negotiated a loan above par and thus realized a large premium in favor of the Treasury; since that time he had redeemed consolidated bonds to the amount of half a million dollars, reducing the public debt by so much, and Mr. Polk announces that the receipts will cover the expenses.[1]

The article indicates that to the conservative *Presse* the contrast between prosperous America and revolutionary Europe was food for envy rather than contempt.[2]

Passing from news reports to editorials, the wealth of material is such here that only excerpts can be given, to show the trend of comment. A considerable number deal with the general value of the American example for France. The showing of the pro-American papers is slight here, their heaviest guns being reserved for special articles.

A conservative paper points out quite early that when it comes to settling the constitutional basis of the republic, there will be those who will say that it is impossible to accept popular government " in the large measure fixed by America." But it is an error to suppose American success along this line determined by her vast territories. That success is even more visible in crowded states like New York than in Texas. " France is republican, she has taught democracy to the whole world; America has practised before us the philosophic theories with which we have covered

---

[1] *Presse,* Dec. 23.

[2] For comment on the Mexican War and the American political situation, *cf. supra*, ch. iii.

society; the time has come to make an application of them to our profit." Liberty of opinion, of conscience, of the press, of association and speech, reduction of governmental functions as far as possible, credit and public works left to individual control, liberty of instruction, free economic competition, a reduced tax-budget make up the program suggested by the paper.[1]

The *Journal des débats* found that " the Constitution of the United States of America is good because under that Constitution America has grown immeasurably in wealth, in power, in consideration in the world." England is also eulogized, " in spite of the vices which theory and even experience easily discover there." [2]

Similarly Émile de Girardin, editor of the *Presse*, announced his candidacy for the Assembly in these terms:

It is by exaggeration, terror, war, bankruptcy and misery that the republic has already perished once in France; it is by good sense, liberty, peace, credit and wealth that the republic was founded in the United States, where it grows each year in power. I understand the republic like Francklin (*sic*), I do not understand it without Washington. If I am wrong not to understand it with citizen Robespierre and like citizen Ledru-Rollin, let me not be nominated and let me be left to the labors of the journals which I direct.[3]

He was taken at his word and was left to his editorial pursuits.

English and American prudence and political firmness were commended by the *Constitutionnel*,[4] which further re-

---

[1] *Courrier français*, quoted in *La Réforme*, Mar. 3. At that early date the radical organ was not as afraid of American example as later, especially as the *Courrier* cleverly asserted that opposition to American methods would be used by the reaction to destroy the fruits of the revolution. And again, *La Réforme* was never socialistic.

[2] *Journal des débats*, Mar. 7.

[3] *Presse*, May 20.   [4] *Constitutionnel*, April 29.

marked on Marrast's disdain of foreign example, as expressed in his report of the constitution, "we had thought that history was the lesson of kings and nations." [1]

A large proportion of the anti-American articles are to be found in the legitimist papers, notably in the *Gazette de France*. Legitimate royalty is, for it, the true, because the ancient, French system. " Let us not lower to the level of imitators the people which is made to serve as model. Let us seek in France and not in America or in England the future of France." [2]   Nothing in the past fifty years is worth copying. "As for the future, we have a choice between the English constitution, the American constitution, the nameless constitution, and perhaps the phalansterian constitution of Fourier. One will permit us to stick to the French constitution." [3]

Two journalists of the English school, Messrs. Thiers and Guizot, in power after the July Revolution, tried to establish the parliamentary government of which they had dreamed under the Restoration, in the *Globe* and the *Constitutionnel*.

Two journalists of the American or republican school are directing the march of the new government.

We shall see if they will be able to establish their theories or if we shall be forced to return to ours, those of the French school, so well characterized by those words of M. Lamartine: Republic at the base, heredity at the summit.[4]

The American republic is not to be imitated, because there " slavery necessitates the federal system." [5]

---

[1] *Constitutionnel*, Sept. 1.

[2] *Gazette de France*, Mar. 6.

[3] *Ibid.*, Mar. 20.   [4] *Ibid.*, Mar. 23.

[5] *Ibid.*, Apr. 15. In the issue of Mar. 30, however, American federalism is cited as suggesting a way by which "the duchy of Savoy, the duchy of the Rhine and Belgium" may be united to France through a system of autonomy.

The *Gazette's* views were given their fullest expression in a long article, headed " The American System."

After having been constituted *à l'anglaise* by M. Guizot, we are to be, it seems, constituted *à l'américaine* by M. de Cormenin. There is question of giving us a single chamber of representatives, with a council of government or senate, and an elective president for three years. . . . The American fashion is still more remote from our nature and our temperament than the English fashion. The right of participating in our own affairs existed among us many centuries before there was any question of the United States. Political liberty is essentially French. In that respect we owe nothing to any one. But what is foreign to us, what we cannot be made to accept without effort and violence are forms of government . . . contrary to our customs . . . to our situation . . . to our traditions, finally to our social constitution.

Were France composed of twenty-six states, independent of one another, except for a few common interests; if she had a vast territory, capable of holding four times the population; if there were no taxes, no fear of continental war and of neighbors with military organization; if everyone could get land for five francs an acre; if the standing army had only 12,500 men; if there were citizens rich, devoted and moderate enough to govern and represent France for 125,000 francs a year, to be ministers for 30,000 and " presidents of states " for 15,000; if we could be feeble and divided, with impunity; if without danger we might exist under the form of a multitude of special associations, independent of each other and of the central government, if our provinces and communes were left to themselves for internal administration, except for a few points of general interest, such as public instruction, navy and great public works; if justice were almost nil; if administration, properly so-called, had neither cohesion nor unity, " we should then say: let us constitute ourselves à *l'américaine*, with an elective president for three years or even for one year; let us form a federal congress with a council of government called senate, and let us so live until time brings other needs." But we have French customs, habits, organizations, interests, etc.

We cannot become Americans then, without peril and without damage. If the English system could not last, if it succumbed to the effort of public spirit, the United States régime would last still less. In mercy, *messieurs constituants,* let us remain French if it is possible; experiments with foreign constitutions cost too dearly,[1]

A still more bitter arraignment appeared two months later. " Our pretended [2] republicans *de la veille* give us to-day as model of government the United States, and they call the cruellest and most abominable despotism, democracy." Then follow statistics of the number of slaves (over two million) and Indians (over three hundred thousand) over whom an oligarchy of whites exercises the most execrable tyranny, having torn the negroes from their homes and their homes from the Indians. " And that is the people which it is wished to give as example to the land of the Franks, which it sufficed to touch in order to be free!" The barons of the Middle Ages were equally free, and if the millions of serfs were uncounted, feudal democracy might be as favorably discussed. " O democratic charlatans, the *Satyre Ménippée* has depicted you!" [3]

Other legitimist papers expressed similar views, though less persistently.

---

[1] *Gazette de France,* June 1.

[2] The adjective is well-advised. The real *républicains de la veille* rarely did so.

[3] *Ibid.,* Aug. 2.

" No one wants for France the Greek or Roman republics, not even that of the United States, which contains
slaves, nor that of Switzerland, more backward in some
cantons than certain European monarchies." [1]

" The example of the United States is often quoted to us,
but without taking the trouble to reflect on the enormous
difference which exists between the situation of the United
States and that of France." The former is federated, the
latter centralized. The former has a positive, prosaic spirit,
no poetical imagination, disdain of glory and honor, an exclusive cult of matter, a passion for money; in the latter,
ambition for honor and power predominates; everyone
dreams of decorations, epaulets and titles. The immense
plains of the former contrast with the crowded ranks of the
latter; every place taken, every land occupied by property-
right. Twenty other differences might be named between
the totally dissimilar situations of France and the United
States." [2]

An ironical review of an article in *L'Ère nouvelle* quotes
that paper as saying that France awaits the hand which
makes moral and political liberty flourish in the United
States; [3] elsewhere doubt is expressed that the leaders of
the republic can measure up to the standard of Washington
and Franklin, and the work of the local " political alchemists " is contrasted with the picture of young America
" committing to the wisest and most illustrious of her citizens the task of drawing up her constitution." [4] Though
expressing such divergent feelings regarding America, the
legitimist journals were agreed in their rejection of the
American example as a general model.

[1] *Assemblée nationale*, Mar. 1.

[2] *Indépendant de l'Ouest* (legitimist), quoted in the *National*, May 4.

[3] *Union*, July 14.

[4] *Opinion publique*, June 21.

Dumas' organ published an article "Concerning the French republic and its comparison with republics which have existed or which still exist." From antiquity, the only thing worth taking was love of country; from the medieval republics, love of art.

As for the republic of the United States, where our law-makers are eternally seeking their inspirations, our utopians their models; as for the republic of the United States, we say, with its federal constitution, its senate and its chamber, its Quakers and its slaves; as for the republic of the United States finally, placed between two immensities, the immensity of the sea which it ploughs with its vessels, the immensity of the desert which it furrows with its colonists, it has surely little to offer us, unless it be its example, its perseverance and its union.[1]

The rest of the article was a long, rhetorical disquisition on the vastness of America as compared with France.

The papers of the left wing had little to say on America in general. Thoré was the chief spokesman.

Shall the French republic be the *sister* of the American re-public, as M. Lamartine said to the minister plenipotentiary of the United States? Shall we have a president with the attributes of a king, and will this president govern France? Shall we have a non-permanent assembly, to leave the full power to the president-king, in the interval between the sessions? . . . If this system has the majority, we are falling back into monarchy. We have already tried, with Philippe, the *best of republics*. Shall we allow ourselves to make another essay of a false republic? Let us at least have the form pure; the essence will perhaps be found in the flagon, and we shall be there to fill it.[2]

A somewhat ominous conclusion.

[1] *Liberté*, May 12.
[2] *Vraie république,* April 30.

Lamennais' constitutional project combined with the decree of Mar. 5, calling for election of the Assembly by departments, seemed to form " a federal establishment very similar to that of the United States of America " and destructive of French unity.[1] So, too, the divisions in the ranks of the Assembly seemed to make it hopeless that the commission would report anything better than " a program of representative or federalist monarchy, after the fashion of England or the United States." [2]

Proudhon published the most philosophic systematized exposition of the radical view under the title, " France has nothing to imitate." There are those, he said, who seem unable to reason except by perpetual comparisons and more or less exact analogies; instead of studying the conditions of their own country, they quote the customs of another, which has purely external likenesses with their own. Such has been the fate of France.

England in particular has been for more than two centuries the political mirage of almost all our publicists, we dare not say our thinkers. . . . Now that France has emerged from the paths of constitutionalism, the publicists have felt the convenience of abandoning or rather changing their warhorse, they have perceived that the republic has buried anglomania. But in so doing, they have made no pretense of despoiling themselves completely of their rage for imitation; they have thus had to offer another type, appropriate to the new state of things, and it is America which has offered them this new theme for hyperboles and commonplaces. America, then, is destined, in the mind of our comparative legislators, to play the same rôle in regard to republican France as England in regard to constitutional France. It is from this new arsenal that innumerable arguments are to be drawn in favor of all the

[1] *Vraie république,* May 6.

[2] *Ibid.,* May 21.

superfluities, useless at least, which it is desired to introduce into the constitution of our young republic. Partisans of indirect election, partisans of two chambers, partisans of the independence of the executive and the legislative power, partisans of the presidency, all these adepts of a modified republic are going to throw the American republic at our heads, as the liberals [1] used to overwhelm us with their Britannic constitutionalism.

The American example proved nothing for France. The American presidency was a needed symbol of unity because of the federal system, but the centralization of France was so complete that she needed the opposite treatment, a democratic organization to preserve her from despotism. Constitutional monarchy and a presidency were thus alike impracticable in France as half-measures; an absolute system was inevitable because of the concentration of political forces, anything else was a fiction and a cheat. As constitutional monarchy in a centralized country must turn into an absolute monarchy, so presidency would become dictatorship. Of the two only possible alternatives, absolute democracy must be the choice to save the country from absolute despotism. The United States presidency would be a sword of Damocles, suspended over the republic's head.

The United States have desired the symbol of unity, not being able to have the thing itself; France must reject the personification of this unity because she possesses the unity in fact, and because she must take care lest this great principle be exploited to the profit of a more or less disguised tyranny.

Hence all imitation should be avoided; France, having to take the initiative, has need of all its originality.[2]

---

[1] The liberal party of Orleanist times, not the government party of 1848, to which the name was not applied contemporaneously.

[2] *Représentant du peuple,* May 1.

Père Duchêne described the newly-reported constitution as " this Americo-Anglo-French piece of work," and took especial umbrage at the creation of a president, instead of confiding the executive as well as the legislative power to the Assembly.[1]

Charivari declared that of the three former presiding officers of the Assembly, M. Buchez had presided like a school-master, M. Senard like a police-court judge, M. Marie like a master of ceremonies, and now came M. Marrast, the first *gentleman* who had sat in the chair, always a republican of distinction, who presented himself today like a president of the United States. " One would have taken him for the veritable M. Polk. The Americans of Paris might be deceived." As for the " rights of capacity " of which he made mention in his speech, the writer was in accord with the speaker " provided he meant to speak of honest folk without intrigue and not to make an advance to M. Thiers, who visibly took the matter for himself, as if we were already at New York." [2]

The Bonapartist paper, with its ultra-radical interpretation of the Napoleonic legend, quoted Thiers' famous saying of 1830,[3] with the comment, " You are neither Americans nor English. Stay at home. Do not question M. Thiers, abortive missionary of a narrow, bourgeois doctrine. You need a constitution of your own make, which smacks of the Terror, which is the chaste fruit of your own entrails." [4]

When it came to the economic aspect of the American system, the conservative papers praised American individualism, the radicals were silent. Garnier-Pagès' report of

[1] *Père Duchêne*, June 22.

[2] *Charivari*, July 25.

[3] *Vide supra*, p. 107.

[4] *Napoléon rêpublicain*, June 16.

certain plans of the executive commission, which involved
government loans to voluntary associations of workmen,
called forth an editorial contrasting those nations in which
the government reserved to itself the direction of industry
with those in which it abstained altogether from such enterprises. The former were undeveloped or servile nations,
the latter those invested with the fullness of the rights of
man. On the one hand were Mehemet-Ali's fellahin, governed like cattle, and the Jesuit-controlled Indians of Para-
guay; on the other the English in Europe, the United States
in America. In those enlightened free nations the government abstained from all manufacture, even that of muni-
tions of war. Any individual could order cannons at Pitts-
burg or in Scotland. The largest American powder factory
was founded by a Frenchman, M. Dupont, in whose family
it remained. A Frenchman who felt a particular drawing
to that business had to exile himself to the banks of the
Brandywine. Thus the monopoly system exercised the
same effect on national prosperity and the development of
the arts as the Edict of Nantes. Only the postal service
was in government hands there and in America, contrary to
the English and French theories which considered it as a
source of revenue, the principle ruled that the receipts should
merely cover expenses.[1]

In a similar spirit, the failures of communistic colonies in
America were cited as justifying the refusal of a later
French administration to recognize certain associations in
their corporate capacity.[2] Dumas reminded the working-
classes that the word " equality " must not be taken too
literally. Equality before the law and before God were
praiseworthy, but inequality must continue in expenditure.
" The workmen of New York are busy only because the

[1] *Journal des débats*, May 20.

[2] *Ibid.*, Oct. 9.

rich are free and tranquil." Those who dream of the happiness of the poor without the liberty of the rich are mad. The rich must continue to give good dinners and beautiful balls in all joy, quiet and liberty for the welfare of the poor. " No liberty without order, no wealth without order and without liberty; those are the key-words of the problem of civilization." [1]

As a set-off to this crass individualism, however, occurs the sentence: " In comparing the history of the republic of the United States with ours, it is impossible not to recognize that if our materials are less republican, our ideas are more democratic." [2]

The same cleavage was maintained in the discussion of the various parts of the political system. Turning from general comment on America as a model to the discussion that arose over her specific institutions, one notes that the same singular silence, previously mentioned, regarding the advantages of the American presidency, continued. Minor points were, however, commended.

The modest establishment of the American executive " in a little, unfrequented city" was praised. The American government does nothing either to encourage or restrain luxury; it limits itself to the proper task of a democratic government, the due administration of the country with conscientiousness, order, simplicity, vigilance and economy.[3]

The American system of pardons, whereby the President or the Governor submitted them to the Senate of the Union or state was noted. It was believed that the executive in France should also have the preliminary advice of a council.[4]

Somewhat grudging use was made of American example

[1] *Liberté*, Mar. 22.

[2] *Ibid.,* May 1.

[3] *Presse,* Oct. 26.

[4] *Ère nouvelle,* June 5.

in connection with the electoral college by a paper that ordinarily found little value in American methods. It was pointed out that the House elected the President only in exceptional cases. Further, no one holding a place of profit in government service could be an elector.[1] This was used in an editorial against Assembly election of the executive.

It was admitted that the United States proved that property could be safe in a republic, but it was felt that popular sovereignty was a less secure guardian of its safety than the principle of heredity.[2]

Another legitimist paper commented on the new constitution:

Numerous loans from the American constitution were expected, tested as it is by a happy experience of more than sixty years. We have sought in vain for a single point of contact. The essential differences between a federal and a unitary republic have without doubt caused the rejection of any sort of assimilation in the least details.[3]

But, curiously enough, the next editorial on the same page contradicts this view: " The new constitution organizes the democratic republic with a president like the United States. We ask, where is Washington?"[4]

The socialist papers left no doubt as to their position. The presidential system was branded as a dangerous heresy. Ministers named by the Assembly should control the executive power, for action follows will, and the arm is agent of the head.

But we are admitting a president, elected by the people, in the fashion of the President of the United States. This, it is said,

[1] *Assemblée nationale*, Sept. 25.
[2] *Opinion publique*, Oct. 22.
[3] *Union*, June 20.
[4] *Ibid.*, June 20.

is the doctrine of the *National,* of the ministry of public instruction and its adherents and of various republicans, versed in political science. Carrel,[1] as will be recalled, strongly sustained the two-chamber theory, having studied the American constitution without sufficiently considering the French spirit.

This president or king, if not in accord with the Assembly, will engage in struggle with it, and you have revolution in permanence or at least in expectation.[2]

Proudhon had another word on the office of president:

It is the idea of M. de Lamennais, supported by the opinion of M. de Lamartine. The decisive argument is the example of the Americans. We have received feudalism from the barbarians, constitutional monarchy from the English; now we are to take presidential democracy from America. Would that we could do something French![3]

As in the commission and the Assembly, the legislative problem called forth a much greater discussion of American precedent. All conservative papers, legitimist, Orleanist, conservative republican alike, supported the bicameral system.

One, commonly anti-American, said: " We likewise think that the national congress should be composed of two elective assemblies like the Congress of the United States and not of two assemblies formed by monopoly and privilege as in England.[4]

And again, when published under another name: " We have, further, the example of two great peoples, whom we consider as our elders in liberty, England and the United States." [5]

[1] Republican leader under the monarchy; killed in duel, 1836.

[2] *Vraie république,* Apr. 4.

[3] *Représentant du peuple,* May 11.

[4] *Gazette de France,* Apr. 18.

[5] *Étoile de la France,* Sept. 26.

The *Union* made a serious study of the value of the Senate as a check on the executive. " In practice, the bicamerists alone can quote examples which have real authority; and the most powerful of all, the example of the United States." No politician of any reputation from the St. Lawrence River to the Gulf of Mexico felt that the republic could have survived without the dual system. But to understand the full value of its meaning, it must be recalled that the Senate has governmental as well as legislative functions. It controls and regulates the central executive. The president can conclude treaties only with its advice and consent; it confirms his nominations of federal officials, is the depository of national traditions, guards the principles of foreign policy which have made the prosperity and power of the United States. Further, it is renewed by thirds, so that if its spirit is modified by the progress of ideas, it is at least never wiped out. In a way, it is the sole permanent power, organized by the American constitution. Without it, every presidential election might be a revolutionary break of continuity. Nor should the Senate's meaning be sought in the federal system. It has the same functions in every state. Everywhere it controls the executive and is the guardian of permanent traditions. Reduced as the executive's powers are, the Americans realized that to leave all important nominations to him alone would be a danger for public liberty. At the same time, they felt that control of the executive could be lodged only in a chamber at once elective and permanent, since all authority proceeds from election and continuity must be safeguarded. The two-chamber question concerns the executive even more than the legislative. So considered, " it borrows from the United States' example an argument whose power is increased by all the interest which attaches to guarantees of liberty." The value of a double deliberation might be contested, but not so necessary a means of defence against executive usurpation.[1]

---

[1] *Union*, July 10.

A certain M. Fabas, spoken of as a *républicain de la veille* and *maître des requêtes* of the council of state, proposed a system which would obviate the dangers of tyranny in case a single chamber were adopted and of conflict between the two chambers of a dual system. " The solution which M. Fabas proposes, a solution which should prevent a struggle between two legislative assemblies, is borrowed from the United States of America." In the State of New York, when the Senate and Assembly do not agree, they unite for a joint vote, the majority of the total vote being decisive. The plan of M. Fabas called for a democratic assembly, elected without eligibility restrictions, a senate of a third or a quarter of the assembly's numbers, a joint vote in case of disagreement, regular and constant intervention of the senate in the exercises of the executive power.[1]

The same paper in a later article dwelt on the capital importance of this legislative question, as indicated by the fact that the United States placed it in the first article of their constitution. Pennsylvania, the only state which had a single chamber at first, soon changed to the dual system. Opposed to the American example stand the unfortunate memories of the senate of the empire and the peers of the recent monarchy. But the correct deduction is "that it is important to make our senate after the pattern of republican senates and not after the pattern of monarchical senates." For nominations by the head of the government, substitute popular elections; for eligibility conditions of birth and wealth, substitute experience. It would be puerile to condemn a good institution out of hatred of a bad one with the same name.[2]

When the cause was all but lost, direct appeal was made to the Assembly.

[1] *Siècle*, Aug. 1.
[2] *Ibid.*, Sept. 4.

It is for you to choose. You may treat history and experience loftily today, you may mock England and its hundred and fifty years of prosperity, despise even the example of the greatest republic in the world, of the American republic! Be tranquil, in their turn history and experience will have their revenge and you will no more change the necessary laws of politics than the laws of the stars.[1]

La Patrie testily declared that if it should show that the dual system had been unanimously adopted by all the democratic peoples of antiquity, and that the United States had been forced to it after an unhappy experiment with the single chamber, the *Bien public* would say as it did of Thiers: " You emerge all dusty from the depths of history." Better so than fresh from one's own notions. It remains for the *Bien public* to prove that the French are infinitely better poised, calmer and wiser than the Americans, and that safeguards necessary to other nations are perfectly useless here, due to the infinite superiority of our moderation, patience and respect for the law.[2]

Commenting on the Duvergier de Hauranne amendment, it pointed out that the bicameral system had behind it the authority of the best publicists of the last fifty years, the witness of the Constituante and the Convention itself, " finally the experience of the most flourishing republic that has ever existed, the United States." Whether the arguments for it would outweigh the parti-pris, the native love of simplicity and adventure, the desire not to be taken for a *républicain du lendemain*, " the fear of resembling America in something," and a false notion of what the republican form required, remained to be seen. It was a doubtful conversion. But the conviction remained that in the end

[1] *Journal des débats*, Sept. 26.
[2] *Patrie*, July 10.

reason and experience would get their rights " and that if France commences like the United States with a single chamber as more popular, it will finish like them by adopting duality as more in conformity with the laws of politics." [1]

Lamartine's rejection of American example as based on federalism was given the usual answer that the states also had the dual system; the point was further made that there are institutions common to all free countries. Dupin proposed the dictatorship, unity and sovereignty of the Assembly, as the base of the republic. " Was it so that the republic of the United States was founded?" [2]

This paper chronicled the adoption of an integral reelection of the Assembly every three years, with the comment: " In the United States, the election of representatives takes place every two years. France is not America, and the wisdom of M. Marrast is not that of Washington." [3]

If all the conservative papers united in favor of the dual system, there was a similar coalition of government and radical papers against it.

It was asserted that,

just as England was quoted ,to us when it was desirable to prove the excellence of the constitutional monarchy, now the United States are cited, where in some respects the spirit of the mother-country lives again in republican institutions and where the two-chamber system is in vogue. Does it not seem that one would thus indirectly renew imitation of the English, proscribed by the February revolution, by placing that imitation under the authority of the name and the example of the American republic?

[1] *Patrie,* Sept. 27.
[2] *Univers,* Sept. 28.
[3] *Ibid.,* Sept. 30.

The English heritage and the federal system, requiring equal representation of each of the states in at least one chamber, explained the dual system in America; its existence in state legislatures was due to historic tradition and the example of the central government. The system might suit America without being in the least fitting for France.[1]

The federal explanation was also given by the *Journal*, in an article headed " The two chambers in the United States," prefaced by the statement that " in the bureaux, at the tribune of the National Assembly, the adversaries of the constitution's article relative to the creation of a single chamber, to defend their opinion and to demand the establishment of two chambers, are continually supporting themselves by the example of the United States." [2]

The Lamartine organ was annoyed because *Le Siècle* objected to its citation of Prussia in support of the single chamber and opposed to it the example of America. The latter was a worse choice. " Is it not indeed a strange thing to want to copy our own new republican constitution from the constitution of the United States, under the pretext that the United States are a republic?" The republic, like the monarchy, is a form of government with infinite combinations. Venice, Sparta, Athens and Rome were republics, but who thinks of taking them for models? The Prussian example is worth while, because it is an affair of today and close at hand. The American constitution goes back more than sixty years, and was made under totally different conditions.[3]

To the radicals, the English and American examples were inconclusive, the former because of aristocracy, the latter because of federalism, freedom from armed neighbors, lack

[1] *National,* July 10.

[2] *Journal,* Sept. 28.

[3] *Bien public,* July 14.

of pretenders supported by rich clientèles, and because historically "the American institution was the product of the old world and bears in itself the social vices of its mother, the monarchy." To give such a constitution to the democratic republic would be an act of folly, if not treason.[1]

A socialist paper wrote:

The partisans of the Britannic tradition of two chambers make, to the profit of their argument, such an abuse of the example of the United States, that it is important to place before the eyes of our fellow-citizens an exposé of the motives which caused the institution of a senate to be adopted by the republicans of the New World.

The federal argument was then employed, after which came a two-column quotation from an essay by M. L. P. Conseil on the Memoirs of Jefferson, quoting his Augean-stable letter of 1794 to Madison and asserting that the real purpose of a second chamber in France was to protect the interests of the great proprietors, which meant the perpetuation of privilege, avarice and ambition.[2]

Dumas' opinions were alike inaccurate, eccentric and contradictory. He wrote: "The law of the United States gives the direct vote to but two chambers, of which one names the other. We behold its effects. Who would desire them for France?"[3]

This remarkable piece of information was followed by an equally unusual suggestion. Starting with the customary statement that "the partisans of two chambers support themselves on the example of the United States, whose prosperity is notorious," he held that social conditions were

---

[1] *Réforme*, Sept. 27.

[2] *Démocratie pacifique*, July 17.

[3] *Liberté*, Mar. 2.

entirely different in the two countries, and then proposed a double executive, copying the consuls of Rome.[1]

A month later he made a complete volte-face, condemning Cormenin for rejecting the bicameral system; "in order not to appear an adept of the English school, he rejects one of the essential elements of the constitution of the United States." So enlightened a man as he must be aware that an omnipotent assembly without counter-weight might go to any extreme of anger or passion.[2]

On the judiciary clause, this paper commented at length, praising the American jury system. urging its application to civil cases, and quoting from Tocqueville, vol. II, ch. VIII, on the point.[3]

In a directly opposite interest, it was urged that Supreme Court judges in America were appointed by the President with the advice and consent of the Senate, permanency of judicial tenure being recognized by the American republic.[4]

The preamble to the American constitution was strongly commended to the Assembly as preferable to the long, controversial declaration adopted by the commission. "It is simple, but it is clear, plain, precise. There is no intellect so dense that it cannot comprehend it; and there is no imagination so perverse that it can logically draw from it dangerous deductions." Good political philosophy consisted in precise demarcation of the goal and in eliminating metaphysical formulas.[5]

If space permitted, a mass of references to American example on other than strictly constitutional questions might be added. They can be only summarized.

[1] *Liberté*, Mar. 5.
[2] *Ibid.*, Apr. 14.
[3] *Ibid.*, Apr. 12.
[4] *Siècle*, May 11.
[5] *Union*, Sept. 7.

It was recognized that an intelligent use of the suffrage required a great extension of elementary education, that the intellectual average might be brought up to the high level it had long held in America;[1] printed ballots on the American model were commended.[2] The division of the population into equal election districts, practised in America, sprang from a state of society which had only towns and plantations, no rural communes. The latter furnished the true political unit for France. Municipal spirit was the germ of public spirit.[3] This occurred in an article favoring indirect election to the Assembly. But further, local self-government found advocates for its own sake. The American and English type of municipal organization was commended.[4] Lamennais' scheme, based on the communal unit, was praised, publicists having " long recognized that the democratic liberty of the United States was founded on the organization of the commune."[5] A week later, however, this paper changed its tone and Lamennais' prohibition of central interference in departmental affairs was condemned as an institution of Swiss cantons or American states.[6]

The reading of the first draft of the constitution disappointed many of both wings; in fact, only the government party (whom we have called liberals) professed satisfaction. One conservative paper declared that a far more rigid monarchy had really been established than under Louis XIV or Napoleon. Liberty of instruction and of conscience had ceased to exist. Other liberties were no better treated. " The citizen of the United States is free, because the

[1] *National*, Mar. 13.

[2] *Gazette de France,* Mar. 9.

[3] *Ibid.*, Mar. 1.

[4] *Revue britannique,* vol. 14, p. 393; vol. 16, p. 238.

[5] *National*, May 5.

[6] *Ibid.*, May 12.

whole power of the state can do nothing against his right. . . . Centralization and liberty are mutually exclusive." In the new plan, the provinces were under the complete control of Paris. The strong executive will almost certainly revive the empire. This would be impossible in the United States, where the force of the central power is nothing in comparison with that of the thirty states. Mr. Polk has no more idea of crowning himself than would a simple citizen under our late dynasty.[1]

The American railroad policy, by which great lines had been built by private capital and the management left in the hands of private corporations, was defended against government construction.[2] A strict limitation of governmental functions in the interest of individual liberty was repeatedly urged. On the other hand, government-ownership advocates found that American example was not wholly against them. It will be said that

the United States, that classic land of liberty, that refuge if it is not the cradle of all democracy, the United States have comprehended that it was necessary to favor, to second great enterprises; America is furrowed with railroads, not one of them belongs to that republic. All belong to companies which have obtained the exploitation of them in perpetuity. This is true only within certain limits, for the politicians of the United States have imposed on the companies the privilege of repurchase.[3]

Ledru-Rollin, opposing the system of a bond required from each newspaper as a guarantee of good behavior, praised the American free press, where the very number of

[1] *Univers,* June 20.

[2] *Journal des débats,* May 22; *Constitutionnel, Univers,* May 22; *ibid.,* June 9; *Opinion publique,* June 22.

[3] *National,* May 30.

conflicting newspapers and the excesses to which they were permitted to run annulled all their power for evil. His view was regarded as ill-founded, because France's centralization would greatly increase the possibility of their harmful influence.[1] The excesses of the American press were reprinted from Capt. Marryatt's diary, in the interest of the financial bond plan.[2] The free-press party drew a very different picture of the American situation from A. Murat's *Esquisses morales et politiques des Etats-Unis de l'Amérique*, Tocqueville's *Démocratie*, and Chassan's *Traités des délits et contraventions de la parole, de l'écriture et de la presse*.[3]

The *Journal des débats* published an article against the clubs which called forth from the government organ in reply an unusually clear statement of the liberal feeling toward the conservatives.

There is much talk there about America, about England, about Washington, about Quincy Adams, and in fact it is France, it is the February revolution, it is the sacred right of meeting, of association, of political discussion, which there has been very evident desire to place in question. Tomorrow, with the same arms, with the same sophistries, the same skill in misrepresenting facts, either the freedom of the press will be attacked or some other element of republican organization, and we shall be altogether astonished, thinking to model ourselves on America, to find ourselves again under the empire of those laws so well exploited by the former patrons of the journal to which we refer.

The statement had been made that no clubs existed in America, that in England they meant something quite different and that no free government could co-exist with them.

[1] *Univers*, Aug. 9.

[2] *Revue britannique*, vol. 16, p. 408.

[3] *République*, Aug 9.

The doctrine is certainly not novel. It is the same which Messrs. Guizot and Duchâtel professed when before the Chamber of 1848, they attacked the reformist banquets with which the left menaced them. Only it presents itself better disguised than it was then, with a republican apparatus and under the unexpected patronage of Washington.

Then followed a long discussion of the freedom of assembly allowed in the American constitution, of Washington's treatment of his political enemies, by appeal to American good sense rather than by force, of the ease with which a newspaper advertisement could call a public meeting, of the party organization and political conventions which took the place of the clubs. The Whigs, Loco-focos, Barnburners and Hunkers were to the Paris clubs as the giant to the dwarf, the block of granite to the dust of the streets.[1]

To which the sharp retort was made:

We published yesterday (*sic*) an article on the rôle that the clubs played in America, and how they no longer play it, thanks to God and thanks to the good sense of the country. The *National* would see in that article a disguised attack on the absolute liberty of the clubs in France. The *National* is deceived in only one point: our attack is not disguised. We did not cite America to conceal our thought; we cited it as an example in support of what we think.[2]

The American system of taxation was expounded with approval.[3]

American religious liberty was loudly praised by the Catholic papers.

Decimated by Muscovite despotism, vilified by Austrian despotism, oppressed by the false liberalism of the so-called con-

---

[1] *National*, July 5.

[2] *Journal des débats*, July 6.

[3] *Ibid.*, July 9.

stitutional princes of Germany, she (the Church) hardly breathed in France and in England where it was sought to make of her an instrument of government. She is entirely free only in the great and glorious republic of the United States.[1]

Catholic success in the United States was considered striking;[2] it was due to the separation of Church and State.[3] It remained for the radical *Charivari* to fling a gibe at the Puritanical American Sunday, and to sound the warning: " Let us beware of making our republic as boresome as the republic of the United States." [4]

In addition to editorial references, special articles were published on America, usually but not always in a favorable sense.

The text of the United States constitution was printed in various newspapers. The *Presse* devoted a page and a third to it, prefacing its article with the significant note: "At the moment when the National Assembly is about to meet, we have thought that the following document, translated by two Americans, would be read with interest, in spite of its length." Then followed a history of the formation and ratification of the constitution, concluding with the statement:

The United States alone present the example of republican, democratic institutions applied with success on a large scale: they alone have put beyond controversy the fact, continually denied, that a nation placed politically and commercially in the first rank among the powers of the world, with a large population, a great area, including a great variety of climates,

[1] *Univers*, Feb. 27. Cf. *ibid.*, May 7, May 29; *Ère nouvelle*, Prospectus, July 29.

[2] *Ère nouvelle*, Sept. 14.

[3] *Liberté*, June 14.

[4] *Charivari*, May 7.

of products and local interests, may be frankly, truly republican, democratic; they alone have proved that a great people may govern itself! . . . At this moment, when France is in agitation, when thrones are falling, when all Europe is in rebellion, and when old populations are preparing to adopt new and better forms of government, it may be useful to know the political and civil institutions which the republic of the United States possesses.

This was signed " W. W. M." Then came a brief account of the nature of the federal government, and finally the constitution in full, with short, explanatory notes.[1]

The *Siècle* printed a history and analysis of the constitution, without comment.[2]

Three months later another summary of the provisions of the federal constitution was given as the first of three articles entitled " Etats-Unis d'Amérique. — Constitutions Americaines." A prefatory note described the great growth of the country. The four states, whose constitutions would be omitted in these articles, Florida, Arkansas, Michigan and Texas, seemed to have copied Missouri.[3] Three of the four retained the plague of slavery. In all the state constitutions the system of checks and balances was maintained, the executive confided to an elective, temporary officer, the bicameral system universal except in Vermont, judges of high rank irremovable, justices of the peace chosen for only a few years.[4] In the second article, the constitutions of Maine and New Hampshire were summarized;[5] in the third, Vermont, Massachusetts, Rhode Island, Connecticut and

---

[1] *Presse*, May 1.

[2] *Siècle*, May 15.

[3] This statement indicates an original intention to publish a greater number of articles.

[4] *Siècle*, Aug. 28.

[5] *Ibid.*, Sept. 11.

New York.[1]	This third article commenced: " A vast re-
public, which for sixty years has given the world a brilliant
proof of the energy and value of democratic institutions, is
the most useful subject of study which one could offer at
this moment to the statesmen of France." The source of
its information was given as an *Essai statistique et politique*
published by A. de Morineau.

A summary of the federal constitution was published as
a quotation from the journal *Droit,* without comment.[2]

Another summary, though incomplete, was printed in
La Liberté, which announced its intention of publishing the
three French republican constitutions and that of the United
States, believing that the Assembly would find " precious
materials " in them. To this was appended an historical
and an analytical comment. The latter emphasized federalism as the dominant principle, dwelt on the dual legislative
system, the mode of election and triple function of the Senate (legislative, judicial in connection with impeachment,
administrative in its surveillance of treaties and nominations), the mode of election and purely legislative function
of the House, the prohibition of members holding other re-
munerative public offices, the duties and powers of the executive. In conclusion it was said: " There may be excellent
things to take from that constitution, but it should be said
that in great part it would not be appropriate to a unitary
republic, as the French republic must be." [3]

A history and analysis of the American constitution appeared as the fourth of a group of articles, " Des constitutions de la France depuis 1791 et de quelques constitutions
étrangères." [4]

[1] *Siècle,* Sept. 17.

[2] *Gazette de France,* Mar. 26.

[3] *Liberté,* May 3.

[4] *Constitutionnel,* Apr. 29.

But in addition to these reprints of the constitution, with or without comment, some of the papers published special series of articles on a much more elaborate scale.

The most important of these were the studies united under the title " Etudes sur la Constitution des Etats-Unis " by Michel Chevalier [1] in the *Journal des débats*. They appeared on May 25, June 6, 15, 22, July 4, 11, 22, Oct. 9, 20, Dec. 7, 12, occupying ordinarily about four columns on the front page.

Chevalier's eulogy of America was quite unbounded, remarkable even in that day of extravagant expressions. In his introductory article, he said:

At this moment when France . . . is occupied in making a republican constitution, all eyes turn toward the United States. This association of flourishing and already populous republics, important for the space they occupy on the map, remarkable for the diffusion they have given to knowledge among them, for the extent of their commerce, the advance of all their industries, the abundance of their capital, is indeed a natural example (*point de mire*) for a great people which is undertaking to constitute itself as a republic.

Its similar civilization, lively sympathy, admirable solution of the problem of welfare, civil and political equality, were all powerful claims to their attention and respect. Its future greatness and importance were incalculable. His most ardent wish for France was that her people might rapidly cover the really great distance between their manner of existence and that of the Americans. " The political mechanism of North America is, of its kind, the most reasonable that men have conceived and applied up to this day. . . . It is, then, not I who will dissuade my compatriots from selecting the United States as model." He only wished to point

---

[1] *Cf. supra*, p. 101.

out how much they would have to do for themselves before " the magnificent instrument of the constitution of the American Union " or one of the states could be really of service to them. They must study how far a constitution *à l'américaine* was permitted to them, " whatever desire we may have to possess one in such conformity with pure reason." [1]

Similar expressions can be found on almost any page of Chevalier's articles. " In regard to law, up to the present we have had a very different attitude from that of the Americans. There is, however, no middle ground: either we must renounce ours to take theirs, or we shall have to renounce liberty." [2] " The struggle now in France is between those who want a republic on the model of the United States, except for the differences which the diversity of national genius requires, and those who consider the terrorist policy of the Convention as the expression of the most elevated, noblest and purest republican policy." If history was to show that this French republic justified what wise men expected of her, she must have abjured the traditions of 1793 and " demanded her inspiration, not from that unhappy epoch, but from the glorious republic which is growing every day on the other shore of the Atlantic; . . . the only patrons in the skies for a modern republic are the Washingtons, the Franklins and the patriotic phalanx who surrounded them." [3]

These are only typical utterances.

Chevalier's interest was social, as well as constitutional, as the following outline of his articles shows.

[1] *Journal des débats*, May 25.

[2] *Ibid.*, June 6.

[3] *Ibid.*, Oct. 10.

I

1. Introduction: America as model.
2. Difference of religion in America and France.
   a. The fact: former Protestant, latter Catholic.
   b. The results: (1) Protestantism conduces to self-government; Catholicism, monarchical and centralizing. (2) Americans more zealous in religion. (3) Resultant purer morals. (4) Good morals produce strong political convictions, *e. g.*, American confidence in republicanism and Anglo-Saxon supremacy. (5) Legal oath religiously binding.
3. Religion superior to philosophy as creative force.
4. Relative decline of Catholic powers.
5. Will 1848 prove a Catholic renaissance?

II

RESPECT FOR LAW

1. An Anglo-Saxon trait.
2. Exceptions: (a) Western America; (b) Aaron Burr; (c) lynch law; (d) waves of crime in cities; (e) political demagogues.   But general rule holds.
3. Law-abiding character of pre-revolutionary protests to George III.
4. Resultant respect for new constitution.
5. Careful provisions for amendment.
6. Difference between " the people " and " the mob."
7. Federal power aids states, but respects their liberty.
8. Supreme Court as guardian of constitution.
9. Dorr rebellion sole example of violence against a constitution.
10. Absence of armed force.
11. How Americans would have handled French crises of 1814, 1830 and 1848.

III

IV

V

THE CLUBS

1. Right of free speech and press guaranteed in constitution; right to bear arms in additional articles.
2. Temperate use of these privileges.
3. Political meetings and banquets; no permanent clubs; possible exception of Tammany Hall.
4. Former menace of political societies:
   (a) Introduced by Genêt after Jacobin model. (b) Genêt's dismissal, but spread of societies. (c) Washington's struggle against them. (d) Adams' Alien and Sedition laws. (e) Died out under Jefferson, from public disapproval rather than legal pressure. (f) No political clubs on French model in England. (g) Self-restraint of Americans. (h) Danger of clubs for France.

VI

TWO CHAMBERS IN CONGRESS

1. The American régime:
   (a) Adams' refutation. (b) Action of Convention of 1787. (c) Adoption of dual system by states. (d) Axiomatic in America today.
2. Prestige of single chamber:
   (a) Turgot; (b) Pennsylvania; (c) fear of English example; (d) dual system adopted in spite of, not because of English example; (e) loose federal authority later changed, on proof of inadequacy.
3. Fact that France is not federal, really an argument for dual system, because of greater mass of legislation required.
4. Equal representation of states, not original cause for dual system in America.

5. Authorities for dual system:
    (a) Adams; (b) Memoirs of members of Convention (esp. Madison); (c) *Federalist.*
6. Arguments of *Federalist:*
    (a) Eminence of Senate guaranteed by (1) smaller number, (2) longer tenure, (3) mode of election; (b) increased security against plots; (c) passions calmed; (d) deeper knowledge of politics; (e) greater stability and sense of responsibility.
7. Method of electing Senate.
8. Bicameral system in larger cities for municipal government.
9. Corner-stone of American system; England; constitution of year III.

VII

HOW THIS CONSTITUTION WAS MADE

1. Differences among colonies.
2. Union against France and later against England.
3. Loose character of Confederation due to dread of tyranny.
4. Financial failure of Confederation after war.
5. Constitution established.
    (a) Its work: it made a nation, though still federal.
    (b) Its success: due to the character of the people.

VIII

PAPER-MONEY; FINANCIAL SYSTEM OF FRENCH CONVENTION

1. Prohibition by Congress of emission of paper by states; joy of Madison expressed in *Federalist.*
2. Depreciation of Continental paper-money during war.
3. Further emission of paper after war; its depreciation.
4. Supreme Court holds Missouri certificates unconstitutional.

5. Opposition to paper-money extends even to banknotes, though these are not real paper-money, being (a) immediately redeemable, (b) taken at will.
6. Jackson tried to establish metal money alone.
7. Bank-notes (a) useful in advancing civilization, (b) failing to provide due guarantees for specie redemption became true paper-money, causing crisis of 1837.
8. Paper-money proposed in France now, but system of assignats and maximum, tried under Revolution, failed.
9. Men of Terror idealized today; in reality, scoundrels.
10. Cambon did not invent assignats, merely used them less disastrously than others; real basis of paper-money the *biens nationaux*, acquired by laws of death and confiscation.
11. Misery under tyranny of Convention.
12. True model not Convention, but American republic; secret of its success, " Love of labor and respect for the laws."

IX

HOW LIBERTY IS UNDERSTOOD AND PRACTISED IN THE UNITED STATES

1. Perverted notions of liberty elsewhere.
2. American freedom of person by habeas-corpus :
   (a) English foundation of principle; (b) general statement in constitution; (c) development in state laws; (d) truth of facts examined, statement of detaining authority not accepted at face-value; (e) parallelism between English and American legislation; (f) partial lack of these guarantees in France, total lack in Turkey; (g) possible suspension of writ in case of public need, so far unused; cases of Burr and Jackson.

3. American customs laws do not permit *visites à corps* [personal examination of suspected smugglers].
4. Imprisonment for debt abolished, even in refusal to honor commercial paper; such refusal would ruin a business man.
5. No domiciliary visits permitted except with much formality.
6. No lodging of troops among citizens required.

X

ELECTION OF THE PRESIDENT

1. Multiple head under Confederation; Congress while in session, committee at other times.
2. President adopted under constitution; fitness of Washington for this post.
3. Constitutional provisions as to President's function.
4. Votes in convention which framed constitution:
   (a) defeat of president's council and of life tenure; (b) adoption of seven-year term, election by Congress, no re-eligibility; (c) revision adopts electoral college, chosen by legislatures; (d) election restored to Congress; (e) present system adopted.
5. Modifying considerations and subsequent developments:
   (a) four-year term thought too short, re-election expected to be the rule; illusion; (b) election by Congress thought to open way for intrigue and executive dependence on legislature; (c) despite quiet and small size of towns, popular suffrage not considered; manner of choosing electors left to each state; (d) South Carolina only state in which people do not now choose electors; some states elect by districts, giving minority representation; usually local pride forces general vote, to make state vote a unit; (e) electors expected to be

calmly independent; now mere party machines; people really decide; (f) inclusion of Senators in estimate of due number of electors, and vote by states when House must decide, concessions to small states.

6. House has decided election twice.
7. Vice-President's function: (a) his deciding vote a concession to states' jealousy of one another; (b) change in election since 1804.
8. Inferior foresight, but superior stability of Americans in constitutional matters.

XI

ELECTION OF THE PRESIDENT. — PREPARATORY DISCUSSIONS. — CONVENTIONS. — FAVOR ENJOYED BY MILITARY CANDIDATES. — SINCERITY OF ELECTIONS

1. Change of electoral college in practice.
2. Designation of candidates:
   (a) by caucus, (b) by convention.
3. The convention:
   (a) rapidity of its action and lack of acquaintance of members a guarantee against cabals; (b) party discipline accepts choice; (c) contrasting party disorganization in France; (d) general excellence of convention's choice.
4. The military presidents:
   (a) due to unequal education in different states and dazzling nature of militarism for uneducated; (b) due to jealousy and calumny of real leaders (e. g. Clay).
5. Electoral frauds:
   (a) growth of cities; (b) immigration of inferior foreign stocks; (c) allegations of fraud in Clay-Polk election; (d) inadequate safeguards of purity of ballot; (e) a real danger for America and even more for

European imitators, Europe's vices being more deeply rooted.

This series of articles by Chevalier attracted wide attention. Its progress was noted and discussed. One paper presented an analysis of the article on the bicameral system.[1] Another remarked:

The *Journal des débats* is still at its studies on the constitution of the United States. Revolutions do not change it, street-battles do not make it interrupt an article once commenced. What we read in its columns in the month of May, we find there at the end of July. M. Michel Chevalier is informing us today how the Yankee constitution was made. The article has four full columns.[2]

A satirical article appeared, entitled *Le Sabbat du Frère Michel*, ridiculing Chevalier's philosophizing on religious conditions, and concluding:

You should not have condemned the constitutional monarchy after only thirty years of experiment. That "only" is adorable! That "only" betrays you, brother Michel; believe us, leave your homilies about Sunday and cease disguising yourself as an Anglo-Saxon to preach in the *Journal des débats*. You are not and you never will be anything but a constitutional royalist, brother Michel Chevalier.[3]

The same paper published a burlesque Chevalier article with the same title as the original, in which the cup-and-saucer story was given as the real origin of the bicameral system and a political evolution represented as taking place in the northern and western states

[1] *Siècle*, July 17.
[2] *Ère nouvelle*, July 23.
[3] *Charivari*, May 26.

toward the ideas of order and conservatism represented by the monarchical formula. . . . It is useless to dissimulate, the Americans have long understood the inconveniences of democracy. Quite a powerful party has even been formed at New Yorck (*sic*) to offer the crown to Prince Louis Napoleon. By a lingering amour-propre the Yankees do not yet dare to raise openly the standard of constitutional monarchy, but the moment is not distant when these last scruples will disappear. *Et nunc intelligite*, you who would found a republic in France.[1]

Chevalier's chair in the Collège de France was suppressed (though before the articles began), and the antipathy of the radicals was so well known that their chief organ felt it necessary to deny as an unworthy calumny the rumors that his dismissal was the reply of Louis Blanc to Chevalier's attacks on his doctrines.[2]

Another series of articles was that by Clarigny in the *Constitutionnel* of June 5, 10, 24, July 3, Sept. 5, 11, Oct. 11, under the title " Des Institutions républicaines en France et aux Etats-Unis."

His general point of view is made sufficiently clear by an extract from his first article in which he expresses his wish to discuss how far this American constitution,

one of the least imperfect works that has proceeded from human hands, is applicable to our state of society with our political customs. . . . What pleases us especially in the constitution of the United States is the minute care, the scrupulous attention that American legislators have employed not to touch human liberty needlessly and to respect as far as possible the fullness of the rights of the citizen. This is the example which our legislators should have perpetually before their eyes. Without speaking indeed of communism and of socialism, which, leading to absolute centralization, are the

[1] *Charivari*, July 12.
[2] *Réforme*, Apr. 16.

very negation of liberty, one cannot disguise the fact that ideas of an exaggerated centralization prevail among the men in power today, and are the dearest dreams of the school which pretends to govern.[1]

The first of the articles was " On the rights of the state." It discussed from the standpoint of political theory the true function of the state, the two opposite dangers, excess of liberty and excess of centralization, the American emphasis on the former, the French on the latter.

The second article, " On the division of powers," expounded autocracy and demagogy (direct popular government) as alike failures, being hostile to the true principle of delegated authority; the centralist school secures equality, but not liberty; power must be divided as well as delegated, the judiciary being co-ordinate with the other two branches; exaggeration of executive power, as in Lamennais' scheme, easily leads to the tyranny of a Jackson, pretending to represent the people against the bourgeoisie, with possible power greater than a king; if the legislative elects the executive, it in turn becomes too powerful; the American constitution is a good example of Montesquieu's sound philosophy; the state constitutions also illustrate it, as Maryland, the Carolinas, Georgia, Virginia, Massachusetts; thus American practice supports the contention of the liberal school.

The third article, " On the legislative power," expounded the advantages of the dual system in preventing the tyranny of a single assembly, delaying hasty legislation, preventing plots and providing stability, closing with Washington's position on the matter.

The fourth article, also " On the legislative power," refuted objections to the dual system (that it had no meaning except in a federal system, being a mere reunion of ambas-

---

[1] *Constitutionnel,* June 5.

sadors, and that if the two chambers are composed of the same elements, one will be useless, if of different elements, one will be aristocratic), replying to the former that the Senate has power of initiating legislation, to the latter, that the dilemma is purely theoretical. The remainder of the article described the organization of American Senates and suggested a possible French arrangement along similar lines (the department being the unit and election made by municipal councils or by representatives of manufacture, agriculture and commerce); the dual system retained eminent men in public life and was well adapted to try impeachments; the council of state was no proper substitute.

The fifth article, " On the executive power," pointed out that the executive must be strong enough to maintain order, yet powerless against liberty, which made its proper organization the greatest difficulty in a constitution; that in Athens the executive perished under demagogy, in Rome it became all-powerful; that the Consulate and the Directory proved the necessity of unity; that an executive council has all the faults of a multiple executive and was eliminated by New York at its first revision; that the American solution of the appointment problem, whereby the President chooses his ministers and personal agents freely, while the Senate confirms judges, diplomats and others having more personal initiative, is a happy one; that a single chamber is not adapted for such confirmation.

The sixth article, continuing the same subject, held that, as in America, the President should command the army and navy, prohibition of such command being no safeguard against usurpation; that except in amnesties he should have power of pardon without intervention of minister of justice or council of state, which brought the case into politics; should have right of receiving ambassadors and negotiating treaties with aid of Senate, right of promulgating laws and of suspensive veto; should be empowered to summon extraordinary sessions of the legislature, rather than leaving it in the hands of a committee of the latter, as in the French project.

The seventh article, concluding the study of this office and ending the series, praised the American executive as an independent, effective power, having unity of person, direct and universal election, a four-year term with indefinite possibility of re-election and a veto against all legislation passed by a bare majority; considered the new French office indefinite, despite universal election and the four-year term, his only clear function being promulgation of laws, with a futile right of demanding a new deliberation; held that the very vagueness of his functions added to the single chamber and centralization might easily lead to usurpation; hence came demand for his election by the Assembly; the arguments in support were the agitation of popular elections, evil effects of party spirit, possible opposition between independent President and Assembly or his tyranny over latter; arguments against were destruction of executive power, separation of powers ignored, inevitable legislative tyranny, these being conclusive; that the four-year interval before re-election in the new project was bad, for mobility of events would preclude re-elections and it was not fitting that the President hold minor offices in the interim; the American four-year term was a mean between that of the House, whose entire renewal gave chance for protest, and that of the Senate, whose permanence meant stability; that re-election was a stimulus to excellence and reward of merit, the tendency of democracies being to shorten terms; repeated arguments against election by the Assembly, pointing out the nominal character of the American electoral college; and ended by showing the importance of the Vice-President in America and his futility under the French project, which debarred him from succession.

Régis de Trobriand had a short series in the *Presse,* called " Etude sur la constitution générale des Etats-Unis d'Amérique," appearing May 12, 13.

The first study was on the legislative power, the second on the executive, both being résumés of the American system rather than elaborate discussions of the Chevalier and Clarigny type.

Trobriand was also an enthusiast and commenced his article thus :

All that concerns the United States is today of high interest. . . . The United States of America are without contradiction the glorious, pure cradle of modern democracy. . . . What is the secret of this unexampled progress? . . . It is the constitution of the state, a magnificent work which has developed all instincts, encouraged all enterprises, safeguarded all rights and given scope to genius of every sort.

Study of this great nation, known here so little because of English jealousy, is of peculiar value at the present; Tocqueville and Chevalier have written on it. The federal system forbids complete application of its constitution here; we shall study only institutions capable of adaptation to our purpose.[1]

A series appeared in *L'Ère nouvelle,* July 17, 23, 30, 31, Sept. 5,[2] under the caption, " Etudes sur la constitution.— Pouvoir exécutif et législatif." While a study of the French constitution, references to the American document are numerous and the second article is practically a comparison of the two. This article contained the interesting passage :

We are hardly out of monarchy; and as if we were slaves,

---

[1] *Presse,* May 12.

[2] This was the sixth article; the fifth is missing.

freshly emancipated, we pretend that there is not on the earth a people which can equal us in popular doctrines and institutions. Up to the present, the example of North America remained for the boldest thinkers, a sort of ideal beyond which vague dreams of our liberty hardly strayed. The success of the United States and their growing prosperity since the war of independence, were the favorite argument and privileged example, which the greatest liberals of Europe placed complacently before the adoration of their thinking. One could not even make them concede what seemed evident to sensible minds, that the republican forms of the Union, because of profound differences of history, customs, territory and national temperament, might be beyond the strength and needs of France. But on the 23rd of February, 1848, all the least anticipated desires of our republicans *de la veille* would have certainly been contented, by permitting them to apply the political forms of North America immediately on French ground. Today their improvised application seems no longer to content anyone among us. What still suffices for the growth and liberty of the United States, long since republican, already suffices no longer for the destinies of France, recently monarchical, which has not yet written the first formula of its new republicanism.

Examples follow at considerable length, the American system of indirect presidential election being contrasted with the new French essay at universal suffrage, " under the radical inspiration of M. Louis Blanc," the age-limit, residence qualification, suspensive veto, constitutional amendment clauses, executive command of army and navy, and two-chamber provisions of the American document compared to their advantage with the corresponding arrangements of the proposed French constitution. " What we have just said suffices to show with what systematic and quite French preoccupation our legislators have determined to differentiate themselves from America." [1]

<hr>

[1] *Ère nouvelle*, July 23.

In addition to studies already mentioned,[1] the *Siècle* printed an " Essai sur les principes démocratiques qui peuvent régir la France républicaine " by Major Poussin. The burden of this essay, as may be supposed, was:

Adopt first the great principles of the American constitution; they have been tested for more than three quarters of a century, in the midst of the most critical as well the most varied circumstances, through which that great nation has been called to pass: they have perfectly responded to the exigencies of war and of peace, to grave party differences, to commercial crises, to territorial jealousies, finally to the radical division of opinion which separates free from slave labor.

These and other considerations commended the adoption of the great American principles, which he proceeded to enumerate as follows: equal rights of all to liberty, security, property, education; popular sovereignty; universal, direct suffrage; the right of bearing arms; universal eligibility to office; incompatibility of legislative and other office; liberty of conscience, separation of Church and State; liberty of teaching; free instruction in all grades; liberty of press and of public meeting; local self-government, the central authority providing for all national services; gradual reduction of the army, but increase of the navy; encouragement of art, industry, agriculture and commerce by periodical reports and national aid; the executive, legislative and judicial departments as provided for in the constitution; trial by jury; no council of state; taxation on uniform, not progressive basis. Then followed a discussion of how far these principles are adaptable to French conditions, in the course of which he refuted the aristocracy argument against the Senate; showed the similarity of customs and character in the two countries, from their common base of popular sov-

[1] *Supra*, p. 284 *et seq.*

ereignty assured by universal suffrage, their common control of public force through the militia idea and their common social equality, based on testamentary laws; indicated that the inferior condition of French labor might be improved by reducing taxes on food-stuffs; suggested that African conquests may be to France what Texas is to America, by giving room for expansion and furnishing new products; insisted that popular education in France must be brought up to the American standard; and concluded: " I maintain that France may receive a democratic organization almost similar to that of the United States, while preserving for the republic the unitary character which constitutes the glory, the power, the prosperity of our country and the fairest title of our nationality!" [1]

Three papers appeared in the *Journal* for Aug. 14, 17, 27, entitled " Les Etats-Unis et la France démocratique," bearing the signature, L. Xavier Eyma. The first two were social rather than constitutional. The opening article stated as a general premise that " at this moment many people in France are turning their attention to the New World," some hoping to borrow illumination from the hearth of liberty, others wondering in terror if a republic is a safe form of government. " I do not wish to say that human perfection has sought refuge in the United States, concentrating there on a few million individuals, to the detriment of the rest of the universe." But it cannot be denied that calmness of reason, love of material and mental order, a patriotism which sacrifices personal to general interests and an ardent national amour-propre are characteristic of Americans and form part of the secret of their national greatness, which deserves careful scrutiny by French students. With this introduction, he discussed the facts of American pros-

[1] *Siècle*, May 26.

perity, its immense energy, the happy relations of social classes, and adduced as cause the immense opportunity for labor and the high esteem in which it was held.

The second paper was a glowing description of elections in the United States, their calmness, lack of serious party conflict, acceptance of the verdict, etc.

The third discussed presidential elections, the electoral college and its evolution into a machine for registering the popular will, re-elections, requirements for office and the convention system, ending with the statement that the interest of the masses was more attached to the state, its constitution being more democratic than that of the Union, which came into little contact with daily life; the educated classes and the press were more interested in federal matters.

Several months later an unsigned article, but apparently by the same author, called " Les Etats-Unis et la France démocratique; Quelques lignes d'histoire " came out, encouraging France by an account of the severe trials through which America passed, her troubles with the Tories and with her first inadequate form of government, before she received " that great and fair constitution which today protects the American Union," and how Washington and Congress never lost hope in Providence or in republican principles.[1]

A study " Du Pouvoir Exécutif " was made by G. Dufour, " Avocat au Conseil d'Etat " in a legal review, in which much use was made of Tocqueville's Démocratie.[2]

Not all of the series of articles so published were friendly to America, however. The most conspicuously hostile was that written by Félix de Courmont, called " Esquisse d'une

[1] Journal, Oct. 23.

[2] Revue de législation et de jurisprudence, Nouv. Série, vol. 10, pp. 141, 142, 330; vol. 11, pp. 40, 41, 59, 60 n.

république," in *L'Opinion publique* for July 3, 9,[1] 12, 29,
Aug. 5, 10. If certain writers were prejudiced in favor of
America, Courmont was no less extravagant in his opposition. He was not only bitterly hostile, but his statements
were often absurdly inaccurate, or grossly exaggerated. He
mistranslated his English quotations, whether by accident
or wilfully. So a passage from Marshall's " Life of Washington," asserting that the constitution was ratified largely
on the character of its makers, he twisted to mean by dint
of personal pressure. A sentence from Harriet Martineau,
reading, " My book comes to an end, but I offer no conclusion of my subject; American society itself constitutes but
the first pages of a great book of events, into whose progress
we can see but a little way, and that but dimly," he translated, " Mon oeuvre touche à sa fin, mais je ne prétendrai
aucune conclusion; la société américaine forme les pre-
mières pages d'un livre gros d'événemens, ces pages sont
obscures et je n'y vois qu'une faible trace destinée au
progrès." [2]

There is no special sequence of thought in his rambling
articles, which deal with social even more than constitutional conditions.

In the first article, Courmont stated his problem as a
study of the question: Is the United States a model of
social progress? Its answer required an examination of the
purity of its political customs and of its family life. Tocqueville gives a false picture, fitting facts to his theories.
Government spies abound in ordinary life, there is the
utmost ease of arrest.

The article of July 9 portrayed the disillusionment of
immigrants, their plunder by swindlers, corruption of magis-

---

[1] Numbered iii in the *Opinion publique;* the issues for July 5, 6, 8
are missing from the file in the Bibl. Nat., Paris.

[2] *Opinion publique,* July 29.

trates, horrors of prisons, legislation favoring the rich, pity and justice being nothing against gold, and the contrasting splendor of Nature.

The next article dealt with the lack of artistic apprecia- tion, the amount of suffering in the United States, Con- gress' denunciation of the Mexican War, an alleged re- quirement of American laws that children be sent from home at the age of nine to make their fortunes,[1] asserted that moral conditions were equal to the most dissolute epochs of antiquity, that debts were commonly repudiated (citing the case of Mississippi and the general bankruptcy law of 1841), that Mexico was invaded from greed, that the financial situation was perilous and electoral conditions corrupt.

The letter of July 29 reviewed the evil social conditions thus presented, and questioned whether the form of gov- ernment could be as perfect as supposed; the root difficulty was a conflict between the aristocratic and democratic ele- ments; a good spirit existed at the time of the Declaration of Independence, but Americans could not get rid of the English taint; the revolution was political not social; liberty insulted by continuance of slavery; the constitution adopted by frauds, the debts of the Confederation so great that tea was taxed and discontent universal until Washington, a pure and great man, presided over the " congrès de Cin- cinnatus," which adopted the constitution; after his death, the banks became headquarters for intrigues of privilege, then came bankruptcy and political corruption; uneven rep- resentation in the House shows an inequality, which makes

---

[1] " Les lois de l'Ohio font un devoir aux pères de famille de renvoyer de chez eux leurs enfants quand ils ont atteint l'âge de neuf ans, à moins qu'ils n'aient une fortune à leur donner. L'état de l'Ohio n'est pas le seul où cette loi existe." This extraordinary statement was re- peated in the Aug. 10 article.

impossible the fraternal spirit and other conditions named by Washington as necessary to the country's existence; the Senate is useless; the dual system came from England, where it arose as a conflict between Saxons and Normans.

On Aug. 5, Courmont depicted the conflict between the ideas of Washington and Adams, representing the English system of money aristocracy; Adams' " Defence " held it a vain idea to base liberty on virtue; " who then can be astonished that in the United States the poor is an object of contempt, virtue a proof of feebleness, and Christian morality the dream of a sick imagination;" America is perhaps good for the Irish, who thus escape the severer English yoke, but ridiculous as a model for France; Aristotle's middle class and the necessary belief in human perfectibility are not found in the United States; there is no universal suffrage; the Senate, chosen by indirect election, does not represent the people; the two chambers were in Adams' view a palliative to liberal ideas, till the time when nominations to the principal posts should be for life and finally hereditary.

The concluding article renewed the discussion of political corruption, supported here as elsewhere by concrete illustrations; stated that the egoist Adams by his maxim that love of democracy and frugality were non-existent in a republic had sown on American soil cupidity, hypocrisy and sacrilegious forgetfulness of family bonds; charged that family affections were replaced by coldness and avarice, that America was a land of perjury and that the jury in civil matters was a farce.

A series of three letters by Aug. Billiard, addressed "Aux auteurs du projet de constitution," was published in the *Réforme*, in which various uncomplimentary references to America were made. "The first condition of making a republican constitution, is to be oneself republican." Is there anything truly republican in the American system, which unites a people's force and intelligence for one or two objects and divides them for the rest, a system productive of egoism rather than fraternity and recalling the " chacun chez soi et pour soi " of a so-called republican member of the commission? [1]

In the third letter, he made the statement: " The delegation of its powers which it [Congress] makes to the President, while it is not in session, is one of the capital vices of the American constitution." [2]

Two letters signed Duverne, *avocat*, appeared in the *Bien public* for July 15 and Aug. 8, directed against the American bicameral system. The first explained it as an imitation of English colonial charters and as due to the jealousy of the small states; the second quoted Jefferson's Augeanstable letter and refuted the arguments for the dual system, much as had been done elsewhere.

The *Constitutionnel*, despite its strongly pro-American position, printed a series of six articles entitled " Les Républicaines " by Alexandre Weill, in which he visited republics, ancient and modern, with unsparing condemnation. In the last of the series he admitted that " the American republic, founded to safeguard national independence, is the only one which, the day after its victory, thanks to Washington, gave thought to liberty." Its conservative administrative system and its great territories have preserved it so far, but democratic elements are entering and trouble is at hand.[3]

In the *Assemblée nationale* appeared an " Examination of the constitutional project," opposing the presidential sys-

[1] *Réforme*, Sept. 22.
[2] *Ibid.*, Oct. 10.
[3] *Constitutionnel*, Aug. 6.

tem as dangerous in view of the absence of checks and balances.

The watchword had been given after Feb. 24th by the friends of the men who dreamed of presidency and dictatorship, perhaps; this watchword was imitation of the United States republic; but in the United States (besides historical, geographic, social differences, which make any comparison with France so impossible), there is a president confronting two chambers, that is to say there is that trinity of guarantees, which assures a true, useful, pacific discussion. Have you transported these guarantees into your constitutional project? Not in the least.

A single assembly, a useless council of state, mean a duel to the death and the despotism of legislative or executive.

The comparison between the French republic and that of the United States is then as false as was that of the representative monarchy of the Bourbons of the older or younger branch with the constitutional aristocracy of Great Britain. The Bourbons of the two branches were lost by a false imitation of English institutions, inapplicable to French civil society, as the present republic would compromise itself by the copy of American institutions, which do not agree with the national character. So much the more, if in copying them, one should leave out the few guarantees they would build up against the excesses of French democracy. . . . Imitations make revolutions. True institutions must be indigenous.[1]

Besides these series of articles, there were many single letters on various phases of the American system.

Lamennais praised the presidential system. For sixty years there had been no attempt at usurpation in America, whose democracy had developed strength daily. " It seems to us that this example has some weight." [2]

[1] *Assemblée nationale*, June 21.
[2] *Peuple constituant*, May 24.

The " Comité Central du Droit National," representing legitimist interests, proposed that the nation be polled on the two-chamber and the executive questions, the latter being phrased thus : " Is it desirable that the president of the republic be named like the President of the United States by the totality of Frenchmen, who should declare in their vote, if it should be for a term, for life or by heredity ?" [1]

F. Saint-Priest, member of the Assembly, defended the validity of American example on the bicameral question, showing that the states and cities employed it as well as the federal government, and quoting from " Adam " and " Levington " (sic) as typical American publicists.[2]

Universal suffrage in America was said by one Ferrari to " lay hold of the boldest projects, to realize them with the suddenness of thought." [3]

A long report on the American public school system by Xavier Eyma was reprinted in the *Atelier* of Apr. 12.

A " former magistrate," writing on the judiciary, called attention " in the interest of liberty " to the fact that " in Turkey the judges are removable; in the United States they are not." [4]

The history of American land speculation was given at considerable length by the *Liberté* of Aug. 27.

American prosperity was traced in part to the non-interference of the state in individual matters and in the untrammelled liberty to work, by Wolowski,[5] J. Magne,[6] and

[1] *Gazette de France*, Apr. 5.

[2] *Union*, Sept. 25.

[3] *Peuple constituant*, Mar. 1.

[4] *Univers*, July 10.

[5] *Siècle*, Mar. 20.

[6] *Revue britannique*, vol. 16, p. 131.

Chevalier.[1]   The latter also showed how the United States, free from the demon of militarism, was able to devote vast sums to material development,[2] while the statistical account of this progress was depicted by Cordier, member of the Assembly, in glowing terms; " already the American Union may be proclaimed heir presumptive of Britannic power." [3]

" An American," in a four-column letter, dated New York, Apr. 29, entitled " La liberté en Amérique," laid great stress on local self-government and the development of business corporations, commending also French interest in the American constitution.[4]

Léon Faucher criticized unfavorably the absence of direct legislative initiative on the part of the American administration.[5]

The religious liberty prevalent in America was praised by Cardinal Bonald, Archbishop of Lyons, in a pastoral circular to the clergy of his diocese,[6] and by Montalembert,[7] while Chevalier's first article in the *Journal des débats* started a controversy between the Protestant *Semeur*, claiming American success as the fruit of Protestant tolerance, and the Catholic *Ère nouvelle*, which in two four-column articles contrasted Bancroft's account of the intolerance of colonial Virginia, Massachusetts and New York [8] with the religious freedom of Catholic Maryland, ascribing the present-day liberty of worship throughout the country to the isolation of the original colonies, the influx of settlers from

---

[1] *Journal des débats*, June 2.
[2] *Revue des deux mondes*, vol. 21, pp. 1083, 1085.
[3] *Gazette de France*, Feb. 29.
[4] *Univers*, June 10.
[5] *Siècle*, Oct. 9.
[6] *Univers*, Mar. 4.
[7] *Ibid.*, Feb. 28.
[8] *Ère nouvelle*, Oct. 23.

all parts of Europe, the necessity of common defense against the French and Indians and later against the English.[1]

Such were the chief special articles in the Paris press on American example. Mention might also be made of a poster, placed on the walls by the "Association pour la liberté des échanges," with the heading " Subsistances publiques. La vie à bon marché," in which it was stated that the average ration of an Englishman was double that of a Frenchman, and that of " a free citizen of the United States " double that of an Englishman; that the governments which love their people have abolished all food taxes and that the hand of a United States legislator would wither before it would sign a law which would increase the price of meat or bread.[2]   The identity of the last clause with language used by Chevalier [3] suggests that the *affiche* was from his pen.

And at the other end of the scale, the members of the Institute listened to Tocqueville reading a paper on a book about Swiss democracy, in which his mode of treatment was to compare the American and Swiss constitutions, to the detriment of the latter.[4]

The most important books on America have already been mentioned.[5]   A complete list will be found in the bibliography. But some reference should be made here to the motives inspiring the publication of a part of this literature and to any fresh contribution of theory it may have made to the subject.

At least a dozen pamphlets were published during 1848 containing the text of the United States constitution, either

---

[1] *Ère nouvelle,* Oct. 30.

[2] *Murailles révolutionnaires,* vol. I, p. 352.

[3] *Revue des deux mondes,* vol. 21, p. 1085.

[4] *Moniteur,* Apr. 14, 18.

[5] *Supra,* ch. iii.

alone or bound with past French constitutions or, very rarely, with those of other countries. The spirit of such publications may be gauged by reference to the preface of several of these collections.

France is about to be called to give itself a republican constitution. It is by study and meditation that preparation should be made for so great and useful a work. . . . Under these circumstances, I have thought it fitting to reunite in one volume all the constitutions which have ruled France since 1789; the declaration of the rights and duties of man and the citizen; the ordinances, decrees, proclamations of the provisional government of 1848 and the constitution of the United States of America. By means of the comparison of their articles, it will be seen what are the great principles which have successively passed through all our constitutions.[1]

But I perceive that I have implicitly settled an important question, that of the adoption by France and its representatives, of the United States form of government; as to that, I have a complete, well settled conviction that we shall be forever happy from such a decision. Therefore I humbly, but with firmness, supplicate my fellow-citizens to make the candidates for the deputation or the national representation explain themselves clearly, and to find out from them if they have fixed ideas on the subject of the constitution to adopt, and of the legislative and executive government which must be founded.[2]

The republic alone is henceforth possible. It exists, it is accepted. It needs only to be founded on rational and durable bases, a great and laborious task which demands experience and foresight, knowledge of ancient and contemporary institutions, especially of national customs and tendencies.[3]

Sometimes the motive was more special, as in the case of

[1] Louis Tripier, *Les Constitutions françaises,* pref.
[2] Fabius Jalaber, *Constitution des Etats-Unis d'Amérique,* p. 24.
[3] J. B. J. Pailliet, *Constitutions américaines et françaises,* p. xxxix.

the anonymous individual who produced his version of the American constitution for twenty-five centimes, with the declaration:

In publishing this translation, which the moderation of its price places within the reach of all readers, our object has been to show that American society, the most democratic of all societies which have ever existed, has recognized the necessity of two chambers: a Senate and a House of Representatives.[1]

Another anonymous translator, in publishing " the immortal work of the Franklins, the Adamses, the Washingtons, which for sixty years has assured the prosperity and well-being of an immense country," notes that "what dominates in this constitution is the existence of three powers, which sustain and fortify one another, but cannot act separately." [2]

Occasionally the motive was less friendly.

We have joined to this constitution [of 1848] those which have preceded it, and under the rule of which we have already lived, God knows how, and that of the United States of America, which has long been given us as the *ne plus ultra* of this species. It goes without saying that we do not intend to judge the merit of the work of the legislators who produced them.[3]

" If we have added to the collection of French constitutions the constitution of the United States, it is to diminish, so far as possible, the number of those who talk on every occasion of institutions about which they know nothing." [4]

Other pamphlets made use of American example, with-

[1] *Const. des Etats-Unis d'Amérique*, p. ii.

[2] *La République des Etats-Unis*, p. 3.

[3] G. de Champeaux, *Constitution républicaine de 1848*, p. ii.

[4] M., *Constitutions de la république française*, p. iii.

out reprinting the entire text, in support of some constitutional point or some ideal reconstruction, borrowing from it as they saw fit.

So Pitray thought it the part of wisdom to take America as model in three matters: the organization of the legislative and executive power, their election by the people, the short duration of their term of office.[1]

Magne laid stress on the threefold division of powers and would have a senate of 240 members elected indirectly by departments for a six-year term, one-third renewed every two years; a house of 480 elected directly every two years by small districts; a president elected directly for five years; a judiciary for life; proper provision for amendments.[2]

Garnier criticized the American Senate's mode of election and mobility as deficient in guarantees of capacity and continuous policy; the lack of legislative membership for ministers of state; the inversion of the initiative and veto, the first of which should belong to the government ordinarily, the second to the assembly. He applauded, however, the single executive, the bicameral system, legislators' ineligibility to other office, removal of the judiciary from politics by releasing it from all penalty except dismissal and by the principle of permanency of tenure, which should be extended by the formation of a real Civil Service.[3]

Chambrun wanted the president to be a neutral power, above parties, holding the balance between the chambers; in this respect the American system was faulty.[4]

America's financial system seemed to one writer to have been conclusive for France.

[1] Pitray, *Que préférer*, p. 7.

[2] J. Magne, "Esquisse d'une constitution" in *Revue britannique*, vol. 15 (6th series), p. 153; published also separately.

[3] A. Garnier, *De l'organization du pouvoir*, p. 19.

[4] A. de Chambrun, *La république réformiste*, p. 16, note.

The English race presents the world the striking example of two nations, equally prosperous and powerful, under two totally opposite régimes. . . . In one, in fact, no common debt, and in consequence, absolute liberty and independence of the citizen with respect to the authorities. In the other, a crushing debt which rallies around the throne all the interests and vital forces of the country. . . . Of these two examples, France has chosen that of the young American republic.[1]

More often the interest was purely constitutional. The single executive and dual legislature as known in America appealed to many.[2] One enthusiast insisted: "The senate of the French republic must be the reproduction of the American Senate. Like the latter, it must participate at once in the legislative, the executive and the judicial power."[3]

By others, the American practice in these matters was condemned.[4] A peculiarly bitter attack on America, chiefly from the social viewpoint, was made by an unreconstructed legitimist, who borrowed the style and even the stories of Félix de Courmont, not always giving due credit to his source. The republic as a form of government was a retrograde step; "'But that of the United States,' some one will say, 'has been maintained and strengthened?' That is true up to now. 'It is a model government,' is added. That is much more contestable." The constitution was established by parliamentary trickery; it would never have been sanctioned by the people, for it hurt too many inter-

---

[1] F. A. Fournier Saint-Auge, *Du rachat de la dette consolidé par l'impot foncier.* Archives Nationales, BB^{30} 320 B.

[2] *E. g.,* H. Colombel, *Quelques réflexions,* pp. 7, 11; A^{te} Nougarède de Fayet, *De la constitution républicaine,* pp. 5, 9.

[3] P. M. Le Mesl. *Considérations,* p. 8.

[4] *E. g.,* L. Cormenin, *Petit Pamphlet,* pp. 15, 30; F. Berriat Saint-Prix, *Plan de constitution,* p. 19.

ests. Federalism, inequality, worship of the golden calf, corruption, lack of art, absence of liberty were among American characteristics.

And one would counsel us to implant the American republic on the soil of the French monarchy? But it would first be necessary to transform French character entirely, to extinguish its spirit, chill its imagination and break its memories. That would be to forbid its glory. Could you grow an Egyptian palm on the coasts of Norway? Could you make a Spanish gipsy out of an English Methodist? Could you build the famous ice palace from the banks of the Neva on the border of the Hellespont? No. All these ideas are absurd, all these chimeras are mad; and we shall be no more American citizens than we could become Persian dervishes.[1]

Courmont, besides the series of newspaper articles, had already written a book in 1847, savagely denouncing America, " that young graybeard which the worm of demagogy is devouring under its purple mantle," yet which was unhappily placed by certain people " not only on an equality with France, but even above our beautiful country." [2]   It is interesting that these two unusually vicious attacks came from the extreme right wing rather than the left.

Mention might also be made of one or two other books, written before the February Revolution. One published in 1842 has the double interest of showing that America was even then suggested as an object of study and that the Orleanists felt very differently about its validity, so long as their own system was in operation.[3]   The author wished to prove " that France is at least the equal of nations which are proposed to it as models by publicists more skillful in the art of speech than in knowledge of facts," nations built

---

[1] Vᵗᵉ D'Arlincourt, *Dieu le veut*, pp. 47-53.

[2] Courmont, *Des Etats-Unis, de la guerre de Mexique*, p. 29 et seq.

[3] On this point, *cf. supra*, p. 244.

on crushing aristocracy or vulgar democracy, and that " to judge by the avidity with which eulogy of the English parliamentary government or the American popular government are received, one would think a great contempt existed for our own institutions; but it is more reasonable to believe in a great ignorance of those same institutions." [1]

On the other hand, in 1832, Murat had already written that practical liberty was obtainable only in the United States. " It is not the constitution and the laws of the United States that I admire and love so much, as the reason that brings it about that the United States have this constitution and these laws. . . . This principle . . . is that which they call in America *self-government.*" The July revolution had made only a small advance. Lafayette understood republican institutions as he did, *à l'américaine.* To Murat these institutions meant destruction of political police, free movement on the part of any citizen, election of representatives by the people, not by a bourgeois aristocracy, an elective senate in place of the Chamber of Peers, initiative of legislators the ordinary method of presenting laws, a real right of petition, responsibility of ministers and inferior employés established, plural office-holding forbidden, commerce freed by abolition of monopolies and octrois, a system of customs duties, protecting industry without forcing it in unnatural routes, a detailed budget, abolition of sinecures and useless expense, cessation of efforts to influence the courts in political cases, something analogous to habeas corpus, mandamus and quo warranto for the protection of liberty, assurance of execution of laws and prevention of usurpation, decentralization of communes, cities and even departments, giving them the right to elect magistrates, dispose revenues, and tax themselves if not interfering with interior commerce, the replacing of the pleasure of gover-

[1] Charles Farcy, *Etudes politiques*, p. 11 *et seq.*

nors by the will of the governed, the adoption of a foreign policy worthy of France, not meddling in the plots of kings, not tying its hands with dogmas of intervention or the opposite, but following its own interests and glory. These hopes were all deceived. " But at present it is the American Union which gives us the best model of government." [1]

This lengthy bill of particulars is interesting as showing that the republicans of Orleanist days gave other reasons for admiring America than those put forth by the *républicains du lendemain* in 1848.

The economic individualism of America and the political self-sufficiency of local communities had always found admirers among French disciples of the Manchester school, however, and were frequently stressed in the later period.

So Laboulaye wrote:

In that country where liberty has given such fine fruits, they are far from charging the government with acting, foreseeing and almost thinking for the citizens; on the contrary, it is to the individual, to the family, to corporations, to communities, to free association that the state commits the greatest part of the social movement, remaining for its part in the higher sphere of general interests, and never descending into those of private interests. *Help yourself,* such is the political and social device of the American. Liberty suffices for everything in that state, where the national workshop, the association subsidized by the government, monopolies, the progressive tax, war on capital, have not yet been invented and where notwithstanding, work is more abundant and the workman better paid, better instructed, more influential than anywhere else; an example doubtless of small value, since socialism has not yet crossed the Atlantic to regenerate the New World on the pattern of ours, and to pour there the torrents of prosperity, with which we are inundated—in the future; but, an example good for meditation nevertheless, by all those alchemists who

[1] A. Murat, *Esquisse morale et politique des Etats-Unis,* pp. vi-xi, xxv.

think to regenerate France, by exhausting for the last four months, the generous blood from her veins, substituting for it the clear water of their theories.[1]

Such was also the whole burden of Dunoyer's treatment; France placed between two republics, toward one or the other of which she must move,

the American republic, and that which February socialism dreamed in France; a republic supremely liberal and another to which liberty is fundamentally repugnant; a republic where everyone is fully his own master and another where the individual is essentially dependent on the community; a republic which leaves as much as possible to private zeal for the initiative in everything and another which affects to leave it the initiative in nothing; etc.[2]

Several collections of letters and memoirs of a later date are also of interest.

The Baron de Barante, Orleanist diplomat and historian, writing to his eldest son, Prosper de Barante, then traveling in America, under date of Paris, July 17, 1848, said: "Work, liberty, prosperity, that is what you see in America, and that is what our revolutionists have destroyed in France. The conditions of a good republic are, morally speaking, the same as those of a constitutional monarchy. The English race has these conditions, we perhaps not." [3]

Another Orleanist statesman and historian, deputy in 1848, the Comte de Rémusat, felt that all liberal statecraft must pattern after American and English example, preferably the latter. " 'No America,' a crowd, which bordered the hedge in front of the grille of the legislative body, cried to us, I remember, one day when we were going into the

---

[1] Laboulaye, *Considérations*, pp. 43, 44.

[2] B. Dunoyer, *La révolution du 24 février*, p. 226.

[3] "Après la révolution de février" in *Revue de Paris*, vol. iii, p. 544.

Constituent Assembly of 1848. That was to cry: 'Long live the unknown!' "[1]

A conversation between provincials of Nantes, whether an individual or a typical occurrence it is hard to tell from the author's account, opened by the assertion of one that everybody is becoming a republican. "Isn't France as capable of governing itself as America?" To which came the reply, "Indeed, we must not be more stupid than the Americans, who have no king and conduct so large a trade."[2]

Quentin-Bauchart, a conservative and later an eminent imperialist, declared that there was no pretence of making the republic of 1848 after the pattern of the United States. There the ministers are the exclusive servants of the President. Not only do they form no part of the assemblies, they do not have the entrée even. The Americans, an eminently practical race, have a system of parliamentary government inconsistent with real republican principles; their government communicates with Congress only by messages, the executive power being completely independent of the other, within its sphere. In 1848 there was nothing of this sort in France.[3]

True as that was of the government party's attitude in 1848, it was not without important exceptions. Louis Blanc, who certainly should have known the real feeling of the Assembly, tells how he suggested abolishing the presidency, which would have cut short all Bonapartist pretensions. This idea met with small favor in the Assembly,

many of whose members regarded the presidency as a bridge thrown over between the republic and royalty. Shall I say it? Even among those who did not have that *arrière-pensée*,

---

[1] Charles de Rémusat, *Politique libérale*, p. 305.

[2] Ch. L. Chassin, *Félicien*, p. 46.

[3] Quentin-Bauchart, *Études et Souvenirs*, p. 217.

the majority found difficulty in conceiving a republic without a president! So much did the example of the United States of America blind them! So little did they comprehend the necessity of entirely subordinating the executive to the legislative power, everywhere that an immense standing army exists.[1]

To conclude this account of the impression made by America on the French mind of 1848, as revealed in literature, it is impossible not to cite the preface to Laboulaye's later history of the United States, largely the reproduction of his lectures of 1849-50 at the Collège de France. In Tocqueville, Chevalier and Laboulaye, more perhaps than in any other three intellectual leaders, enthusiasm for America became an absorbing passion.

As for me, in 1848, it was from the history of the United States that I had sought instruction. What had led me to that study was what I knew in general of the American constitution, and of the difficulties which liberty had had to conquer in the New World before performing its miracles there; and the more closely I viewed that great spectacle, the more I was struck by it as by a revelation. These were our faults and our sufferings, but with what courage and what wisdom the Americans had extricated themselves from the peril, and what a difference in their fashion of understanding and establishing liberty! One would have said that in the French constitutional project, our modern Lycurguses had expressly taken the opposite of American ideas and that their work was a denial of Washington's wisdom, a defiance hurled at the experience of ages. It was then that in a profound disquietude and sadness, I wrote, in July, 1848, the *Considérations sur la Constitution*, and that the feeling of danger drove me to join

---

[1] L. Blanc, *Hist. de la rév. de 1848*, vol. 2, p. 124. *Cf.* p. 326 *et seq.* for further remarks on the American executive, which he expected to make the substance of a speech during the constitutional debate, had he not been earlier proscribed.

to that publication the following letter, addressed to General Cavaignac by a man unfortunately too little known for him to listen to me in the midst of party cries and fury. . . . Named professor,[1] my duty was marked out [*écrit*]. It was to make America known to France, and to demand of it examples and assistance for the approaching storm. I began that study, therefore, with ardor and I neglected nothing to make a complete exposé of the events which had so direct an interest for us. Bancroft gave me the history of the colonies, which is the subject of this first volume; Story gave me the history of the constitution, but to these two authors, my constant guides, to whom I owe whatever value there is in this work, I added everything I could find from original documents and biographies. . . . As for me, I attached myself to it with passion and I do not know which instructed me more, the history of the colonies or that of the Revolution or the fashion in which that admirable constitution was made, that has given the United States an unexampled prosperity, and which after sixty years is younger and more popular than ever. . . . Such was the object of my course; such was the picture that I tried to fill in. More than once it seemed to me that the audience shared my ideas; but as for me, I lived in them, and it seemed to me that no publication could be more useful than a book in which America should speak to France, and communicate to it its own experience. Of small import was the author's merit, provided his work contained the substance of American ideas, and on this point which required only labor, I thought myself in position to satisfy the reader.[2]

[1] Of Comparative Legislation at the Collège de France, 1849.

[2] E. Laboulaye, *Histoire politique des Etats-Unis,* vol. 1, pp. iii-vi, xvii. The book was about to be published early in 1851, when the question of constitutional revision came up and the author wrote his *Révision de la constitution,* proposing a solution borrowed from the American system. The ensuing political upheavals postponed the larger work until 1855, when it was published without change from the original version.

CHAPTER VIII

CONCLUSIONS

It remains to sum up briefly the extent and trend of the influence exerted by American precedent on the French Assembly of 1848. In general, it is clear that the influence on the government party, the liberal republicans who controlled the Assembly, was slight. It was accordingly slight on the constitution which they framed.

A comparison of the two documents suggests analogies between the French Articles 26, 28, 36, 43, 44, 45, 48, 50, 52, 53, 54, 55, 58, 60, 64, 72, 87, 109, in whole or in part, and corresponding provisions in the American constitution. But in many cases this resemblance is no doubt accidental. Unless there is direct evidence in the arguments used in the commission or on the floor of the Assembly, influence cannot safely be predicated.

The incomplete record of the commission's discussions shows American example to have been urged on the suspensive veto [1] and the executive's appointment of the highest judicial court.[2] Of these, the first was modified, the second rejected. On the latter point, however, the Assembly reversed the commission's decision. Negatively, the alleged failure of the American system of immediate reeligibility to the presidential office seems to have been decisive in causing the defeat of that plan in the commission.[3]

[1] Supra, p. 157.
[2] Supra, p. 162.
[3] Supra, p. 158.

In the Assembly, it was asserted by a member of the commission that American precedent had been considered in fixing the basis of legislative representation.[1] A belief that such had been the case in regard to the Assembly's duty to choose among the five highest candidates for president, in case of no popular choice,[2] and in regard to the president's message,[3] was also asserted without contradiction.

It may almost certainly be added that the presidential office and the four-year term were due to American example. For this there is the evidence of the debate in the Assembly[4] and of contemporary discussion outside.

Beyond this, little can be said with assurance. American precedent may have been a factor in determining other issues, but there is no direct evidence that such was the case.

This meager result by no means indicates the amount of reference to American example, however, as is abundantly evident from the foregoing study. Without attempting to enumerate all the points on which that example was vainly urged, it is plain that the bicameral legislative system called forth by far the greatest number of references. The chief arguments against its use in this connection were the federal system and the assertion that it was itself an imitation of the aristocratic English model. The favorite reply to the former was that each American state used the dual system and that Pennsylvania had adopted it on discovering its necessity, while the greater volume of business and the greater need of checks and balances made it even more essential in a centralized government; to the latter, that America adopted it in spite of, rather than because of England, and that it could be so organized as to eliminate the

---

[1] *Supra*, p. 183.
[2] *Supra*, p. 192.
[3] *Supra*, p. 212.
[4] *Supra*, pp. 187 *et seq.*

danger of aristocracy. Indirect election, as illustrated in the American electoral college, was one of the alternatives suggested to a direct popular choice of the executive. This received less attention than the other alternative, election by the Assembly.

The absence of a bill of rights in the preamble to the American constitution was regarded with favor by a minority, though a counter-argument was found in the amendments by those who favored such a declaration. The example thus neutralized itself.[1]

The nature of the features most admired in the American system, the arguments used in their support and, above all, the known political attitude of those most interested in their adoption show unmistakably the character of the influence. With hardly any exception, it was conservative in politics, individualistic in economics. The liberals were cold, the radical republicans and socialists actively hostile. The former derived their strength from their majority in the Assembly and were anxious to maintain its power unimpaired by the addition of a second chamber; their great inconsistency was their defeat of the Grévy and Leblond amendments and their fatuous confidence that they would dominate future Assemblies, both errors arising from a mistaken judgment of the political temper of France at large. Whatever misgivings they had on this point found utterance in Lamartine's fatalistic *Alea jacta est.* Their adoption of the American executive sprang from the necessities of their position midway between monarchists and radicals. To avoid a reaction, they must not stir up unhappy memories of Convention and Directory; to avoid dominance by the Paris mob, they must establish universal suffrage. As republicans *de la veille*, who had come into

[1] *Supra*, pp. 165 *et seq.*

power through popular disgust at the restricted franchise, the doctrine of universal suffrage appealed to them for its own sake as a symbol of pure republican theory. Whether or not they felt assured that their confidence in the people would be practically justified, political conditions required them to make the venture.

The radical republicans opposed the American executive as well as the legislative example, because their political model was Jacobinism and their strength lay among the small shopkeepers of Paris. Ledru-Rollin's despatch of commissioners into the provinces in a hopeless endeavor to educate the peasantry in republican principles is evidence of his perfectly correct judgment of the situation. As matters stood, the provinces would never support Paris radicalism; the only chance for radical success lay in an all-powerful Assembly on the model of the Convention.

The socialists, desiring a complete reconstruction of society, could have no interest in a political system, which history had linked so closely with economic individualism.

But whatever slight hope of success the radical elements might have had was destroyed by the June insurrection. Just as Shays' rebellion in Massachusetts, embodying the vague discontent of the debtor class, helped to convert the stabler interests to the necessity of a strong national constitution, so this last upheaval of February idealism, impractical but dangerous, immeasurably strengthened the forces of conservatism. The full extent of the reaction was destined to destroy the republic; it was only partially embodied in the constitution of 1848. The short life of this unhappy document was due in part to its compromise character; it was not the product of a strong, consistent policy; the rival impulses of February and June, struggling for the mastery, each left their mark upon it. The drift after June was steadily conservative; the only question was how far it would go before the constitution received its final form. Not that new elections had returned the conservatives to power. The liberals were still in control, but they were under the shadow of a great fear. It may be fairly said that the constitution was framed by timidity. Fear of a possible Bonaparte despotism bore its part in the creation of a single chamber; fear of a socialist Convention brought forth a powerful executive in counterpoise. Thus two strong powers were placed vis-à-vis, but both annoyingly robbed of free action. The chamber had no control over the army nor the civil service; the president was not immediately re-eligible. The juxtaposition of two strong, dissatisfied powers produced an unstable equilibrium; the attempted checks (a council of state in one case, impeachment in the other) were illusory. Revolution became probable from whichever side happened to develop a strong, unscrupulous leader; it chanced that a Bonaparte appeared rather than a Robespierre. Had the president been given the right of re-election or had the chamber been given control of the army (in other words, had timidity not tried unduly to shackle strong men with petty bonds which they could and would break), the republic might have lived.

It is clear, then, that the constitution, like most political documents, was the product of circumstances rather than of dispassionate reflection, and that the liberals, even had they been more inclined to the American system than they were, would have felt themselves practically estopped from introducing it. Its friends, then, must come from the conservatives, who had no interest in the favor of Paris and no fear of a strong executive.

An interesting cleavage among the conservatives is, however, apparent. The legitimists were almost as opposed to American example as their opponents of the Left. Their royalist principles were too deeply rooted to allow any republican admirations, though they might and did make use of republican institutions, once founded, for their own advantage. Since their dynasty had not been in power immediately before the February Revolution, they escaped some of the odium attaching to the unfortunate Orleanists and could seek popularity by joining in the reprobation of the fallen system without discarding their own tenets. Realizing the conservative temper of the provinces, they could hope for an eventual restoration without adopting more than the thinnest republican disguise, when, indeed, they were willing to do even that. Their attachment to the Catholic establishment caused them to detest the American free church system, despite Lacordaire's propaganda.

The foregoing analysis leaves the ex-Orleanists as the pro-American party par excellence. Voltairean in religion, the absence of a state Church harmonized with their philosophic convictions. Having no loyalty to Henri V, and no hope of immediately restoring their own line, they were willing to try republicanism. The Orleanist dynasty had had too accidental a beginning and too brief a career to inspire sentimental affections, nor was its history adapted to develop them. The constitutional monarchy had been itself the adaptation of an alien form of government, as the legitimists never tired of pointing out, and could readily yield to a similar experiment. Anglo-Saxon models had always appealed to this party; they might hope to preserve the essentials of their system, by merely exchanging an English king for an American president. The bicameral system, indirect election, the suspensive veto were all part and parcel of the system of checks and balances to which they were deeply committed. Equally hostile to an absolute king and an absolute democracy, they sought support for their plutocratic interests in an upper chamber, of non-hereditary character. Their strength lay in the upper middle class, the great financial interests which had dominated the late régime; they had prospered by economic individualism and were willing to show enthusiasm for any political system that would protect and leave them alone. Such a system they believed they had found in America. Its strength, too, lay in the free, vigorous development of material resources; its government fostered the growth of industry and commerce. The Orleanists had two ideals of statecraft, order and liberty. Since their wealth lay in fluid capital, rather than in land as did that of the legitimists, public security and confidence were of even greater importance for them; their paper fortunes might be shattered by a turn of the Bourse. Liberty to carry on their undertakings without being hampered by government interference was only less essential. They, therefore, desired a strong government, but not too strong in any part; a system able to protect the country's peace from external and internal foes, but so adjusted by checks and balances that neither despot nor democrat could use it as an instrument of oppression. Jeffersonianism, as time had developed it, was a system made to their hand. From interest and conviction, the former supporters of the Orleanist monarchy welcomed American constitutional example; its theory and observed practice accorded so well with their views that they urged it unceasingly as a model for France. They failed because the February wave had not yet spent itself. If they had succeeded, there would have been no Second Empire.

APPENDIX

CONSTITUTION OF 1848

Préambule

En Présence de Dieu et au Nom du Peuple Français
L'Assemblée Nationale Proclame:

I. La France s'est constituée en République. En adoptant cette forme définitive de gouvernement, elle s'est proposé pour but de marcher plus librement dans la voie du progrès et de la civilisation, d'assurer une répartition de plus en plus équitable des charges et des avantages de la société, d'augmenter l'aisance de chacun par la réduction graduée des dépenses publiques et des impôts, et de faire parvenir tous les citoyens, sans nouvelle commotion, par l'action successive et constante des institutions et des lois, à un degré toujours plus élevé de moralité, de lumières et de bien-être.

II. La République française est démocratique, une et indivisible.

III. Elle reconnaît des droits et des devoirs antérieurs et supérieurs aux lois positives.

IV. Elle a pour principe la liberté, l'égalité et la fraternité. Elle a pour base la famille, le travail, la propriété, l'ordre public.

V. Elle respecte les nationalités étrangères, comme elle entend faire respecter la sienne, n'entreprend aucune guerre dans des vues de conquête, et n'emploie jamais ses forces contre la liberté d'aucun peuple.

VI. Des devoirs réciproques obligent les citoyens envers la République et la République envers les citoyens.

VII. Les citoyens doivent aimer la patrie, servir la République, la défendre au prix de leur vie, participer aux charges de l'État en proportion de leur fortune; ils doivent s'assurer, par le travail, des moyens d'existence, et, par la prévoyance, des ressources pour l'avenir; ils doivent concourir au bien-étre commun en s'entr'aidant fraternellement les uns les autres, et à l'ordre général en observant les lois morales et les lois écrites qui régissent la société, la famille et l'individu.

VIII. La République doit protéger le citoyen dans sa personne, sa famille, sa religion, sa propriété, son travail, et mettre à la portée de chacun l'instruction indispensable à tous les hommes; elle doit, par une assistance fraternelle, assurer l'existence des citoyens nécessiteux, soit en leur procurant du travail dans les limites de ses ressources, soit en donnant, à défaut de la famille, des secours à ceux qui sont hors d'état de travailler.

En vue de l'accomplissement de tous ces devoirs, et pour la garantie de tous ces droits, l'Assemblée nationale, fidèle aux traditions des grandes assemblées qui ont inauguré la Révolution française, décrète, ainsi qu'il suit, la Constitution de la République.

CONSTITUTION

CHAPITRE PREMIER

DE LA SOUVERAINETÉ

Article premier. La souveraineté réside dans l'universalité des citoyens français.

Elle est inaliénable et imprescriptible.

Aucun individu, aucune fraction du peuple ne peut s'en attribuer l'exercice.

CHAPITRE II

DROITS DES CITOYENS GARANTIS PAR LA CONSTITUTION

2. Nul ne peut être arrêté ou détenu que suivant les prescriptions de la loi.

3. La demeure de toute personne habitant le territoire français est inviolable; il n'est permis d'y pénétrer que selon les formes et dans les cas prévus par la loi.

4. Nul ne sera distrait de ses juges naturels.—Il ne pourra être créé de commissions ni de tribunaux extraordinaires, à quelque titre et sous quelque dénomination que ce soit.

5. La peine de mort est abolie en matière politique.

6. L'esclavage ne peut exister sur aucune terre française.

7. Chacun professe librement sa religion, et reçoit de l'État, pour l'exerçice de son culte, une égale protection. Les ministres, soit des cultes actuellement reconnus par la loi, soit de ceux qui seraient reconnus à l'avenir, ont le droit de reçevoir un traitement de l'État.

8. Les citoyens ont le droit de s'associer, de s'assembler paisiblement et sans armes, de pétitionner, de manifester leurs pensées par la voie de la presse ou autrement.—L'exercice de ces droits n'a pour limites que les droits ou la liberté d'autrui et la sécurité publique.—La presse ne peut, dans aucun cas, être soumise à la censure.

9. L'enseignement est libre.—La liberté d'enseignement s'exerce selon les conditions de capacité et de moralité déterminées par les lois, et sous la surveillance de l'État.—Cette surveillance s'étend à tous les établissements d'éducation et d'enseignement, sans aucune exception.

10. Tous les citoyens sont également admissibles à tous les emplois publics, sans autre motif de préférence que leur mérite, et suivant les conditions qui seront fixées par les lois. Sont abolis à toujours tout titre nobiliaire, toute distinction de naissance, de classe ou de caste.

11. Toutes les propriétés sont inviolables. Néanmoins l'Etat peut exiger le sacrifice d'une propriété pour cause d'utilité publique légalement constatée, et moyennant une juste et préalable indemnité.

12. La confiscation des biens ne pourra jamais être rétablie.

13. La Constitution garantit aux citoyens la liberté du travail et de l'industrie.

La société favorise et encourage le développement du travail par l'enseignement primaire gratuit, l'éducation professionnelle, l'égalité de rapports entre le patron et l'ouvrier, les institutions de prévoyance et de crédit, les institutions agricoles, les associations volontaires, et l'établissement, par l'Etat, les départements et les communes, de travaux publics propres à employer les bras inoccupés; elle fournit l'assistance aux enfants abandonnés, aux infirmes et aux vieillards sans ressources, et que leurs familles ne peuvent secourir.

14. La dette publique est garantie.—Toute espèce d'engagement pris par l'Etat avec ses créanciers est inviolable.

15. Tout impôt est établi pour l'utilité commune.—Chacun y contribue en proportion de ses facultés et de sa fortune.

16. Aucun impôt ne peut être établi ni perçu qu'en vertu de la loi.

17. L'impôt direct n'est consenti que pour un an.—Les impositions indirectes peuvent être consenties pour plusieurs années.

CHAPITRE III

DES POUVOIRS PUBLICS

18. Tous les pouvoirs publics, quels qu'ils soient, émanent du peuple. Ils ne peuvent être délégués héréditairement.

19. La séparation des pouvoirs est la première condition d'un gouvernement libre.

CHAPITRE IV

DU POUVOIR LÉGISLATIF

20. Le peuple français délègue le pouvoir législatif à une Assemblée unique.

21. Le nombre total des représentants du peuple sera de sept cent cinquante, y compris les représentants de l'Algérie et des colonies françaises.

22. Ce nombre s'élèvera à neuf cents pour les assemblées qui seront appelées à reviser la Constitution.

23. L'élection a pour base la population.

24. Le suffrage est direct et universel. Le scrutin est secret.

25. Sont électeurs, sans condition de cens, tous les Français

âgés de vingt et un ans, et jouissant de leurs droits civils et politiques.

26. Sont éligibles, sans condition de domicile, tous les électeurs âgés de vingt-cinq ans.

27. La loi électorale déterminera les causes qui peuvent priver un citoyen français du droit d'élire et d'être élu.—Elle désignera les citoyens qui, exerçant ou ayant exercé des fonctions dans un département ou un ressort territorial, ne pourront y être élus.

28. Toute fonction publique rétribuée est incompatible avec le mandat de représentant du peuple. Aucun membre de l'Assemblée nationale ne peut, pendant la durée de la législature, être nommé ou promu à des fonctions publiques salariées dont les titulaires sont choisis à volonté par le pouvoir exécutif.—Les exceptions aux deux paragraphes précédents seront déterminées par la loi électorale organique.

29. Les dispositions de l'article précédent ne sont pas appliquables aux assemblées élues pour la revision de la Constitution.

30. L'élection des représentants se fera par département, et au scrutin de liste.—Les électeurs voteront au chef-lieu de canton; néanmoins, en raison des circonstances locales, le canton pourra être divisé en plusieurs circonscriptions, dans la forme et aux conditions qui seront déterminées par la loi électorale.

31. L'Assemblée nationale est élue pour trois ans, et se renouvelle intégralement.—Quarante-cinq jours au plus tard avant la fin de la législature, une loi détermine l'époque des nouvelles élections. Si aucune loi n'est intervenue dans le délai fixé par le paragraphe précédent, les électeurs se réunissent de plein droit le trentième jour qui précéde la fin de la législature.

La nouvelle Assemblée est convoquée de plein droit pour le lendemain du jour où finit le mandat de l'Assemblée précédente.

32. Elle est permanente. Néanmoins, elle peut s'ajourner à un terme qu'elle fixe.

Pendant la durée de la prorogation, une commission, composée des membres du bureau et de vingt-cinq représentants nommés par l'Assemblée au scrutin secret et à la majorité absolue, a le droit de la convoquer en cas d'urgence.

Le Président de la République a aussi le droit de convoquer l'Assemblée. L'Assemblée nationale détermine le lieu de ses séances. Elle fixe l'importance des forces militaires établies pour sa sûreté, et elle en dispose.

33. Les représentants sont toujours rééligibles.

34. Les membres de l'Assemblée nationale sont les représentants, non du département qui les nomme, mais de la France entière.

35. Ils ne peuvent reçevoir de mandat impératif.

36. Les représentants du peuple sont inviolables.—Ils ne pourront être recherchés, accusés, ni jugés, en aucun temps, pour les opinions qu'ils auront émises dans le sein de l'Assemblée nationale.

37. Ils ne peuvent être arrêtés en matière criminelle, sauf le cas de flagrant délit, ni poursuivis qu'après que l'Assemblée a permis la poursuite.—En cas d'arrestation pour flagrant délit, il en sera immédiatement référé à l'Assemblée, qui autorisera ou refusera la continuation des poursuites. Cette disposition s'applique au cas où un citoyen détenu est nommé représentant.

38. Chaque représentant du peuple reçoit une indemnité à laquelle il ne peut renoncer.

39. Les séances de l'Assemblée sont publiques.—Néanmoins l'Assemblée peut se former en comité secret, sur la demande du nombre de représentants fixé par le règlement.—Chaque représentant a le droit d'initiative parlementaire; il l'exercera selon les formes déterminées par le règlement.

40. La présence de la moitié plus un des membres de l'Assemblée est nécessaire pour la validité du vote des lois.

41. Aucun projet de loi, sauf les cas d'urgence, ne sera voté définitivement qu'après trois délibérations, à des intervalles qui ne peuvent pas être moindres de cinq jours.

42. Toute proposition ayant pour objet de déclarer l'urgence est précédée d'un exposé des motifs.—Si l'Assemblée est

d'avis de donner suite à la proposition d'urgence, elle en ordonne le renvoi dans les bureaux et fixe le moment où le rapport sur l'urgence lui sera présenté.—Sur le rapport, si l'Assemblée reconnaît l'urgence, elle le déclare et fixe le moment de la discussion.—Si elle décide qu'il n'y a pas urgence, le projet suit le cours des propositions ordinaires.

CHAPITRE V

DU POUVOIR EXÉCUTIF

43. Le peuple français délègue le pouvoir exécutif à un citoyen qui reçoit le titre de Président de la République.

44. Le Président doit être né Français, âgé de trente ans au moins, et n'avoir jamais perdu la qualité de Français.

45. Le Président de la République est élu pour quatre ans, et n'est rééligible qu'après un intervalle de quatre années.

Ne peuvent, non plus, être élus après lui, dans le même intervalle, ni le vice-président, ni aucun des parents ou alliés du Président jusqu'au sixième degré inclusivement.

46. L'élection a lieu de plein droit le deuxième dimanche du mois de mai.—Dans le cas où, par suite de décès, de démission ou de toute autre cause, le Président serait élu à une autre époque, ses pouvoirs expireront le deuxième dimanche du mois de mai de la quatrième année qui suivra son élection.

Le Président est nommé au scrutin secret et à la majorité absolue des votants, par le suffrage direct de tous les électeurs des départements français et de l'Algérie.

47. Les procés-verbaux des opérations électorales sont transmis immédiatement à l'Assemblée nationale, qui statue sans délai sur la validité de l'élection et proclame le Président de la République.

Si aucun candidat n'a obtenu plus de la moitié des suffrages exprimés, et au moins deux millions de voix, ou si les conditions exigées par l'article 44 ne sont pas remplies, l'Assemblée nationale élit le Président de la République, à la majorité absolue et au scrutin secret, parmi les cinq candidats éligibles qui ont obtenu le plus de voix.

48. Avant d'entrer en fonctions, le Président de la République prête au sein de l'Assemblée nationale le serment dont la teneur suit:

En présence de Dieu et devant le peuple français, représenté par l'Assemblée nationale, je jure de rester fidèle à la République démocratique, une et indivisible, et de remplir tous les devoirs que m'impose la Constitution.

49. Il a le droit de faire présenter des projets de loi à l'Assemblée nationale par les ministres.—Il surveille et assure l'exécution des lois.

50. Il dispose de la force armée, sans pouvoir jamais la commander en personne.

51. Il ne peut céder aucune portion du territoire, ni dissoudre, ni proroger l'Assemblée nationale, ni suspendre en aucune manière l'empire de la Constitution et des lois.

52. Il présente chaque année, par un message, à l'Assemblée nationale l'exposé de l'état général des affaires de la République.

53. Il négocie et ratifie les traités.—Aucun traité n'est définitif qu'après avoir été approuvée par l'Assemblée nationale.

54. Il veille à la défense de l'État, mais il ne peut entreprendre aucune guerre sans le consentement de l'Assemblée nationale.

55. Il a le droit de faire grâce, mais il ne peut exercer ce droit qu'après avoir pris l'avis du Conseil d'État.—Les amnisties ne peuvent être accordées que par une loi. Le Président de la République, les ministres, ainsi que toutes autres personnes condamnées par la Haute Cour de justice, ne peuvent être graciées que par l'Assemblée nationale.

56. Le Président de la République promulgue les lois au nom du peuple français.

57. Les lois d'urgence sont promulguées dans le délai de trois jours, et les autres lois dans le délai d'un mois, à partir du jour où elles auront été adoptées par l'Assemblée nationale.

58. Dans le délai fixé pour la promulgation, le Président de la République peut, par un message motivé, demander une nouvelle délibération.

L'Assemblée délibère : sa résolution devient définitive ; elle est transmise au Président de la République.

En ce cas, la promulgation a lieu dans le délai fixé pour les lois d'urgence.

59. A défaut de promulgation par le Président de la République, dans les délais déterminés par les articles précédents, il y serait pourvu par le président de l'Assemblée nationale.

60. Les envoyés et les ambassadeurs des puissances étrangères sont accrédités auprès du Président de la République.

61. Il préside aux solennités nationales.

62. Il est logé aux frais de la République, et reçoit un traitement de six cent mille francs par an.

63. Il réside au lieu où siège l'Assemblée nationale, et ne peut sortir du territoire continental de la République sans y être autorisé par une loi.

64. Le Président de la République nomme et révoque les ministres.

Il nomme et révoque, en conseil des ministres, les agents diplomatiques, les commandants en chef des armées de terre et de mer, les préfets, le commandant supérieur des gardes nationales de la Seine, les gouverneurs de l'Algérie et des colonies, les procureurs généraux et autres fonctionnaires d'un ordre supérieur.

Il nomme et révoque, sur la proposition du ministre compétent, dans les conditions réglementaires déterminées par la loi, les agents secondaires du gouvernment.

65. Il a le droit de suspendre, pour un terme qui ne pourra excéder trois mois, les agents du pouvoir exécutif élus par les citoyens.

Il ne peut les révoquer que de l'avis du Conseil d'Etat.

La loi détermine les cas où les agents révoqués peuvent être déclarés inéligibles aux mêmes fonctions.

Cette déclaration d'inéligibilité ne pourra être prononcée que par un jugement.

66. Le nombre des ministres et leurs attributions sont fixés par le pouvoir législatif.

67. Les actes du Président de la République, autres que ceux par lesquels il nomme et révoque les ministres, n'ont d'effet que s'ils sont contresignés par un ministre.

68. Le Président de la République, les ministres, les agents et dépositaires de l'autorité publique, sont responsables, chacun en ce qui le concerne, de tous les actes du gouvernement et de l'administration. Toute mesure par laquelle le Président de la République dissout l'Assemblée nationale, la proroge ou met obstacle à l'exercice de son mandat, est un crime de haute-trahison.—Par ce seul fait, le Président est déchu de ses fonctions; les citoyens sont tenus de lui refuser obéissance; le pouvoir exécutif passe de plein droit à l'Assemblée nationale. Les juges de la Haute Cour de justice se réunissent immédiatement, à peine de forfaiture; ils convoquent les jurés dans le lieu qu'ils désignent, pour procéder au jugement du Président et de ses complices; ils nomment eux-mêmes les magistrats chargés de remplir les fonctions du ministère public.—Une loi déterminera les autres cas de responsabilité, ainsi que les formes et les conditions de la poursuite.

69. Les ministres ont entrée dans le sein de l'Assemblée nationale; ils sont entendus toutes les fois qu'ils le demandent, et peuvent se faire assister par des commissaires nommés par un décret du Président de la République.

70. Il y a un vice-président de la République nommé par l'Assemblée nationale, sur la présentation de trois candidats faite par le Président dans le mois qui suit son élection.—Le vice-président prête le même serment que le président.—Le vice-président ne pourra être choisi parmi les parents et alliés du président jusqu'au sixième degré inclusivement.—En cas d'empêchement du président, le vice-président le remplace.—Si la présidence devient vacante par décès, démission du président, ou autrement, il est procédé dans le mois à l'élection d'un président.

Chapitre VI

du conseil d'état

71. Il y aura un Conseil d'État, dont le vice-président de la République sera de droit président.

72. Les membres de ce Conseil sont nommés pour six ans par l'Assemblée nationale. Ils sont renouvelés par moitié, dans les deux premiers mois de chaque législature, au scrutin secret et à la majorité absolue.—Ils sont indéfiniment rééligibles.

73. Ceux des membres du Conseil d'État qui auront été pris dans le sein de l'Assemblée nationale seront immédiatement remplacés comme représentants du peuple.

74. Les membres du Conseil d'État ne peuvent être révoqués que par l'Assemblée, et sur la proposition du président de la République.

75. Le Conseil d'État est consulté sur les projets de loi du gouvernement qui, d'après la loi, devront être soumis à son examen préalable, et sur les projets d'initiative parlementaire que l'Assemblée lui aura renvoyés.—Il prépare les réglements d'administration publique : il fait seul ceux de ces réglements à l'égard desquels l'Assemblée nationale lui a donné une délégation spéciale.—Il exerce, à l'égard des administrations publiques, tous les pouvoirs de contrôle et de surveillance qui lui sont déférés par la loi.

La loi réglera ses autres attributions.

Chapitre VII

de l'administration intérieure

76. La division du territoire en départements, arrondissements, cantons et communes est maintenue. Les circonscriptions actuelles ne pourront être changées que par une loi.

77. Il y a : 1° dans chaque département, une administration composée d'un préfet, d'un conseil général, d'un conseil de préfecture ;

2° Dans chaque arrondissement, un sous-préfet ;

3° Dans chaque canton, un conseil cantonal ; néanmoins, un

seul conseil cantonal sera établi dans les villes divisées en plusieurs cantons ;

4° Dans chaque commune, une administration composée d'un maire, d'adjoints et d'un conseil municipal.

78. Une loi déterminera la composition et les attributions des conseils généraux, des conseils cantonaux, des conseils municipaux et le mode de nomination des maires et des adjoints.

79. Les conseils généraux et les conseils municipaux sont élus par le suffrage direct de tous les citoyens domiciliés dans le département ou dans la commune. Chaque canton élit un membre du conseil général.—Une loi spéciale réglera le mode d'élection dans le département de la Seine, dans la ville de Paris et dans les villes de plus de vingt mille âmes.

80. Les conseils généraux, les conseils cantonaux et les conseils municipaux peuvent être dissous par le président de la République, de l'avis du Conseil d'État. La loi fixera le délai dans lequel il sera procédé à la réélection.

Chapitre VIII

DU POUVOIR JUDICIAIRE

81. La justice est rendue gratuitement au nom du peuple français.

Les débats sont publics, à moins que la publicité ne soit dangereuse pour l'ordre ou les moeurs ; et, dans ce cas, le tribunal le déclare par un jugement.

82. Le jury continuera d'être appliqué en matière criminelle.

83. La connaissance de tous les délits politiques et de tous les délits commis par la voie de la presse appartient exclusivement au jury.—Les lois organiques détermineront la compétence en matière de délits d'injures et de diffamation contre les particuliers.

84. Le jury statue seul sur les dommages-intérêts réclamés pour faits ou délits de presse.

85. Les juges de paix et leurs suppléants, les juges de première instance et d'appel, les membres de la Cour de Cassation et de la Cour des Comptes, sont nommés par le président de la

République, d'après un ordre de candidature ou d'après les conditions qui seront réglées par les lois organiques.

86. Les magistrats du ministère public sont nommés par le président de la République.

87. Les juges de première instance et d'appel, les membres de la Cour de Cassation et de la Cour des Comptes, sont nommés à vie.—Ils ne peuvent être révoqués ou suspendus que par un jugement, ni mis à la retraite que pour les causes et dans les formes déterminées par les lois.

88. Les conseils de guerre et de revision des armées de terre et de mer, les tribunaux maritimes, les tribunaux de commerce, les prud'hommes et autres tribunaux spéciaux, conservent leur organisation et leurs attributions actuelles jusqu'à ce qu'il y ait été dérogé par une loi.

89. Les conflits d'attribution entre l'autorité administrative et l'autorité judiciaire seront réglés par un tribunal spécial de membres de la Cour de Cassation et de conseillers d'État, désignés tous les trois ans en nombre égal par leurs corps respectif.—Ce tribunal sera présidé par le ministre de la justice.

90. Les recours pour incompétence et excès de pouvoirs contre les arrêts de la Cour des Comptes seront portés devant la juridiction des conflits.

91. Une Haute Cour de justice juge, sans appel ni recours en cassation, les accusations portées par l'Assemblée nationale contre le président de la République ou les ministres.

Elle juge également toutes personnes prévenues de crimes, attentats ou complots contre la sûreté intérieure ou extérieure de l'État, que l'Assemblée nationale aura renvoyées devant elle.—Sauf le cas prévu par l'article 68, elle ne peut être saisie qu'en vertu d'un décret de l'Assemblée nationale, qui désigne la ville où la Cour tiendra ses séances.

92. La Haute Cour est composée de cinq juges et de trente-six jurés.—Chaque année, dans les quinze premiers jours du mois de novembre, la Cour de Cassation nomme, parmi ses membres, au scrutin secret et à la majorité absolue, les juges de la Haute Cour, au nombre de cinq, et deux suppléants. Les cinq juges appelés à siéger feront choix de leur président.

Les magistrats remplissant les fonctions du ministère public sont désignés par le président de la République, et, en cas d'accusation du président ou des ministres, par l'Assemblée nationale.

Les jurés, au nombre de trente-six, et quatre jurés suppléants, sont pris parmi les membres des conseils généraux des départements.

Les représentants du peuple n'en peuvent faire partie.

93. Lorsqu'un décret de l'Assemblée nationale a ordonné la formation de la Haute Cour de justice, et, dans le cas prévu par l'article 68, sur la réquisition du président ou de l'un des juges, le président de la Cour d'Appel, et, à défaut de Cour d'Appel, le président du tribunal de première instance du chef lieu judiciare du département, tire au sort, en audience publique, le nom d'un membre du conseil général.

94. Au jour indiqué pour le jugement, s'il y a moins de soixante jurés présents, ce nombre sera complété par des jurés supplémentaires tirés au sort, par le président de la Haute Cour, parmi les membres du conseil général du département où siégera la Cour.

95. Les jurés qui n'auront pas produit d'excuse valable seront condamnés à une amende de mille à dix mille francs, et à la privation des droits politiques pendant cinq ans au plus.

96. L'accusé et le ministère public exercent le droit de récusation comme en matière ordinaire.

97. La déclaration du jury portant que l'accusé est coupable ne peut être rendue qu'à la majorité des deux tiers des voix.

98. Dans tous les cas de responsabilité des ministres, l'Assemblée nationale peut, selon les circonstances, renvoyer le ministre inculpé, soit devant la Haute Cour de justice, soit devant les tribunaux ordinaires, pour les réparations civiles.

99. L'Assemblée nationale et le président de la République peuvent, dans tous les cas, déférer l'examen des actes de tout fonctionnaire, autre que le président de la République, au Conseil d'État, dont le rapport est rendu public.

100. Le président de la République n'est justiciable que de la Haute Cour de justice.—Il ne peut, à l'exception du cas

prévu par l'article 68, être poursuivi que sur l'accusation portée par l'Assemblée nationale, et pour crimes et délits qui seront déterminés par la loi.

Chapitre IX

DE LA FORCE PUBLIQUE

101. La force publique est instituée pour défendre l'État contre les ennemis du dehors, et pour assurer au dedans le maintien de l'ordre et l'exécution des lois.—Elle se compose de la garde nationale et de l'armée de terre et de mer.

102. Tout Français, sauf les exceptions fixées par la loi, doit le service militaire et celui de la garde nationale.—La faculté pour chaque citoyen de se libérer du service militaire personnel sera réglée par la loi du recrutement.

103. L'organisation de la garde nationale et la constitution de l'armée seront réglées par la loi.

104. La force publique est essentiellement obéissante. Nul corps armé ne peut délibérer.

105. La force publique, employée pour maintenir l'ordre à l'intérieure n'agit que sur la réquisition des autorités constituées, suivant les règles déterminées par le pouvoir législatif.

106. Une loi déterminera les cas dans lesquels l'état de siège pourra être déclaré, et réglera les formes et les effets de cette mesure.

107. Aucune troupe étrangère ne peut être introduite sur le territoire français sans le consentement préalable de l'Assemblée nationale.

Chapitre X

DISPOSITIONS PARTICULIÈRES

108. La Légion d'honneur est maintenue; ses statuts seront revisés et mis en harmonie avec la Constitution.

109. Le territoire de l'Algérie et des colonies est déclaré territoire français, et sera régi par des lois particulières jusqu'à ce qu'une loi spéciale les place sous le régime de la présente Constitution.

110. L'Assemblée nationale confie le dépôt de la présente

Constitution et des droits qu'elle consacre, à la garde et au patriotisme de tous les Français.

Chapitre XI

DE LA REVISION DE LA CONSTITUTION

III. Lorsque, dans la dernière année d'une législature, l'Assemblée nationale aura émis le voeu que la Constitution soit modifiée en tout ou en partie, il sera procédé à cette revision de la manière suivante.

Le voeu exprimé par l'Assemblée ne sera converti en résolution définitive qu'après trois délibérations consécutives, prises chacune à un mois d'intervalle et aux trois quarts des suffrages exprimés. Le nombre des votants devra être de cinq cents au moins.

L'Assemblée de revision ne sera nommée que pour trois mois.

Elle ne devra s'occuper que de la revision pour laquelle elle aura été convoquée.

Néanmoins, elle pourra, en cas d'urgence, pourvoir aux nécessités législatives.

Chapitre XII

DISPOSITIONS TRANSITOIRES

112. Les dispositions des Codes, lois et règlements existants, qui ne sont pas contraires à la présente Constitution restent en vigueur jusqu'à ce qu'il y soit légalement dérogé.

113. Toutes les autorités constituées par les lois actuelles demeurent en exercice jusqu'à la promulgation des lois organiques qui les concernent.

114. La loi d'organisation judiciare déterminera le mode spécial de nomination pour la première composition des nouveaux tribunaux.

115. Après le vote de la Constitution, il sera procédé, par l'Assemblée nationale constituante, à la rédaction des lois organiques dont l'énumération sera déterminée par une loi spéciale.

116. Il sera procédé à la première élection du président de la République conformément à la loi spéciale rendue par l'Assemblée nationale le 28 octobre 1848.

BIBLIOGRAPHY

A.—Contemporary Works

1. Reports of debates
   a. Constitutional Commission:
   Procès-verbal. Ms. in archives of Chamber of Deputies, Paris. 2 vols.
   b. Assembly:
   Compte-rendu des séances de l'Assemblée Nationale. Paris, 1849. 10 vols. in 4°.
   Table analytique du compte rendu. Paris, 1850.
   Le Moniteur universel. May-Nov., 1848.
   c. U. S. Congress:
   Congressional Globe, vol. 17 (1st session, 30th Congress).

2. Newspapers
   a. Legitimist:
   L'Assemblée nationale. Mar. 1-June 25 (suspended) ; Aug. 7-Dec.
   La Gazette de France. Suspended Aug. 24; issued as *Le Peuple français,* Aug. 30-Sept. 6; as *L'Etoile de la France,* Sept. 14-Oct. 24; reappears in original form, Oct. 25.
   L'Opinion publique. May-Dec.
   L'Union monarchique.[1]
   b. Conservative republican:
   Le Constitutionnel.
   Le Journal des débats.
   La Patrie.
   c. Liberal republican:
   Le Bien public. May 24-Dec.
   Le Journal. July 28-Nov. 1.
   Le National.

[1] Unless otherwise indicated, file in *Bibliothèque Nationale,* Paris, runs unbroken throughout the year. In other cases, months here given refer to 1848 only. *Cf.* ch. vii for further details.

d. Radical republican:

Le Charivari.
Le Peuple constituant. Feb.-July 11.
La Réforme.

e. Socialist:

L'Ami du peuple. Feb. 27-May 14.
L'Atelier. Published irregularly; sometimes weekly, usually monthly.
La Démocratie pacifique.
Le Père Duchêne. April-June; suspended June 25; resumed for five numbers in August.
Le Populaire.
Le Représentant du peuple. Apr. 1-Aug. 24 with occasional intermissions; continued from Sept. 1 as *Le Peuple.*
La République.
La Vraie république. Mar. 26-June 24; Aug. 8-21.

f. Bonapartist:

Le Napoléon républicain. June 11-25.
Le Petit Caporal. June-Dec.; suspended during July. This and preceding, radical in sentiment.

g. Catholic:

L'Ère nouvelle. April-Dec.
L'Univers.

h. Personal organs:

L'Evénement. Aug.-Dec.
La Liberté. Mar. 1-June 26; Aug. 7-Sept. 2; Nov. 8-Dec. 31.
La Presse. Suspended from June 25 to Aug. 7.

i. Reviews:

Le Mois. March-Dec.
Revue britannique. Feb. number contains an article from the *Edinburgh Review*, "Des progrès de la civilisation commerciale en Amérique depuis la découverte de Ch. Colomb jusqu'en 1846," treating largely of the tariff, agriculture and immigration, eulogistic of American liberty. July number has article, "Des causes de la prospérité des Etats-Unis d'Amérique" by J. Magne (for his sketch of constitution, see below). Other articles on advantages of a transcontinental railroad over a Panama canal, on life in the Far West, negro slavery, Emerson, a pacifist book by Charles Sumner, etc.
Revue des deux mondes. Articles on America are chiefly literary criticisms.

Revue de législation et de jurisprudence. Laboulaye's *Considér-ations* first published in Aug. number.

Revue nationale. Suspended in July for lack of bond. Several uncomplimentary allusions to American slavery.

j. Foreign publications:

London Times.

New York Evening Post.

Phila. Public Ledger.

Washington Daily National Intelligencer.

Niles' Register, vol. lxxiv.

3. Collections of constitutions

Anonymous. *Constitution des Etats-Unis d'Amérique.* 16mo. Imp. de Crapelet. Paris, 1848. The preface praises the bicameral system, indirect election to the senate, the president with his four year term, suspensive veto, executive nomination rather than election to posts in the civil service, the system of checks and balances, the property qualification for suffrage in most American States; in lieu of the latter, however, it demands only an ability to read and write.

Anonymous. *République des Etats-Unis d'Amérique. Sa constitu-tion avec les divers amendments depuis son origine.* 8vo. Paris, April, 1848. Incomplete paraphrase chiefly of legislative sections.

Balbo, I. P. *Constitutions républicaines du globe.* Contains those of France, United States, Delaware, St. Domingo, Italy, Venice, Genoa, San Marino, Germany, Bavaria, Switzerland, canton of Vaud. Paris, 1848.

Champeaux, G. de. *Constitution républicaine de 1848 précédés des Constitutions françaises . . . et suivie de la constitution améri-caine.* Paris, 1848.

Jalaber, Fabius. *Constitution des Etats-Unis d'Amérique, traduite sur l'ouvrage original et suivie d'observations tirées en majeure partie de l'ouvrage de M. Destutt de Tracy.* Nantes, 1848. Tracy was a friend of Jefferson; the work referred to is a com-mentary on Montesquieu, which he wrote in 1807 in the United States and published there in 1811.

M. ————. *Constitutions de la république française annotées et suivies de la constitution des Etats-Unis d'Amérique.* Paris, 1848.

Pailliet, J. B. J. *Constitutions américaines et françaises.* Paris, 1848.

Tripier, Louis. *Les Constitutions françaises depuis 1789 et y com-pris les décrets du gouvernement provisoire de 1848, suivies de la constitution des Etats-Unis d'Amérique.* Paris, 1848.

Dupin, André Marie J. J. (Dupin aîné). *Constitution de la répub-lique française accompagnée de notes sommaires.* Paris, Jan. 1849

Author a member of the constitutional commission. He comments favorably on the American presidential message and the
permanent tenure of the judiciary.

Teulet, A. F. *Recueil de constitutions françaises depuis 1791, et
constitutions des Etats-Unis d'Amérique avec table méthodique.*
Paris, 1851.
Apparently reprint of an earlier edition. Table of contents men-
tions federal constitution and state constitutions of Mass., Penn.,
Del., Md., Vt., and S. C.
Pages allotted to state constitutions are taken up in this edition
by const. of 1848.

4. Political books and pamphlets

Anonymous. *Catéchisme républicain par le Père André, suivi des
conseils pour faire fortune et de la science du Bonhomme Richard
par Franklin.* 4th edition, 91st thousand. Paris, 1833-48.
In French Revolutionary Pamphlets, vol. 2, Columbia Univ. Lib.
Republican pamphlet; alludes to American example.

Anonymous. *Projet d'une constitution de la république, en sept
articles, par un citoyen qui s'est donné la peine de lire et de
comparer toutes les constitutions de la France et des pays étrangers
depuis 1788.* Paris, 1848.
Calls for a lower house elected by general vote for three years
on basis of population, a senate chosen from a list of notabilities
by general vote for nine years, renewed by thirds, a president for
three years popularly elected, a council of ministers named and
revocable by the president, a council of state named and revocable
by him acting in conjunction with the ministers.

d'Arlincourt, Vte. *Dieu le veut.* Paris, 1848.
Legitimist plea for Henry V; went to 64 editions by 1850; bitterly
hostile to U. S.

Barthélemy, A. M. *À M. J. K. Polk, président des États-Unis
d'Amérique.* Paris, 1848.

Berriat Saint-Prix, F. *Plan de constitution, avec indication des
sources et des motifs.* Paris, 1848.
Democratic standpoint; U. S. example rejected because of federalism and bicameral system.

Bonis, Améd. *Les Queues de chevaux ou lettre de la jeune
Amérique à la France républicaine.* Paris, 1848.
Trivial eulogy of republicanism.

Brougham, Lord. *Letter to the Marquess of Lansdowne on the
late revolution in France.* London, 1848.
Argues for two chambers, alluding to American and English
example.

Chambrun, Adelbert de. *La République réformiste et la république révolutionnaire.* Paris, 1848.
Ex-monarchist, who hopes that American and English experience will not be unheeded by France.

Colombel, H. *Quelques réflexions concernant la constitution.* Nantes, 1851.
Appeared first in the *Courrier de Nantes*, May 14, 1848. Quotes American example four times in an essay of 16 pages; no other country quoted.

Cormenin, L. M. *Petit pamphlet sur le projet de constitution, par Timon.* Paris, 1848.

Emar, Louis. *La Constitution comme je la voudrais avec des débats imaginaires.* Paris, 1848.
Praise of the high standard of American diplomats.

Garnier, Adolphe. *De l'organisation du pouvoir.* Paris, 1848.
Appeared first in *La Liberté du penser*, June 15, 1848. To be found in French Political Pamphlets, Z1, Columbia Univ. Library. Author a professor of philosophy at the Sorbonne; ch. iii, *De la constitution américaine*, examines American methods from a conservative, generally favorable standpoint; no other foreign system studied.

Laboulaye, E. *Considérations sur la constitution.* Paris, 1848.
Appeared first as article in *Revue de législation et de jurisprudence*, Aug. 1848.

Lamartine. *Trois mois au pouvoir.* Paris, 1848.

Le Mesl, P. M. *Considérations sur la partie du projet de constitution qui concerne l'organisation du pouvoir exécutif et du pouvoir législatif.* Paris, 1848.
Asserts that there are only two parties, that of order and stability, that of disorder and anarchy; France must study the example of the United States.

Magne, J. *Esquisse d'une constitution. Ce que la France républicaine pourrait, avec avantage, emprunter aux institutions des États-Unis.* Paris, 1848.
Appeared first in *La Revue britannique*, May, 1848.

Morton, Georges. *Lettre d'un citoyen des États-Unis d'Amérique sur la présidence de la république française.* Paris, Nov. 1848.
In Cavaignac interest.

Nougarède de Fayet, Ate. *De la constitution républicaine à donner à la France et du danger d'une assemblée unique.* Paris, 1848.

Pitray. *Que préférer? une assemblée unique omnipotente ou une législature composée d'une chambre des représentants, d'un sénat et d'un président?* Bordeaux, 1848.
Author a refugee from St. Domingo to the U. S.; citizen there

for 22 years; French citizen again for 28 years. Adds as appendix Washington's opinion, found in his letter as Pres. of the Const. Convention to the Pres. of Congress, Sept. 17, 1787.

Regnon, H. de. *À M. de Cormenin, prés. de la commission de la constitution.* Nantes, 1848.
Open letter, in Catholic interest, advocating " la liberté d'une république plutôt fédérative qu'unitaire, comme celle des États-Unis."

Saint-Auge, F. A. Fournier. *Du rachat de la dette consolidé par l'impôt foncier.* Paris, 1848.
Pamphlet in Archives Nationales.

Saint-John, P. B. *French Revolution in 1848.* New York, 1848.
Sympathy with republic, but dislike of socialism.

Saint-Priest, F. *Question des deux chambres.* Paris, 1848.
Author a member of Assembly. American example invoked in favor of bicameral system.

Stern, Daniel. *Lettres républicaines.* Paris, 1848.

Constitutionnelisky, C. S. *Considérations ... sur la mesure de liberté ... que nous devons au ... siècle des constitutions ('48-'52).* Montauban, 1854.

Dunoyer, Barthélemy C. P. Jos. *La Révolution du 24 février.* Paris, 1849.

Guizot. *De la démocratie en France.* Paris, 1849.

Laboulaye, E. *De la constitution américaine et de l'utilité de son étude. Discours prononcé le 4 déc. 1849, à l'ouverture du cours de législation comparée.*
Appeared first in *Revue de législation et de jurisprudence,* Dec. 1849.

Rendu, A. *Les Deux républiques ou États-Unis et France.* Paris, 1850.
Shows continuance of interest in American example after constitution-making period.

5. Works on the United States

Beaumont, G. de and Tocqueville, A. de. *Système pénitentiare aux États-Unis et de son application en France.* Paris, 1831; 3rd ed. 1845.

Chevalier, Michel. *Lettres sur l'Amérique du Nord.* Paris, 1836; 2nd ed. 1837.
Histoire et description des voies de communication aux États-Unis. Paris, 1840-41. 2 vols.

Courmont, F. de. *Des États-Unis, de la guerre du Mexique et de l'île de Cube.* Paris, 1847.

Farcy, Charles. *Études politiques. De l'aristocratie anglaise, de*

la démocratie américaine, et de la libéralité des institutions françaises. Paris, 1842.
Violent disapproval from standpoint of Guizot Orleanist before the revolution.

Guizot. *Washington, Etude historique.* Paris, 1839.

Murat, Achille. *Esquisses morales et politiques des États-Unis de l'Amérique du Nord.* Paris, 1832.

Poussin, G. T. *Considérations sur le principe démocratique qui régit l'union américaine.* Paris, 1841.

De la puissance américaine. 3rd ed., enlarged. Paris, 1848.

Travaux d'améliorations intérieures, projetés ... par le gouvernement général des États-Unis d'Amérique de 1824 à 1831. Paris, 1834.

Tocqueville, A. de. *La Démocratie en Amérique.* Paris, 1835, 3 vols.
A tenth edition published in 1848.

6. Collections of documents

Archives Nationales. Cartons BB[30]299-320 contain a mass of printed and unprinted matter relative to 1848, including reports, petitions, addresses, letters, etc., mostly of little value.

Anonymous. *Les Affiches rouges.* Paris, 1851.

Les Murailles révolutionnaires de 1848. Paris, 1867.
Two collections of revolutionary posters.

7. Miscellaneous

Jefferson, Thomas. *Writings.* (Ford ed.) New York, 1892-99. 10 vols.

Lowell, J. R. *Biglow Papers, First Series.* Many editions.

Moses, Myer. *Full Annals of the Revolution in France, 1830. To which is added, A Full Account of the Celebration of said Revolution in the City of New York, on the 25th November, 1830; Being the Forty-seventh Anniversary of an event that restored our citizens to their homes, and to the enjoyment of their rights and liberties.* New York, 1830.

Thomas, Emile. *Histoire des ateliers nationaux.* Paris, 1848. (Marriot ed. Oxford, 1913).

Tocqueville, A. de. *Correspondance.* Vols. 5-7 of *Oeuvres complètes.* Paris, 1866.

B.—SECONDARY WORKS

1. Memoirs and histories by contemporaries

Babaud-Laribière, L. *Histoire de l'Assemblée nationale constituante.* Paris, 1850. 2 vols.

Barante, Baron de. "Après la révolution de février." In *La Revue de Paris*, vol. iii, pp. 309-335, 539-568. Paris, 1899.

Barrot, Odilon. *Mémoires posthumes.* Paris, 1875. 4 vols.

Beaumont-Vassy, Vicomte de. *Histoire de mon temps, 1830-51.* 1st series, vol. 4. Paris, 1858.

Blanc, Louis. *Histoire de la révolution de 1848.* Paris, 1870. 2 vols.

Carnot, Hippolyte. *Memorial d'. Bibliothèque de la société d'histoire de la révolution de 1848,* vol. viii.

Castille, H. *Histoire de la seconde république française.* Paris, 1855. 4 vols.

Chase, Lucien B. *History of the Polk Administration.* New York, 1850.

Chassin, Ch. L. *Félicien. Souvenirs d'un étudiant de '48.* Paris, 1904.

Corkran, J. F. *History of the National Constituent Assembly.* New York, 1849.

Garnier-Pagès. *Histoire de la révolution de 1848.* Paris, 1866. 8 vols.

Guizot. *Mémoires pour servir à l'histoire de mon temps.* Paris, 1875. 9 vols.

Laboulaye, E. *Histoire politique des États-Unis* (1620-1789). Paris, 1855-66. 3 vols.

Lamartine. *Histoire de la révolution de 1848.* Brussels, 1849. 2 vols.

Marx, Karl. *Der Achtzehnte Brumaire des Louis Bonaparte.* Hamburg, 1869.
Published originally in *Die Revolution,* a New York monthly, in 1852.
The history of the second republic, viewed as a contest of classes.

Mitchell, Donald G. *The Battle Summer.* New York, 1850.

Normanby, Marquis of. *A Year of Revolution; from a journal kept in Paris in 1848.* London, 1857. 2 vols.

Quentin-Bauchart. *Etudes et souvenirs sur la deuxième république et le second empire.* Paris, 1901.

Rémusat, Charles de. *Politique libérale.* Paris, 1860.

Rush, Richard. *Occasional Productions, Political, Diplomatic and Miscellaneous. Including among others, a glance at the court and government of Louis Philippe and the French Revolution of 1848.* Philadelphia, 1860.

Stein, Lorenz. *Geschichte der sozialen Bewegung in Frankreich.* Leipzig, 1850. 3 vols.

Stern, Daniel. *Histoire de la révolution de 1848.* Paris, 1878. 2 vols.

Tocqueville, A. de. *Souvenirs.* Paris, 1893.

2. Later works

Berton, H. "La constitution de 1848" in *Annales de l'école libre des sciences politiques*, vol. 12, pp. 673-712; vol. 13, pp. 343-374.

Bourne, H. E. "American constitutional precedents in the French National Assembly" in *American Historical Review*, vol. 8, pp. 466-486.

Chaboseau, A. "Les constituants de 1848" in *La Révolution de 1848*, vol. 7, pp. 287-305, 413-425; vol. 8, pp. 67-80.

Dodd, W. E. *Expansion and Conflict* (Riverside Hist. of U. S., vol. 3). Boston, 1915.

Dolléans, E. *Robert Owen*. Paris, 1907.

d'Eichthal, Eugène. *Alexis de Tocqueville, et la démocratie libérale. Etude suivi de fragments des entretiens de Tocqueville avec Nassau William Senior* (1848-1858). Paris, 1897.

Foville, A. de. *La Transformation des moyens de transport*. Paris, 1880.

Hamel, E. *Histoire de France depuis la révolution jusqu' à la chute du Second Empire*. Paris, 1883-93. 10 vols.

Hélie, F. A. *Les Constitutions de la France*. Paris, 1875.

La Gorce, P. de. *Histoire de la seconde république française*. Paris, 1898. 2 vols.

Levasseur, E. *Histoire des classes ouvrières et de l'industrie en France de 1789 à 1860* (1st ed. 1867). Paris, 1903. 2 vols.

McMaster, J. B. *History of the People of the United States from the Revolution to the Civil War*. New York, 1885-1913. 8 vols.

Marcel, R. P. *Essai politique sur Alexis de Tocqueville*. Paris, 1910.

Michel, H. "Note sur la constitution de 1848" in *La Révolution de 1848*, vol. 1, pp. 41-56.

Müller, Wilhelm. *Political History of Recent Times*. New York, 1882. Translation of *Politische Geschichte der neuesten Zeit*.

Pierre, V. *Histoire de la république de 1848*. Paris, 1873-1878. 2 vols.

Rammelkamp, C. H. "The French Constitution of 1791 and the United States Constitution; a Comparison" in *South Atlantic Quarterly*. Vol. 2, p. 56, et seq.

Renard, Georges. *La République de 1848*. Paris, 1906. Vol. ix of *L'Histoire socialiste*, Jean Jaurès ed.

Rhodes, J. F. *History of the United States from the compromise of 1850 to the final restoration of home rule at the South in 1877*. New York, 1893-1906. 7 vols.

Richardson, James D. *A Compilation of the Messages and Papers of the Presidents*. Washington, 1897. 10 vols.

Rittiez, F. *Histoire du gouvernement provisoire de 1848*. Paris, 1866. 2 vols.

Rosenthal, Lewis. *America and France: influence of the United States on France in the 18th century.* New York, 1882.

Seignobos, Ch. "Histoire politique de la France contemporaine depuis 1848" in *Revue des cours et conférences,* Nov. 1907-July, 1908.

Histoire politique de l'Europe contemporaine. Paris, 1897.

Spuller, E. *Histoire parlementaire de la seconde république.* Paris, 1891.

Tchernoff, J. *Le parti républicain sous la monarchie de juillet.* Paris, 1901.

Von Holst, H. *John C. Calhoun.* Boston, 1884.

Wassermann, Suzanne. *Les Clubs de Barbès et de Blanqui en 1848.* (*Bibliothèque d'histoire moderne, fascicule xii*). Paris, 1913.

Weill, G. *Histoire du parti républicain en France de 1814 à 1870.* Paris, 1900.

C.—BIBLIOGRAPHIES AND WORKS OF REFERENCE

1. Bibliographies

Bibliographie de la France; journal général de l'imprimerie et de la librairie: 1st series, 1811-1856; 2nd series, 1857-present.

Brière et Caron. *Répertoire de l'histoire moderne de la France.* Paris, 1898-1903 incl.
Hiatus till 1910, being covered by two volumes in preparation. Continued by Caron et Burnand, *Répertoire,* 1910-1912. For subsequently published works, *cf. Revue d'histoire moderne,* and its annual *Répertoire méthodique. Cf.* also *La Révolution de 1848,* published every two months since 1904 by the *Société de la Révolution de 1848,* under editorship of G. Renard.

Caron, P. *Bibliographie des travaux publiés de 1866 à 1897 sur l'histoire de la France depuis 1789.* Paris, 1912.

Caron, P. "Les sources manuscrites parisiennes de l'histoire de la révolution de 1848 et de la deuxième république" in *Revue d'histoire moderne et contemporaine,* vol. 6, pp. 85-119.

Catalogue de l'histoire de France. Bibliothèque Nationale, Paris. Vols. 4, 7 and 11 (suppl.).

Larned, J. N. *The Literature of American History* (Am. Lib. Assoc. Annotated Lists). Boston, 1902.

Le Soudier. *Bibliographie française.* 1st series, catalogues of French publishers to 1900; 2nd series, 1900-1909.

Lorenz, O. *Catalogue général de la librarie française,* esp. vol. 7. 1840-1912; monthly supplements, 1912-1915.

Poole's *Index to Periodical Literature,* esp. vol. 1.

2. Lists of newspapers

> Hatin, E. *Bibliographie historique et critique de la presse périodique française.* Paris, 1866.
> *Histoire politique et littéraire de la presse en France.* 8 vols. Paris, 1859-1861.
> Izambard, H. *La presse parisienne.* Paris, 1853.

3. Biographies of representatives

> Alhoy, M. *Biographie parlementaire des représentants du peuple à l'assemblée nationale constituante de 1848.* Paris, 1848.
> *Dictionnaire des parlementaires français, comprenant tous les membres des assemblées françaises et tous les ministres français depuis le 1er mai 1789 jusqu'au 1er mai 1889.* Adolphe Robert, Edgar Bourloton, Gaston Cougny, editors. Paris, 1891. 5 vols.
> Lesaulnier, C. M. *Biographie des 900 députés à l'assemblée nationale par ordre alphabétique de départements.* Paris, 1848.
> *Biographie des représentants du peuple à l'assemblée nationale constituante, avec un tableau des députations par départements. Par les rédacteurs de Notre Histoire.* Paris, 1848.

4. Miscellaneous.

> *Almanach nationale.* Paris, 1848.
> *Assemblée nationale constituante. Impressions. Projets de lois, propositions, rapports, etc.* Paris, 1849. 16 vols. in 8vo, and 5 vols. in 4°.
> Carrey, E. *Recueil des actes du gouvernement provisoire de 1848.* Paris, 1848.
> *La Grande Encyclopédie.* Paris, 1886-1903. 31 vols.